Women in Early Medieval China

Women in Early Medieval China

Bret Hinsch

ROWMAN & LITTLEFIELD
Lanham • Boulder • New York • London

Published by Rowman & Littlefield
An imprint of The Rowman & Littlefield Publishing Group, Inc.
4501 Forbes Boulevard, Suite 200, Lanham, Maryland 20706
www.rowman.com

Unit A, Whitacre Mews, 26-34 Stannary Street, London SE11 4AB, United Kingdom

British Library Cataloguing in Publication Information Available

Library of Congress Cataloging-in-Publication Data

Names: Hinsch, Bret, author.
Title: Women in early medieval China / Bret Hinsch.
Description: Lanham : Rowman & Littlefield, [2018] | Series: Asian voices |
    Includes bibliographical references and index.
Identifiers: LCCN 2018020869 (print) | LCCN 2018040057 (ebook) | ISBN
    9781538117972 (Electronic) | ISBN 9781538117965 (cloth : alk. paper)
    ISBN 9781538158326 (pbk: alk. paper)
Subjects: LCSH: Women—China—History—Middle Ages, 500-1500. |
    China—History—220-589. | China—History—Sui dynasty, 581-618.
Classification: LCC HQ1147.C6 (ebook) | LCC HQ1147.C6 H56 2018 (print) |
    DDC 305.40951/016—dc23
LC record available at https://lccn.loc.gov/2018020869

∞™ The paper used in this publication meets the minimum requirements of
American National Standard for Information Sciences—Permanence of Paper
for Printed Library Materials, ANSI/NISO Z39.48-1992.

Printed in the United States of America

A long period of calamity or decay must have checked the industry, and diminished the wealth, of the people; and their profuse luxury must have been the result of that indolent despair which enjoys the present hour and declines the thoughts of futurity.

—Edward Gibbon,
The Decline and Fall of the Roman Empire

There is no document of civilization that is not at the same time a document of barbarism.

—Walter Benjamin

Contents

Chronology of Medieval Chinese Dynasties and Eras

Eastern Han	25–220
Three Kingdoms	220–280
Western Jin	265–317
Sixteen Kingdoms	304–439
Eastern Jin	317–420
Northern and Southern Dynasties	420–589
Northern Wei	386–534
Western Wei	535–557
Eastern Wei	534–550
Northern Zhou	557–581
Northern Qi	550–577
Liu (Former) Song	420–479
Southern Qi	479–502
Liang	502–557
Chen	557–589
Sui	581–618
Tang	618–907

Introduction

The dramatic rise and fall of dynasties have long provided Chinese writers with plentiful material for crafting entertaining fiction. For the millions of women and men living at the time of cataclysmic events, however, these upheavals presented immense challenges. War and chaos altered the lives of myriad people, often in unexpected and terrible ways. The fall of the Eastern Han dynasty in the early third century, after a long stretch of national unity, marks the beginning of the period covered in this book. Dynastic collapse plunged China into tumult and division that lasted for centuries. Instability stands out as the hallmark of the age. Millions died or fled their homes, governments collapsed, important families fell into ruin, and ancient verities dissolved. Yet cataclysm also unleashed a remarkable surge in creativity, forcing people to reassess their lives and change the ways they thought, acted, worshipped, spoke, and wrote. In spite of the era's importance, confusion and fragmentation make it perhaps the most difficult period for historians of China to comprehend. Faced with a baffling succession of dynasties, kingdoms, pretenders, foreign invaders, and petty warlords, even specialists have trouble coming to grips with this muddle.[1]

The Han dynasty had given China four centuries of unity under a sophisticated administrative system. But no dynasty was ever permanent, and during the second century government fell into decay. Institutions gradually failed and the economy regressed. Imperial relatives and palace eunuchs, equally selfish and shortsighted, fought for control of a failing state, treating their foes with increasing cruelty. As administration sank into a mire of hopeless decadence, the wealthy and educated turned away from politics in disgust. In the year 220 the dynasty formally came to an end.

The Han dynasty had accustomed the populace to national unity, so everyone expected a talented general to quickly subdue his rivals and reunite the realm. The subsequent Jin dynasty initially intended to create a strong government capable of reuniting China and holding together the world's biggest polity. However, a series of untalented rulers sat atop the anemic Jin regime, which remained weak and divided. This ill-fated dynasty reached a nadir under Emperor Hui (r. 301–307). Foolish and probably mentally ill, he shocked courtiers with a stream of outrageous statements. The simpleton even suggested that his starving subjects should nourish themselves by eating meat porridge.[2] Incapable of making rational decisions, he plunged the state into complete disarray.

Foreign tribesmen to the north and west took note of the tottering dynasty's obvious weakness. Although Chinese mistakenly considered pastoral peoples perennially intent on invasion, in fact nomadic chieftains preferred a strong China that could afford to buy peace by showering them with lavish gifts.[3] Mired in internal feuds, the feeble Jin could not marshal sufficient resources to pacify the adjacent steppe. Unable to extort resources in the usual manner, warriors on horseback swept down from the north and invaded China. In 311 a coalition of nomadic warriors captured the capital, killed the crown prince and senior ministers, and massacred the populace. As they wasted both cities and countryside, throngs of terrified refugees streamed southward in search of safety. This immense exodus of people from the north included some of the most prominent families, hollowing out the traditional northern homeland of Chinese culture and elevating the south to new prominence. Forced to flee their northern homeland, Jin remnants reconstituted a rump state in the south. North China fell to the Tuoba (Tabgach) clan of Xianbei nomads, who founded the Northern Wei dynasty (386–534). The establishment of China's first conquest dynasty set an important precedent. In the centuries that followed, foreign conquerors ruled over at least part of China for about half of the nation's subsequent history.

This first experience of life under foreign rule humiliated and traumatized conquered Chinese. A sophisticated agricultural civilization had come under the domination of a much simpler pastoral society. Although life in the north regressed in some ways, the Tuoba managed to establish a stable government, putting an end to 150 years of chaos. Even so, they faced many challenges. Most importantly, they had to ameliorate the basic conditions of life in their impoverished and depopulated realm. In response, they experimented with new administrative practices. They also sought to revive the economy by restoring irrigation networks and distributing abandoned fields to able bodied adults—women as well as men. Although Wei institutions often differed from previous norms, in general they suited the new conditions.

As the Tuoba created a new type of society and government, administration in the north and south diverged. In the south, the Eastern Jin and its successor dynasties considered themselves the legitimate heirs of Chinese civilization, so they tended to follow Han dynasty precedents in their workings. Yet despite their claims of orthodoxy, the southern dynasties never fully restored order, and they faced periodic uprisings and banditry.[4] China remained divided between north and south until the Sui dynasty reunited the nation in the late sixth century.

The era of disunion in between the unified Han and Sui dynasties goes by various names. Chinese usually refer to it by a verbose appellation: Wei, Jin, North, and South Dynasties. Others emphasize only the most important regimes and call it the Six Dynasties. Scholars have long debated whether this era represents an extension of antiquity or the beginning of a new kind of society. The influential Japanese historian Naitō Konan (1866–1934) persuasively argued that this era constituted a fundamental rupture from the past and should be considered a medieval society.[5] He noted that after the fall of Han, the landed gentry ossified into a hereditary aristocracy, initiating a new social structure. Many historians now accept Naitō's interpretation and classify this era of disunion as China's early medieval era.

The official histories paint a grim picture of life in this age of chaos. Invaders and bandits slaughtered entire communities and enslaved the inhabitants of others. People fled their homes in panic, uncertain where to run. Some places teemed with starving refugees, while regions once known for their productive fields became desolate wastelands. In one border region of Jin, military service was so harsh and dangerous that when people bore a son they often did not even bother to raise him.[6]

Nevertheless, chaos stimulated rapid change, giving rise to fresh ideas and opportunities. Societies in a state of upheaval often move forward very quickly. The masterful French historian François Guizot (1787–1874) considered Europe's frequent episodes of war and disorder a useful engine of progress.[7] He contrasted Europe's energizing chaos with the supposed torpor of China and India. He believed that in those countries, stability had devolved into stultifying traditionalism. Indeed, during the Han era a stifling sense of cultural orthodoxy had long suppressed the imagination of the era's leading minds, so the dynasty's collapse unleashed pent-up creativity. Thinking people experimented with novel ideas and ideologies and used new literary genres to discuss unprecedented topics. The ferment and experimentation of the early medieval era transformed Chinese civilization in fundamental ways.

Extended division led the north and south to develop differently.[8] In the north, stronger regimes provided more stability, allowing the economy to recover somewhat. The breakdown of traditional order allowed the conquerors to fuse Chinese and steppe customs, creating a multicultural society. Over time, the Tuoba adopted a sedentary way of life and gradually embraced the culture of subjects. For example, in 496 the Wei emperor ordered the Xianbei to exchange their long surnames for shorter versions that sounded more Chinese.[9] Outside the capital, however, many Xianbei resisted this unpopular decree, and the government eventually rescinded it. The Xianbei dispute over surnames illustrates how sinicization raised emotionally charged issues. The extent to which each Xianbei clung to tradition or embraced Chinese alternatives varied considerably according to situation and temperament.[10] This mixing of cultures affected Chinese as well, and they adopted many steppe customs. But because the Xianbei found China's high culture completely alien, they disregarded it, and the intellectual and literary output of the north went into steep decline.

Most southern emperors displayed weakness and incompetence, casting a shadow of perpetual uncertainty over the region. Nevertheless, in some respects the south benefitted from what the Roman historian Livy dubbed the revenge of the losers.[11] Traditionally Chinese had dismissed the south as marginal and unimportant. Poetry depicted the entire region as recalcitrant, licentious, and semi-civilized.[12] Among northerners, these stereotypes persisted. One northern writer mocked the south as a malarial swamp full of insects and frogs. The tattooed inhabitants lacked proper ritual, music, or law. They spoke absurd languages. Their behavior was insolent and violent. In sum, he considered southerners little better than birds and beasts.[13]

Stung by accusations of cultural inferiority, the southern elite strove to preserve China's grand cultural tradition. Instead of conceiving of themselves in ethnic or political terms, they stressed a common Chinese culture as the foundation of their identity.[14] At first, northern refugees hated life in the south. They felt disconcerted and depressed by an unfamiliar landscape and strange customs. Some tried to make the best of their predicament. The poet Wang Can (177–217) sought inspiration in the exotic beauty of southern landscapes.[15] Even so, he never really felt at home and suffered from homesickness and insomnia. Yet, over time erudite northern families assimilated into southern life, enriching their new homeland by raising the level of culture to new heights.

The conquest of the north by rough warriors on horseback challenged how people perceived the relative worth of each region. Southerners questioned traditional assumptions of northern superiority. Instead of worshipping the north as the cradle of Chinese civilization, they began to regard it as an inhospitable foreign land, ransacked of its former glory and devoid of classical tradition. The outspoken social critic Ge Hong (283–343) considered southern culture superior as their customs aligned more closely with China's ancient traditions.[16] He resented the adoption of northern fashions and derided the north for decadence and savagery.

In both north and south, the elite had to adapt to changed circumstances.[17] In contrast with the social mobility of the Western Han dynasty, early medieval society calcified into a rigid hierarchy. Among the lower elite, some families rose or declined in importance. However, the greatest families of the early medieval era usually maintained high status for centuries. For example, the family of the noted author Yan Zhitui (531–591) remained prominent for twenty generations.[18] Even though these families lacked a title, they enjoyed hereditary privilege, and so historians consider them an aristocracy. By and large, the early medieval aristocracy did not derive their status from favors shown by the emperors. Instead the great families in each region claimed superiority based on long genealogies and repeated intermarriage with similarly exalted peers. These aristocrats condescended toward the common people, regarding them as little better than slaves.

The Japanese historian Michio Tanigawa (1925–2013) emphasized that the ascendancy of the early medieval aristocracy relied not just on birth and wealth but on high culture as well.[19] The elite flaunted their mastery of Confucian, Daoist, and Buddhist learning to cultivate an air of preeminence. Some families became renowned for their expertise in classical scholarship or arcane ancient ritual. Others preferred the imaginative speculations of Daoist metaphysics. And as learned monks translated an increasing number of Buddhist sutras from Sanskrit, some of the great families devoted themselves to Indian learning.

In this era, the uppermost elite became obsessed with reputation. Their good name became a key source of power. An aristocrat might even decline to serve in office if he felt it would compromise his social standing. So rather than relying solely on wealth or ideology, the aristocrats also employed psychological means to control society.[20] Due to their pedigree and cultural accomplishments, they demanded deference from social inferiors. In return, they protected and guided their communities. Although the elite ruthlessly exploited those beneath them, they also endeavored to hold together local society and foster harmony and stability.

Changes in the administrative system made it even more important for the elite to cultivate a distinctive culture.[21] During the late Eastern Han, when corrupt eunuchs dominated government, many gentry turned away from the sterile moral platitudes of political Confucianism in disgust. In place of ethics, they embraced "pure criticism" (*qingyi*) and used pithy phrases to sum up the character of prominent individuals. When judging other people, participants in this movement focused on memorable personal traits instead of adherence to Confucian morals. The Wei dynasty nine ranks (*jiupin*) system gave this discourse political significance. Under this arrangement, leading aristocrats judged candidates for office according to prevailing cultural standards. As high culture became linked to worldly success, an ambitious man had to embrace the values, taste, and behavior of his peers if he hoped to serve in office.

In spite of the importance of culture and education to the elite, this era stands out as a low point for Confucian learning. Classical scholarship declined markedly in both quantity and quality as the learned turned their attentions to alternative modes of thought. Nevertheless, the ancient learning still retained some prestige. Leading families continued to study the old canon because classical erudition, having become rare, distinguished them as unusually learned. The elite educated their children in the Confucian classics and referred to these ideas in their own writings. For example, discussions of family management applied Confucian ideals to practical matters of daily life.

Rulers also continued to encourage Confucian scholarship. During the Han dynasty, Confucianism became China's official political ideology. Close association with the state allowed this school of thought to flourish for centuries. However, by becoming intertwined with government, Confucianism declined in tandem with the dynasty that promoted it. Even so, medieval rulers recognized the usefulness of a body of thought that extolled loyalty to the state as a prime virtue.[22] One ruler declared that among the three major teachings, Confucianism stands first, Daoism second, and Buddhism third.[23] As the reputation of Confucianism went into general eclipse, political utility guaranteed its survival. Nevertheless, Confucianism declined compared to other doctrines. Warlords and aristocrats felt alienated from teachings that restricted their autonomy by emphasizing obedience to the emperor.[24] They often downplayed Confucianism out of self-interest. And many educated people criticized mindless devotion to old books and arcane rites. Creative minds rejected restrictive ethical rules and instead reveled in a new sense of intellectual and emotional possibility.

The Confucian scholarship produced during this era unintentionally attested to the decline of this school of thought. The writings of Huangfu Mi (215–282) exemplify the decay of traditional learning. Although his peers considered Huangfu an erudite classicist, later scholars derided him as a sloppy mediocrity. The renowned Tang commentator Yan Shigu (581–645) dismissed Huangfu's historical investigations as worthless.[25] And the Song dynasty writer Zhao Dingchen (b. 1068) pointed out Huangfu's flagrant errors and cursed him as a "rotten scholar" (*furu*).[26] Confucianism may not have died, but it had clearly degenerated.

Daoism replaced Confucianism in the affections of many educated people. However, medieval Daoism diverged from the ancient teachings of *Laozi* and *Zhuangzi*, presenting many new ideas. Scholars interpreting old texts interjected their own speculations about cosmology, giving rise to an abstruse form of metaphysics called Dark Learning (*xuanxue*) or Neo-Daoism. For many educated people, elaborate metaphysical theories served as a kind of escapism. Discussing intangible conjectures liberated them from restrictive Confucian ethics, and they exulted in the resulting intellectual and emotional freedom. Metaphysics also provided a safe refuge at a time when politics often brought frustration, failure, or even death.

The rise of Buddhism also sent thinkers in new directions. At first Chinese had little understanding of Buddhist doctrine, and the early version of the faith differed little from credulous wizardry. But as believers studied a stream of new translations from Sanskrit and Pali, they were shocked to discover foreign ideas as profound as their own. Not everyone welcomed this influx of foreign ideas and values. Some teachings clashed with mainstream ethics, prompting critics to deride this religion as alien, heterodox, and immoral. Yet in spite of this criticism, Buddhism spread rapidly and became extremely popular among all levels of society. Untainted by the failures of Confucianism, Buddhism promised solace and liberation. This influx of subcontinental ideas spurred deep contemplation and intellectual creativity.

Few medieval thinkers can be classified as purely Confucian, Daoist, or Buddhist, as they did not consider these teachings incompatible. Many books and essays blithely fused ideas from rival strains of thought.[27] An openness to synthesis allowed Confucianism to maintain a degree of influence. An educated man would often study the old books, observe some traditional virtues, and make a show of adhering to the rites. Yet he might also embrace Daoism, valuing its nonconformity. And he likely practiced some Buddhist ceremonies as well. Although these three ways of thought had distinctive and even contradictory content, each served a different purpose. Confucianism provided a cornucopia of classical erudition. Daoism empowered the individual. And Buddhism promised liberation from suffering. Useful in different ways, these three ways of thought coexisted and intermingled.

Literature also entered an exciting new phase. Some of the old styles of writing endured. Historians largely hewed to Han dynasty precedents in writing about female matters. The standard histories mention empresses, princesses, and exceptional women, and some works devote chapters to a particular female role.[28] Instead of portraying women as unique individuals, historians tended to position them within conventional historical or ethical frameworks, thereby reducing women to standardized archetypes. In other respects, however, literature changed dramatically. In the final decades of the Eastern Han, literary conventions underwent a dramatic shift. During the Jian'an reign period (196–220), war and pandemonium brought widespread suffering. However, this dislocation had an unexpectedly positive effect on aesthetics. As chaos battered traditional restraints, poets found the freedom to explore new and more realistic themes. In particular, they probed the inner life of the individual, making literature far more subjective and introspective.

This sudden shift in the style and focus of poetry led to a reconsideration of the basic role of literature. By the end of the sixth century, critics had elevated literary theory to a high level of refinement.[29] Previously, literature had largely served as a medium for expressing social and political norms. Writers won acclaim for eloquently expressing conformist views. In contrast, the new literature rejected blunt ideology. Writers began to see their art as an autonomous realm of discourse, to be appreciated in its own right as a purely aesthetic or individualistic pursuit. Divorcing literature from politics made writing more relevant to the concerns of this new age. When educated members of the aristocracy became disenchanted with politics, they often turned to literary creation and connoisseurship for consolation. The new writing frequently expressed novel ideas, including a keen attention to female matters.[30] Literary works portrayed women in inventive ways, offering insights into their lives and psychology.

During this era it became common to commemorate a deceased family member by engraving a stone tablet with a long epitaph. These documents provide detailed information about individual women not mentioned elsewhere.[31] A man named Lu Tui explained why so many families composed epitaphs for deceased women. When asked why he wrote an obituary for his mother but not his father, he explained, "Surely it must be because a man's virtue is displayed in his conduct of affairs, while a woman's excellence, unless it be the subject of an obituary, would never be made public."[32] Although epitaphs often provide details from a woman's life and describe it at length, these sources have some drawbacks.[33] Most commemorate members of the elite, so they do not necessarily represent the lives of ordinary women. Also, epitaphs employ highly formulaic language to portray the deceased in the best possible light, so they do not necessarily convey true feelings or actions. Yet in spite of these shortcomings, commemorative inscriptions reveal many important facts that would otherwise have remained unrecorded. For example, according to these documents, the average age of death for elite women varied from 43.33 to 52.88, as opposed to between 44.2 and 51.7 for men.[34] Many of these women died due to complications from pregnancy or childbirth.

A surge in writing about female concerns reveals new details absent from earlier records. Many texts emphasize the essential inequality of patriarchal society. Although restrictions had loosened, people still treated the sexes very differently, and some women found these petty inequities hard to endure. A poem gives voice to a woman lamenting her oppression.[35]

Pity me! my body is female,
My lowly state hard to describe.
. . .
A girl is born, there is no celebration,
She is not her family's prized jewel.
Grown up, she hides deep in her room,
Veils her head, too shy to look on others.
The tears she sheds at marrying into another town
Are sudden like a cloudburst of rain.

Numerous texts also detail the terrible suffering of women in an age of incessant violence. Authorities considered women the weaker sex and called for them to be treated more leniently than men. Legal codes included provisions for women to receive gentler treatment during detention, sentencing, and punishment.[36] Nevertheless, when order collapsed, marauding soldiers abused and slaughtered the populace at will. During one of these episodes, "warlords killed several thousand men and women."[37] Another time, soldiers reportedly captured one hundred thousand people and subjected them to horrific mistreatment. Only two or three thousand survived.[38] History and literature record numerous episodes of terrible suffering such as a woman captured by bandits who died in captivity or the northerner from a good family who fled south and became a concubine to survive.[39] Sometimes a pregnant woman had so little food that she feared she could not carry her baby to term.[40]

Yet in spite of injustices and dangers, rapid social change brought new opportunities. Generally speaking, the decline of Confucian propriety gave people of both sexes more leeway to pursue pleasure and enjoy life. Women could visit Buddhist temples, go fishing, climb mountains, and travel to scenic riversides. Excursions featured food and drink, music, and singing.[41] And due to changing mores, the sexes casually mingled far more than before.[42] They even openly expressed affection without embarrassment. Poetry expressed romantic sentiments that would have scandalized Han dynasty readers.

As China remained divided, female life in each region took on distinct characteristics. The north received considerable influence from the steppe.[43] Pastoral traditions allowed women considerable autonomy. Living in tents, they could not possibly remain hidden from the eyes of men. Nomadic women spent most of the day outside, performing domestic tasks, and even herding animals and hunting. They rode horses and practiced archery. And because steppe clans arranged marriages for political benefit, some women participated in tribal politics. Influence from steppe customs weakened some native Chinese practices, increasing the independence of northern women. Instead of remaining demurely hidden within the home and depending on their menfolk, they took it on themselves to deal with government officials, seek redress through lawsuits, and handle family matters.[44]

In contrast, the southern aristocracy continued to hold classical culture in high regard, so Confucianism and ritual retained more authority in that region. As a result, they still expected women to seclude themselves in the home and defer to male kin. Yet even in the south, constraints declined.[45] Most visibly, separation of the sexes became far less stringent than before. Some women exposed themselves to the public gaze, traveled to scenic spots, and mingled with men in social settings. When a visitor arrived at another man's home, he assumed that he would be introduced to his host's wife. And as education became more common among elite women, their horizons broadened. The most talented women traded quips and barbs with male counterparts in cultured salons. The field of medicine also minimized differences between the male and female. Physicians continued to assume that people of each sex had both yin and yang elements that need to be kept in harmony to ensure good health, so medicine still took a relatively androgynous view of the body. Only after the Tang dynasty would ideas about human biology become highly gendered.[46]

Early medieval society and culture underwent many other shifts as well, marking it as a period of rapid transition. This dynamic context conditioned many aspects of female life. The fall of Han brought rupture and uncertainty, and women sought ways to thrive amid changing circumstances. To appreciate how early medieval women lived, what they wanted, and how they understood themselves, the historian must determine how they fit into the intricate social mosaic of the complicated age of division.

1

Family

As the primary institution and social space, family circumstances conditioned the lives of both sexes. But because a bride typically left home to join her husband's household, marriage had a far greater impact on women than on men. Social upheavals during the period of disunion brought many changes to family life, forcing brides to face unprecedented situations. Chinese had traditionally defined family largely in terms of property. A group of people who collectively owned and worked a plot of land and lived off its produce constituted a family.[1] Because property passed down the male line, wives could seem like interlopers. In theory, when a woman first conducted ancestral rites in honor of her husband's forebears, she officially joined his family.[2] However, *Family Instructions for the Yan Clan (Yanshi jiaxun)* by Yan Zhitui (531–591) emphasizes the importance of blood as the basis of kinship. He warned that solidarity between father and sons unifies the family while the entrance of female outsiders through marriage divides it.[3]

Kinship became far more complex in this era. Centuries before, Qin dynasty regulations encouraged people to live in nuclear families, as the government found it easier to control small domestic units. Limited resources had also kept most families small, and households of about five members remained standard through the Western Han.[4] During the early medieval period, most people continued to live in small families consisting of three to five people. For the wealthy, however, family life changed significantly. During the Eastern Han, as political institutions frayed and society became increasingly chaotic, distant relatives banded together to safeguard their common interests. As a result, some families became larger and more complex.[5] Moralists encouraged this trend by praising large families as ideal.[6]

As kinship groups expanded and traditional customs frayed, some men practiced bigamy.[7] Officials sometimes found it politically expedient to have two or more wives, and even some monarchs had more than one empress. Sometimes a man ended up with more than one wife due to war and upheaval. Others simply enjoyed having more than one wife. Members of complex families sometimes got along well. An official named Li Chong (450–498) had six brothers born to four different mothers.[8] They owned the family property in common and continued to live together after their father died, having accepted their communal life and convoluted kinship ties.

Yet complicated family arrangements could also give rise to discord. The unfortunate case of Li Hongzhi (d. 484), a Wei official, reveals both the pragmatic mindset of the time and also the problems raised by complicated marital arrangements.[9] His first wife, surnamed Zhang, helped him manage his property, and over time the family became wealthy. After Li became successful, he took a second wife, named Liu Fang. Thereafter he maintained two separate households. However, his wives and children could not accept this arrangement. The wives ended up suing one another, and his children threatened violence against their half-siblings.

Aristocratic households sometimes expanded to enormous proportions, with more than a hundred people residing together in a gigantic compound.[10] These groupings might include distant relatives such as cousins and nephews as well as assorted concubines, dependents, and slaves. A high death rate, bigamy, and frequent divorce and remarriage could make family relations even more convoluted. A large family might include a step-mother, children whose mother had died, sons of multiple wives, and so on.[11] Even if everyone in a household got along fairly well, problems might still arise. In one representative case, a man had married two women in succession, resulting in a complex household. When he died, the children of each wife demanded that he be buried with their mother, sparking an awkward conflict over the funeral.[12]

Anthropologists conventionally argue that polygyny generally tends to degrade the position of wives within the family.[13] Large family size has also been associated with decreased female status. A study of one hundred nonindustrial societies found that wives in nuclear families generally enjoyed more power within the home than those in extended kinship groupings.[14] However, these blanket assertions cannot capture the nuances and compromises of real life. In early medieval China, large families were organized in different ways, and each woman dealt with her particular situation somewhat differently, resulting in a wide range of outcomes. Overall, women living in large households played key roles at home and people valued their contributions to a family's collective success.[15]

Due to war and pandemonium, many spouses became involuntarily separated.[16] Sometimes a man abandoned his wife and even his mother and children to flee from danger.[17] In such cases, a husband might end up in the south while his wife remained in the north. Also, the capture of enemy wives and mothers became a prime goal of warfare, resulting in numerous broken families.[18] In other cases, a man would leave his wife or children with a rival as hostages and fail to redeem them.[19] Whatever the cause of separation, if a man found himself parted from his wife, he usually took a new spouse. When peace was restored, a remarried man sometimes returned home to confront his first wife and deal with the consequences of bigamy.[20]

A man sometimes simply abandoned his wife. If she had children, she might suddenly find herself the head of a rump family. In such a situation, a woman did whatever was necessary to survive. One mother married off her daughter to an undesirable spouse in return for immediate aid.[21] Other women returned to their natal family to seek the support of blood kin.[22] As a result of involuntarily separation, some spouses eventually ended up buried in different places, a situation that elicited concern.[23]

Many families practiced cross-cousin marriage. During the Han dynasty, people had sometimes married their cousins. These unions usually took place among kin who did not have reciprocal mourning obligations, so according to ritual regulations their marriage did not constitute incest. Early medieval aristocrats sometimes married a cousin as a way of wedding someone of similar background, an important goal in a severely hierarchical society. But not everyone looked upon cross-cousin marriage favorably. Northern governments repeatedly banned the practice. This prohibition may have been intended to prevent the native Chinese elite from using cross-cousin unions as an excuse to avoid marrying with the imperial line and steppe nobility.[24]

As north and south remained divided for centuries, kinship organization in each region evolved in reaction to their distinct economic, political, and social conditions, resulting in very different practices.[25] Many nomadic customs differed dramatically from Chinese traditions, spurring innovations in the north.[26] People of the same surname could marry in contravention of the rites.[27] And children sometimes chose their own spouses.[28] Some differences were extremely stark. Traditionally, a Tuoba groom could take a bride by capturing her from her family. Kidnapping a bride or conducting a sham fight between the families of bride and groom represented a kind of de facto marriage ceremony on the steppe.[29] Some Tuoba seized women as brides during the Northern Wei, much to the dismay of ethnic Chinese.

More frequently, Xianbei held a formal wedding marked by the presentation of a betrothal gift from the groom's family to that of the bride. However, this custom could cause problems. In a poor pastoral society, many men did not have enough property to pay for a wife. So instead of presenting wealth to his fiancée's family, a prospective groom could perform bride service instead, temporarily working for his bride's clan to procure her in exchange for his toil. The Tuoba considered bride service a way to test a man's spirit as well as fair compensation to the bride's family for the loss of her labor.[30]

Steppe peoples also traditionally practiced levirate.[31] When a man died, a brother or another blood relative might marry his widow to keep her with the family. Having paid for her through brideprice or bride service, the family did not want to lose a useful worker. Although northern governments periodically attempted to stamp out levirate because it contravened Chinese norms, the practice nevertheless endured.[32]

The declining influence of Confucian propriety further affected marriage customs. During the Eastern Han, the most important families followed the ritual canon to gain prestige and maintain domestic harmony.[33] Ancient ritual set down very clear marriage regulations. Even after the fall of Han, these rules retained an air of orthodoxy. Imperial edicts repeat Confucian platitudes about marriage, calling it the "beginning of way of humanity" and a way to inculcate righteousness in both spouses.[34] Nevertheless, the influence of the ancient marriage rites declined during the era of disunion. Some weddings became extremely crude, with the guests asking the bride lewd questions and expecting her to entertain them with bawdy replies.[35]

No ritual code survives from the early medieval era. The influence of the rites over marriage seems to have varied considerably by region and class.[36] Some places continued to uphold aspects of the ritual canon and Han dynasty customs. Aristocrats and southerners more often upheld ancient traditions. In contrast, foreign customs had considerable influence on the north. Many northerners embraced steppe customs regarding family and marriage, and even the weddings of ethnic Han featured horses and tents.[37]

Generally speaking, as the rites waned, skepticism toward traditional values increased, giving spouses more room for self-expression. Some young people even questioned the perennial custom of arranged marriage and demanded to choose their own spouse. Usually the groom took the initiative, but some women could be extremely assertive.[38] After the wedding, spouses interacted far more freely than before. Wives used informal pronouns to address their husbands, fostering a new sense of intimacy.[39] Couples expressed strong feelings to one another and spoke candidly.[40] Sometimes a wife might even criticize or tease her husband.[41]

When people ignored the rites, no clear rules guided married life, making conjugal relationships more flexible and ambiguous. As spouses drew closer, they were also far more likely to fall into discord.[42]

Han dynasty authorities considered family matters the purview of ritual. But during the Six Dynasties, the state became far more active in regulating the domestic realm. Authorities upheld many traditional precedents.[43] As before, judges enforced gender hierarchy, emphasized filial piety, and demanded that wives be distinguished from concubines. Officials continued to consult the ancient classic *Springs and Autumns* (*Chunqiu*) when deciding domestic disputes, so Confucianism still shaped jurisprudence. Nevertheless, Confucianization of the law remained piecemeal.[44] As before, a woman who injured her husband would be punished more severely than if she had hurt an unrelated man, in line with basic Confucian values.[45] However, ancient ethical works often offered no guidance on matters of contemporary concern. As jurists addressed new social conditions, they adjusted the law accordingly, prohibiting child marriage and legalizing cross-cousin unions.[46] In an effort to strengthen the family and ensure marital harmony, the law also dealt with domestic violence in detail.[47]

The elite married their peers to confirm their privileged status. During the Eastern Han, the gentry arranged marriages with other prominent families to augment their power. Many of the most important warlords of the late Eastern Han emerged from families that had used marriage relations to build up a confederation of allies.[48] During the succeeding Three Kingdoms era, with society in flux, the elite did not value pedigree as much as before. Instead they sought talented in-laws who were most likely to succeed amid turbulence.[49] With the advent of the Western Jin, official service once again became a prime measure of social standing. The composition of the elite solidified and status became largely hereditary. This resulting aristocracy largely intermarried with one another to maintain their unique status and exclude outsiders.[50] Families allied by marriage often became extremely close and acted in concert to increase their collective power.[51]

Clans also played a major role in early medieval society. Although clans had been important in antiquity, large kinship groupings fragmented into small families during the Eastern Zhou. Amid the deteriorating conditions of the Eastern Han, clans reemerged to dominate local society.[52] In a time of unrest, people had little trust in strangers and found it safer to cooperate with extended relatives. Clan members presumably shared a common ancestor. At the very least, they had the same surname.[53] As people with the same surname often lived in proximity, they could easily organize a clan. Pooling resources and taking joint action allowed large groups of kin to pursue their collective interests, meet challenges, and aid

Figure 1.1.   Woman in a loose-fitting garment.

members in need.[54] In some areas, clans became so powerful that the state could not control them and they became the de facto local government.[55] The rising importance of clans shifted the marriage calculus. A wedding did not just link two families. It could also serve as a bridge between two powerful clans.

Aristocrats could publicly demonstrate their prestige by marrying well.[56] For parvenus, marriage with a major family signaled their acceptance into the upper elite.[57] Because marriage confirmed status, the elite practiced class endogamy. Members of the greatest families married one another generation after generation.[58] This strategy paid off. Families that carefully selected spouses with high backgrounds could maintain their high standing for centuries.[59] Some repeatedly wed close relatives to create an ironclad bond among a small but highly prestigious kin group.[60] Others took the opposite approach, casting their nets wide and allying with the elites of various places.[61]

Because officials usually came from high backgrounds, aristocratic marriage carried political consequences, and so the government regulated certain aspects of these unions.[62] Most importantly, the state prohibited marriage between aristocrats and people of low status, as mésalliance would challenge the status quo and degrade the office-holding class.[63] In fact, these rules were unnecessary as the elite usually sought to marry those of similar background to maintain their reputation. High-ranking families in the north and south sought different qualities in a marriage partner. Southern aristocrats wanted a spouse whose family had comparable wealth and genealogy. Leading southern families sometimes even hesitated to marry their daughters to the emperors of dynasties founded by usurping generals, regarding them as lowly upstarts.[64] In contrast, northerners put more value on the relative power wielded by each side.[65]

Although the great families held themselves aloof and usually wed within a small circle, different groups inevitably mixed. Southern aristocrats sometimes married commoner nouveaux riches, uniting money with prestige.[66] In an age of endless warfare, southern gentry might condescend to take a spouse from a military family in return for protection.[67] And in the north, some nomadic families became highly sinicized. They intermarried with the Chinese elite, educated their sons in the classics, and served in the bureaucracy.[68] For example, the Lu family entered China as invading warriors together with the Tuoba.[69] They soon abandoned militarism, embraced Chinese culture, and began to produce educated offspring competent to serve in the bureaucracy. Instead of taking spouses from the military elite, they preferred to marry with Chinese or acculturated steppe families. The women who passed between pastoral and ethnic Han families played a major role in cultural exchange, transmitting ideas, values, and customs between ethnic groups.

War and upheaval had depopulated many areas, decreasing the number of farmers and soldiers. To remedy this situation, rulers encouraged people to marry and bear children.[70] If a young person had not wed by the usual age, a local official might step in to expedite a union.[71] However, most people did not need much encouragement to get married, as establishing a family brought economic benefits and allowed spouses to assume respected social roles. Because of the importance of marriage to social identity, families even conducted posthumous weddings for children who had died before marrying.[72]

Couples tended to marry relatively young. Young men underwent the capping ceremony (*guan*) marking the onset of adulthood at age fifteen, earlier than most eras, allowing them to marry sooner.[73] According to epitaphs from the north, brides usually married between the ages of eleven and eighteen.[74] A poem sums up the ideal schedule:[75]

> Nevergrieve at thirteen could weave fine silk,
> At fourteen picked mulberry at the top of south lane,
> At fifteen she married, became a wife in the Lu family.
> At sixteen she gave birth to a boy named A-hou.

In one sample of forty-two marriages, the average woman's age at the time of marriage was 16.7 years. Other studies confirm that early marriage was common, although some women remained unmarried at age twenty.[76] The average husband was about nine years older than his wife.[77]

Some girls married before age fourteen. A bride was unlikely to wed before her pinning (*ji*) ceremony, which marked official entry into adulthood.[78] And the law theoretically prohibited child marriage.[79] Even so, some people still married very young. Because the marriages of imperial relatives had political significance, their union was often arranged early for maximum benefit, and they sometimes wed while still children. Folksongs also mention early marriage, suggesting that ordinary people sometimes married young as well.[80]

The bride's family eagerly awaited the betrothal gift, so they wanted to marry off their daughters as soon as possible. Families often finalized engagements while the fiancés were still children or even before their birth.[81] Moreover, steppe peoples traditionally married young, and their customs influenced China. In such a violent age marked by uncertainty, it seemed prudent to marry and bear children while young.[82] However, not everyone welcomed early marriage. The parents of one ambitious young man arranged for him to marry when he was seventeen. He did not yet want to be tied down with a wife and children because he feared that this burden would ruin his prospects, so on the wedding day he fled.[83]

Prior to the Song dynasty, bridewealth usually outweighed dowry in value. In this era, betrothal gifts tended toward generosity, particularly if the groom came from a lower background than the bride.[84] The Xianbei traditionally expected considerable bridewealth, and this outlook affected Chinese marriage customs. Betrothal gifts became increasingly expensive, leading to hardship among the families of grooms.[85] Governments made periodic efforts to limit the costs of weddings, but these measures failed.[86] Officials also tried to prevent marriages across class lines, as wealthy parvenus offered huge betrothal gifts to attract aristocratic brides. To address this problem, the government compiled official genealogies of aristocratic families, classifying them according to rank and setting limits on betrothal gifts for people on each rung of the hierarchy.[87] However, these efforts had little impact and weddings remained extremely expensive. Some families even had to take out loans so that their sons could marry an appropriate partner.

Although the aristocracy preferred to marry within a tight circle of similarly exalted families, high bridewealth gave affluent arrivistes an opportunity to obtain a daughter-in-law from higher up on the social scale, resulting in some social mixing and mobility.[88] When a great family needed an influx of wealth to restore their fortunes, they could marry beneath them in return for a huge betrothal gift, thereby maintaining the family's position for one more generation.[89] However, this sort of mésalliance could be awkward, as a woman from a higher-ranking family was more likely to be assertive or jealous.

Partly in reaction to this practice, writers increasingly emphasized the importance of a daughter-in-law's obedience to her husband's parents in the name of filial piety, shifting the domestic dynamics of power. Over the centuries, the rubric of filial piety had steadily expanded. This concept initially developed out of ancestor worship, as people accustomed to revering deceased forebears began to show similar respect to living elders.[90] At first filial piety regulated relations between fathers and sons, but people soon extended it to include both parents.[91] Beginning in the Eastern Han, women became integrated into filial discourse. The focus remained on men, but people increasingly expected women to carry out similar expressions of devotion. Many characters in tales of female filiality lack brothers, implying that they took on stereotypically male ethical obligations out of necessity.[92] However, unlike men, the scope of a woman's filial piety went beyond her own parents to encompass her husband's parents as well.[93] Although this value system might seem to degrade women's position in the family, it also brought benefits, stabilizing the family and allowing the wife to integrate with her husband's kin more smoothly.

Filial virtue provided women with new opportunities. By serving and obeying her parents and parents-in-law, a woman could prove herself virtuous and thereby gain respect. Narratives about model women often mention solicitude toward a parent-in-law to attest to their goodness. In particular, writers frequently depicted the ideal woman diligently attending to her husband's mother.[94] The poor reputation of mothers-in-law made this attentiveness seem even more outstanding. Popular stories describe a wicked mother-in-law abusing her son's wife in appalling ways.[95] Considering the demonization of mothers-in-law, any woman who willingly submitted to her husband's mother seemed a paragon of virtue.

Ancient Chinese writings had little to say about filial women or the good daughter-in-law, so people turned to Buddhist texts for inspiration. This era witnessed a huge output of Buddhist texts, comprising translations, forgeries, and original works. It became common to look to this huge body of wisdom for guidance on pressing social issues, so Buddhists provided advice on the issue of female filial piety. The *Scripture on Young Woman Yuye (Yuye nüjing)* set out the proper behavior of a daughter-in-law in an aristocratic family.[96] This short text was originally written in Pali and five translations appeared in Chinese. None of the Chinese versions came from major translators, marking it as a popular text rather than part of the central canon. This scripture demands that a daughter-in-law exhibit filiality and loyalty toward her husband's family even if this required her to sacrifice her own interests. Because the Chinese translations employ

Confucian terminology, they turn an ostensibly Buddhist scripture into a treatise on Confucian ethics. This popular devotional work seems to have had an impact on ethical views. Due to the popularity of Buddhism, even if a woman knew little about the Chinese classics, she could still absorb Confucian-style teachings about filial piety while studying her religion.

The extension of filial piety to include parents-in-law brought a woman closer to her husband's kin. Nevertheless, since antiquity a woman's primary loyalty had rested with her natal family and she retained a strong bond with blood relatives after her wedding.[97] Parents could even exert authority over a married woman.[98] Given these dual ties, a wife's position in the kinship network rested somewhere between her birth family and marital relations.[99] A revealing vignette sums up the prevailing mindset. When one woman's blood relatives were about to be exterminated, she decided to die with them, pronouncing that if her family were wiped out, "How could I live?"[100] A woman might even prioritize the interests of blood family over those of her husband. When one man accused his wife's father of plotting rebellion, she grabbed a knife and threatened to kill him.[101]

In some respects, the law treated a woman as a member of her husband's family.[102] However, the state also considered a married woman part of her natal family. Regulations regarding group punishment exhibit this conflicted identity. Since ancient times, officials had punished a group of affiliated people for the crimes of a single individual as a way to deter misdeeds. Entire families or even neighborhoods could suffer for the crimes of one member. As a result of this practice, a wife could be enslaved or exiled if her husband committed a crime.[103] And popular opinion also considered a woman an extension of her husband, so sometimes a man would kill a man's wife to exact vengeance upon him.[104] However, a married woman might also be held responsible for offenses committed by her blood relatives, putting her in double jeopardy. One woman was threatened with death after her brother rebelled.[105] Another was sent into exile near the border with Korea after her father's execution.[106]

Because married women retained membership in their natal family, they sometimes visited their parents.[107] And while some widows continued to reside with their in-laws, it seems that most moved back to their own family.[108] When chaotic conditions separated a woman from her husband, she frequently returned home to live with her own kin, bringing along her children. When detested conquerors forced a man to serve their regime as an official, he might send his wife and children to live with her family for safety. Sometimes he would then take a second wife and start a new family. Deliberately dividing families seems to have been a pragmatic strategy to ensure the survival of at least some kin during this violent and uncertain age.[109]

Men did not discourage their wives from remaining close to their blood relatives.[110] On the contrary, they saw in-laws as potentially useful allies and actively cultivated close relationships with them. Families allied by marriage often cooperated for mutual well-being.[111] When one side prospered, the other often benefited.[112] Many children also had strong relationships with maternal kin. Some people sometimes considered their maternal relatives almost as important as those of their father's line and made little distinction between maternal and paternal grandparents.[113] Many men also had extremely close ties with their maternal uncles.[114]

Even as wives remained close to the family of their birth, the relationship between spouses became more intimate than before, bringing about a major shift in the nature of Chinese marriage. Of course, not every couple got along well. Violent husbands abused their wives and temperamental women terrorized their husbands.[115] But overall, the marital bond strengthened. People increasingly thought of husband and wife as two parts of a single unit. As before, a man's rank determined that of his wife.[116] However, the conventions for naming women changed. Instead of referring to a married woman by her natal surname, people increasingly referred to her as the "wife of" her husband. The chapter on model women in *Records of the Latter Han (Hou Hanshu)* identifies 70 percent of them by both natal surname and given name. But *Records of Wei (Weishu)* names only 12 percent of female paragons this way, identifying the remainder as the wife of a certain man.[117]

Just as the wife became more closely linked to her husband, a man's identity also increasingly encompassed his wife. Beginning in the third century, men's epitaphs provided increasing amounts of information about their wives. These inscriptions often mentioned a woman's natal surname and her age at the time of her husband's death.[118] One man felt so close to his wife that before he committed suicide he poisoned her so that they could depart the world together.[119] He assumed that he and his wife ought to share the same fate.

During the Han dynasty, when the ritual canon regulated marital relations, couples strove to maintain an air of formal decorum. As the rites declined in influence, husbands and wives began to interact more casually and marital relationships became increasingly egalitarian.[120] When one husband rebuked his wife for disrespectfully addressing him with an informal pronoun, she disarmingly replied that she spoke to him so casually because she loved him.[121] Another man who had to leave home on official business did not want to leave his wife, and the couple exchanged despondent poems and letters while apart.[122] While poetry about a widow's longing for a dead husband had circulated for centuries, men now began to express the pain they felt on losing a beloved wife. When convention

forced a man to end his official mourning after one year, he wrote a poem
to express his continuing despondency:[123]

> By ritual rule, as I am taught,
> I state the end of mourning at your tomb,
> But at the altar suffer pain,
> As if my inmost heart were drawn.

Marital relations had clearly undergone a major shift. Candid emotions
increasingly replaced ritual artifice in regulating conjugal relations.

Burial customs symbolize the close link between spouses. People believed that a couple should remain together even after death.[124] Placing
them in the same tomb ensured their eternal inseparability. As during the
Han, joint spousal burials remained most common.[125] Aristocratic couples
shared a square or rectangular tomb with one or two chambers.[126] Spouses
rarely died at the same time, so mourners usually had to open the joint
tomb to insert the second body.[127] In one case, husband and wife died
thirty-six years apart, and the tomb had to be reopened after this lengthy
interval. Not all women were buried with a husband. Certain women
had an individual tomb, including second wives, concubines, nursemaids, unmarried women, those who predeceased their husband, some
empresses and princesses, and women who had been separated from
their husbands.[128] Nuns were usually cremated and their ashes placed in
a stupa or temple.

Love emerged as a major theme of married life. In embracing romance,
Six Dynasties poetry departed from the impersonal decorum of Han dynasty literature. Poets looked beyond Han propriety to seek inspiration
in the ancient *Classic of Poetry (Shijing)*, which includes numerous poems
about love and thwarted desire. More than 90 percent of surviving folksongs from the Southern Dynasties describe love. The influential anthology *New Songs from a Jade Terrace (Yutai xinyong)* also took romance as the
primary theme.[129] Although men wrote the poems in this collection, they
often took on a female literary persona and described matters from the
perspective of an imaginary woman. The editor notes in the introduction
that he compiled it specifically for women, showing that he considered
romantic poetry suitable for female eyes.[130]

These love poems do not describe ordinary women. Instead they focus
on a beautiful high-born lady ensconced amid otherworldly luxury. Love
is the center of her life, and she longs for an absent man. "My love is close
to you / As shadow follows form."[131] Propriety ruled out descriptions of
sexual acts, so poets employed elaborate symbolism and allusion to create
an erotically charged atmosphere.[132] Silk evokes sensuality, lotus stands in
for female genitalia, and the elegant boudoir exudes sexuality.

In the earliest poems, the protagonist personifies ideal femininity. Yet in spite of apparent perfection, her lover's absence makes her miserable. Later poems evoke the dramatic pining lover of the ancient *Songs of Chu (Chu ci)*, portraying the lovelorn woman as a pathetic victim of uncontrolled passions.[133] She is so distraught that she cannot even groom herself properly. A ravishing beauty has degenerated into a sickly wretch with tangled hair and smeared makeup. Her opulent bedroom has become a dusty mess. This melancholy woman spends her meaningless days yearning for an absent lover who never appears.[134]

> I'll always love you
> However long we're parted.
> My love's distance is like a drought.
> Alone, standing still,
> My heart taut inside me,
> I stare at clouds gone, gone far away,
> Stare at birds flown, flown into nothingness.
> Useless staring always ends like this:
> Pearl tears that won't be wiped dry.

Effusive Liang dynasty love poetry gave women permission to vent their passions. But at the same time, it promoted a conservative view of female identity, embracing the traditional belief that only a man can make a woman feel whole.

Unmarried people sometimes fell in love, and folksongs describe marriage as the culmination of premarital attraction.[135] But romance did not necessarily evaporate after the wedding day. Unlike the romantic literature of some cultures, such as tales of courtly love from the European Middle Ages, Chinese accepted that spouses could also feel strong affection for one another. The happy marriage had a foundation of mutual love. The woman in one poem frames her marriage in romantic terms:[136]

> When I first married you,
> Melon tendrils were locked in close embrace.
> I leaned my poor frame against you,
> As if clinging to Mount Tai.

Nor were loving sentiments limited to women. A husband could also feel strong love for his wife:[137]

> Great love wed us in the past,
> Vows of fidelity bound us to the Three Gods.
> I keep my heart metal and rock firm—
> How could I be ruined by common fashion?
> Lovely eyes pass by, but I don't look,

Slender waists are nubile in vain.
What shall I use to pledge my deep affection?
I look up and point at that pole-star!

Literature even projected conjugal love onto the supernatural. The popularity of stories about strange events made anomaly tales a major literary genre. Many of these stories describe a handsome young man encountering an amorous female ghost. Critics contend that these tales act out male sexual fantasies. Reading these stories allowed men to daydream about loving a woman without the restraints of social convention.[138] Sometimes a mortal man wed a female ghost, projecting this romantic fantasy onto marriage. This literature depicts extramarital romance as fleeting and frustrating, thereby casting marriage as an arrangement that allows romance to endure.[139] However, marriages between human and ghost could be awkward. Most pressingly, the mixed couple faced the question of where they ought to live. Sometimes the man inhabited the ghostly realm with his beloved wraith, while in other stories they lived in the mundane world.[140]

In antiquity, China lacked true divorce. Because women could not own land, a wife usually did not dare leave her husband, however difficult her circumstances, as she would find it difficult to survive on her own. A man who felt unsatisfied with his marriage did not have to undertake any formal procedures. He simply absconded or cast his wife out of the house.[141] But as state institutions became increasingly complex, the government began to regulate divorce. Initially administrators wanted to keep household registers up to date for tax purposes. Over time, however, officials regulated divorce to ensure a just dissolution of the marriage and foster social stability. After the fall of the Han, when women became more independent and confident, divorce seems to have become more common.[142] Most information about divorce from this period concerns the elite. Ordinary couples were probably much more likely to stay together out of economic necessity.[143]

As in antiquity, medieval writings describe divorce from the male perspective as *qi* (casting off).[144] If a man fell in love with a concubine and divorced his wife, in contravention of ritual norms, the state apparatus might intervene.[145] Otherwise, he could usually divorce his wife freely without government interference. And under most circumstances, a woman could leave her husband. However, a woman married to a soldier might be denied the right to divorce. Life in military households on the borders could be harsh, and soldiers there found it difficult to find a spouse. Governments punished soldiers' wives who absconded to help maintain stable garrisons in strategic areas.[146]

Couples separated for a various reasons. Straightforward incompatibility could precipitate divorce. A man also sometimes divorced his wife because he had fallen in love with someone else.[147] In an era that idealized romance, men did not necessarily feel obligated to remain with an unloved wife. And sometimes couples had different ideas about their relationship, giving rise to friction. In particular, princesses tended to believe that a husband should treat them with deference, while their husbands asserted patriarchal privilege. Sometimes a princess divorced a husband who failed to live up to her expectations and returned to the palace. For example, one woman left her husband because people ridiculed him for his foolishness.[148]

The unstable conditions of this period also precipitated separations. Sometimes a man simply abandoned his wife and fled to safety alone.[149] Couples also divorced due to political expediency.[150] An up-and-coming official might renounce his wife so that he could promote his career by marrying a princess.[151] Women related to a defeated general could also find themselves suddenly divorced, as ambitious men suddenly cast off their wives to seek a marriage alliance with the newly ascendant power.[152] Shifting coalitions among leading families also precipitated divorces. When two officials found themselves aligned with opposing factions, they would divorce one another's women.[153]

Poetry provides insights into how people regarded divorcees.[154] Although men wrote these poems, they speak from a female point of view. They wrote in a time-tested style. Many ancient poems describe the plight of abandoned women, portraying them as angry and regretful. Six Dynasties poets emulated this tone. Society put a high value on loyalty, so some poems describe the divorced woman as remaining faithful to the man who had cast her away, making her a martyr to virtue worthy of empathy and respect. The divorced woman who did not remarry could supposedly survive by weaving cloth for sale, but such a life would surely have been very difficult.[155]

Literary depictions of divorced women explore a spectrum of conflicted emotions. Some female characters wax philosophical on the inconstancy of fate: "Natural law has its shifts and turns, / Moral law lacks saving constancy."[156] Inevitable or not, an abandoned woman considered herself a shameful failure: "I do not pity my poor rejected body, / But fear the blueflies' gossip."[157] If a marriage had produced a child, the divorcee considered it an important consolation. But if she had not borne offspring, she looked back on the failed union as completely fruitless:[158]

> The childless wife must be sent home.
> With child she is the moon that sails the skies,
> Childless she's like a falling star.

At least she could take comfort from the wisdom that she had gained from confronting hardship: "Who says a divorced woman is pathetic? / A divorced woman's feelings grow more mature."[159]

Concubines also had an extremely uncertain place in society. In antiquity, the rites limited a man to one wife, and monogamy remained the standard rule thereafter. Even so, a man with sufficient means would often keep several women in his household, giving rise to concubinage. These women were called *qie* or *jiqie*. *Ji* referred to a female performer, so the compound *jiqie* acknowledged that some concubines served the wealthy as in-house entertainers.[160] The state paid little attention to concubines except to distinguish them from wives and prohibit a man from promoting a concubine to the status of wife, measures intended to prevent domestic discord.[161] Custom regulated the relationship between concubine and master. Marriage began with a proper wedding that included a betrothal gift.[162] Otherwise, a woman entered the house as a concubine. Steppe peoples had traditionally lacked concubinage, so northerners were less interested in differentiating between wife and concubine.[163] If both women came from respectable backgrounds, northerners might not distinguish between them.[164]

A man could take a concubine in various ways. Some of these women took part in a simplified wedding ceremony, giving them a status lower than a true wife yet higher than most concubines.[165] Others were captives handed out as booty of war.[166] In one case, a warlord killed a man and then gave his daughter to a childless supporter to bear him a son.[167] Most concubines were purchased, making them little different from slaves. Concubines did not necessarily remain with one master for life. They could be sold or exchanged between men, so these women had little control over their own fate.[168] Men took a concubine for various reasons. Some just wanted a sexual plaything.[169] Others sought trained singers, musicians, or dancers to serve as household entertainers. Some men brought in a concubine to bear children.[170] And a widower who did not want to remarry might take a concubine to oversee domestic duties in the household.[171]

During the Han dynasty, even the wealthiest men usually kept only a few concubines. In contrast, some medieval aristocrats assembled huge harems with hundreds of women. The growing number of unattached women provided a huge pool of potential concubines.[172] Chaos had forced numerous women to flee their homes. A woman uprooted from her community, with menfolk dead or missing, might become a concubine or servant to survive. Also, while military victors often executed surrendered men, they enslaved captured women or handed them out to supporters, further increasing the number of concubines.

In this impoverished age, keeping numerous concubines became a status symbol. Particularly in the south, elite men assembled large harems to flaunt their wealth and status.[173] Southern aristocrats sometimes maintained hundreds of female performers and attractive female attendants. Even wealthy eunuchs took multiple concubines to attest to high rank.[174] An author describes how a Jin dynasty official used his harem to intensify the opulent atmosphere in his mansion. "His concubines numbered in the hundreds, and they all were draped in silks and embroideries and had ear ornaments made of gold and kingfisher plumes."[175]

Because the number of concubines in a man's home symbolized his status, sumptuary measures sought to tie the number of concubines to a man's social station. In the north, regulations specified the number of concubines permitted for officials of each rank.[176] But ambitious aristocrats did not hesitate to flout these rules. Of course, wives resented having so many beautiful young rivals in their home, so the rise in concubinage fueled jealousy and domestic discord.[177] Multiple concubines also challenged male endurance. One sickly man drove dozens of his slave women and concubines out onto the street after he realized that sexual dissipation had ruined his health.[178]

The lives of these women varied considerably. Some masters maintained their concubines in comfortable circumstances, either to show off their own wealth or out of affection or respect. Wealthy men sometimes took a woman from a good background as a concubine. Serving as a concubine in a luxurious mansion might seem preferable to being the wife of someone with a much lower standard of living. In one such case, a woman raised by a princess in luxurious surroundings became the concubine of a wealthy man. It was expected that a man would treat this sort of concubine well.[179] In another case, a woman from a good family consented to become the concubine of a powerful warlord to gain benefits for her family.[180] Everyone involved in this arrangement seems to have assumed that this relationship would be courteous. Moreover, some concubines displayed intelligence and virtue, earning them respect and good treatment.[181] A woman who bore a son or captured her master's affections could also raise her position in the household.[182]

Some men valued their concubines and treated them with affection and loyalty. Men fleeing danger sometimes abandoned a wife so that they could escape more quickly. But others brought along not just their wife but concubines as well.[183] When a man loved his concubine, he would try to shield her from his wife's jealousy.[184] Sometimes an indulgent official even allowed a favored concubine to interfere in affairs of state or solicit bribes.[185] If a man had a close bond with a concubine, when she died he might honor her with an elaborate burial and carefully composed epitaph.[186] And a favored concubine might reciprocate good treatment with

loyalty. When one warlord suffered defeat, his favorite concubine committed suicide.[187]

Although some men treated their concubines well, this seems to have
been exceptional. Masters usually treated these women as chattel, to be
used and disposed of according to whim. Concubines differed little from
slaves and were bought, sold, traded, and given away.[188] When a man
died, his heirs inherited his concubines. If none of his progeny wanted
these women, they would be sold off.[189] Not surprisingly, concubines usually held a lowly place in the household.[190]

Customs regarding concubinage varied according to region. Northern
concubines had a lower status than those in the south. And society looked
upon the sons of concubines very differently in these two places. Under
the southern dynasties, although the sons of wives took precedence over
men born to concubines, these two groups nevertheless had similar status
and opportunities.[191] For example, the mother of Ruan Fu (278–326), a
distinguished official, was a slave from the western regions.[192] In contrast,
northerners considered it disgraceful to have been born to a concubine,
and the sons of these women suffered insults and humiliation.[193] Sons of
concubines who had previously been slaves or entertainers held a particularly lowly status.[194] Because the sons of concubines had such a debased
status in the north, men there did not like to use these women to bear
them an heir. They much preferred to have children by a wife. If a northern widower lacked sons, he would often remarry. Some men remarried
several times just to avoid having sons born to a concubine. Due to serial
remarriage, a new wife might be younger than her step-sons, fueling ten-
sions within the family.

Even in the south, a mother's standing in the household affected her
children's status. If a concubine had a close relationship with her master,
her children would probably receive better treatment. Likewise, the position of a concubine's son influenced her status. If the son of a concubine
distinguished himself in government service, he brought honor to his
mother and raised her social standing.[195] The diversity of concubinage
highlights the complicated, changing, and often conflicted web of relationships within the household. As the conditions of medieval society
evolved, people had to creatively adapt to maintain a stable and successful family.

2

Mothers

During the Six Dynasties, the bond between mother and child intensified, making motherhood an even more important aspect of female identity than before. The shift stemmed in part from nomadic influences, as mothers had a particularly strong presence in steppe families. Chinese embraced this foreign value system, thereby giving mothers more influence over their sons.[1] Art and literature increasingly featured mothers and celebrated their importance.[2] The language used in epitaphs also documents the rising cult of motherhood. And mourners routinely lauded a deceased woman as a paragon of maternal virtue (*mude*) who observed the rites of motherhood (*muyi*).[3]

The bond between mother and child did not depend on her status as the father's wife. They had a separate relationship with one another, so even after a couple divorced, a mother maintained a tie with her children.[4] Writers also reaffirmed the classical maxim that a widow's social rank followed that of her son. This assumption had become standard during the Eastern Zhou and remained in force during the Han, so medieval authorities accepted it as an established principle.[5] Even if a man had been born to a concubine, his rise would affect his mother's position.[6]

Maternal virtue came to be seen as a key ethical achievement on par with the moral attainments of highly cultivated men.[7] In recognition of the importance of good mothering, a man might attribute his success to the woman who raised him.[8] The bond between mother and child intensified to an almost mystical degree. When one elderly woman heard that her son had been besieged, she began to lactate. She considered this an inauspicious sign, and indeed her son was eventually defeated.[9] Motherhood had become so prestigious that even men sometimes claimed maternal virtue. A righteous official could be praised as treating the people under his jurisdiction the way a loving mother cares for her baby.[10]

In many respects, son and mother constituted a discrete social unit. For example, an emperor could honor a man by granting his mother an imperial audience.[11] But the close identification of mother with son had a darker side as well. A mother could be punished for a son's crimes, and capturing an enemy's mother became an important goal of warfare.[12] Sometimes a captured mother received polite treatment, but others were killed, sometimes in a gruesome manner. One man murdered a rival's mother by scalding her to death with boiling wax.[13] A son's foe might even desecrate his deceased mother's body. The skeleton of one rebel leader's mother was exhumed and scattered as a way of humiliating him.[14]

Rhetoric about filial piety intensified and shifted focus. Writers increasingly stressed the obedience of son to mother, further strengthening their bond. They portrayed a mother's love and her child's filial piety as complementary virtues.[15] Popular opinion did not condemn a grown man who remained dependent on his mother. To the contrary, he stood out as a model of filial virtue.[16] In the north, a child could even cover up a mother's crime with impunity, as filial piety took precedence over the law.[17]

Although mothers enjoyed a revered place in the collective imagination, reality was more complicated. While some mothers willingly sacrificed themselves for the sake of children, not all women lived up to this demanding ideal. Infanticide remained common. A mother might kill or abandon her baby if the family could not afford to raise it or if an inauspicious omen tainted the birth. And ineffective contraception and dangerous abortion techniques made infanticide a form of birth control.[18] The failure of so many women to live up to the maternal ideal made the loving mother seem all the more admirable.

The early medieval era marks a highpoint for scholarship on the *Classic of Filial Piety (Xiao jing)*.[19] This ancient text likely dates to the fourth century before the Common Era. It became popular during the Han, when scholars considered it a significant statement on ethics. Six Dynasties emperors patronized scholarship on this text, resulting in numerous works of annotation and commentary.[20] With so many people studying the *Classic of Filial Piety*, scholarship diverged into rival schools, sparking lively debate. Thinkers contemplated fraught moral topics, such as conflicts between the Confucian virtues of *ren* (kindness toward unrelated people) and *xiao* (duty to senior kin).[21] Short and written in simple language, the *Classic of Filial Piety* also served as a popular textbook. Children studied it before progressing to more difficult texts.[22]

Filial piety became an important political ideology in this era. As Han dynasty institutions withered, Cao Cao sought to channel the respect for filial piety toward the weakened state.[23] He reconstructed the foundations of government by reviving the early Western Han idea that the state constitutes an expanded version of the family. One memorial describes the emperor as both the father and mother of the people.[24] Under this patrimonial scheme, the ruler took on the role of *pater familias* with a personal tie to his subjects. In this way, the government used filial piety to inspire loyalty to the state. Officials compared the roles of parent and child with that of ruler and minister. Just as a man owes obedience to a parent, so too must he submit to the emperor's authority.

Other medieval schools of thought also embraced filial piety. Religious Daoists absorbed filial ideals from secular society and integrated them into their ethical doctrine, promoting them under the guise of religion.[25] Buddhism provided the most innovative and influential advocacy. Buddhist enthusiasm for filial piety emerged in reaction to persecution. Because monks and nuns left home, making them unable to provide for elderly parents, critics accused them of selfish cruelty. To counter these charges, Buddhism assimilated secular filiality and augmented it with new ideas on the subject.[26] Unlike Confucian writings, which had traditionally focused on the paternal bond, Buddhists emphasized the relationship between mother and son as the core of filial piety.[27] According to the Buddhist viewpoint, a father should be respected but a mother ought to be loved.[28] They also recast filial piety as a manifestation of compassion, envisioning the filial child as akin to a bodhisattva.

Buddhists also introduced new ways children could express filial commitment.[29] Buddhist writers portrayed saving a sinful mother from the torments of hell as the ultimate manifestation of filial virtue. They encouraged men to engage in religious practice so that they could devote their accumulated merit to their mother, thus potentially saving her from perdition. Scholars translated relevant works on filial piety from Sanskrit and also created new texts that could cast it as a Buddhist virtue.[30] The story of an Indian man named Uttara became particularly popular. Uttara saw a terrifying vision of his deceased mother, whom he realized had been transformed into a hungry ghost because of her sins.[31] By making offerings to monks on her behalf, Uttara generated enough merit to allow her to be reborn in a beautiful heaven full of lotuses. Other Buddhist stories of filial heroism became popular, culminating in the story of Mulian, a filial son who used religious practice to save his mother from hell.[32]

Discussions of filial behavior of all sorts, religious and secular, became increasingly common and appeared in literature, epitaphs, and biography. According to these narratives, the virtuous man respected and obeyed his parents, mother as well as father, making filial piety a component of ideal masculine identity.[33] Aside from providing moral guidance, this virtue had practical ramifications as well.[34] The aristocracy displayed this virtue to claim the moral high ground. They also promoted it as a way to reinforce the basic social bonds of rural society, which had frayed during centuries of chaos. Villagers already identified age with status, so promoting an age-based hierarchy used traditional thinking to stabilize the established order. Upholding filiality as a prime social bond had a profound effect on the social fabric. For example, the relationship between step-mothers and step-sons seems to have become more amicable than before, as step-sons treated their fathers' new wives as surrogate mothers worthy of respect and obedience.[35] Given the complexity and fragmentation of so many households, harmony between step-mother and step-son went a long way toward fostering family harmony.

Law and administrative measures also reflected filial values.[36] A Northern Wei edict declared, "Of the three thousand crimes, none is greater than unfiliality." Those guilty of this offense could be publicly humiliated by having their head shaved.[37] A mother whose son had abandoned her could sue him for support.[38] Under some early medieval law codes, a son could be executed for plotting to kill, beating, or even just cursing a parent.[39] The eight highest officials in the Wei government once memorialized that a man convicted of hurting his mother deserved to be torn apart between chariots.[40] And according to the Jin code, if a man arranged for someone to assault his parent, he would receive a harsher punishment than the perpetrator.[41] However, jurists sometimes had to confront conflicting moral priorities. In one perplexing case, when a woman killed her husband, their son did not report the crime. Officials had trouble deciding whether he should be lauded for protecting his mother or condemned for betraying his father.[42]

A growing sensitivity to the pain and dangers of childbirth helped shift the focus of filial piety toward mothers. Women often died during delivery, which largely accounts for the frequency of male remarriage.[43] To address this problem, medical texts explained pregnancy and childbirth in detail, making gynecology into a sophisticated branch of medicine. An expectant mother undertook elaborate preparations.[44] She drank herbal potions to safeguard her pregnancy and ease childbirth. Wealthy families set up a room or tent for delivery, sometimes erected in an auspicious place to elicit supernatural protection. Detailed charts specified the location of delivery tents, squatting positions, and where to bury the placenta. People considered the fetus a human being and took great pains to see that it was carried to term. Under the Northern Wei, a pregnant woman condemned to death would not be executed until after she had delivered.[45]

Rising devotion to mothers affected female status. The power of motherhood made some women extremely confident and commanding. A historian who describes one woman as "strong and stern" notes that she was extremely strict with her sons.[46] When one man was defeated in battle, his mother became so angry that she fell ill. She condemned him on her deathbed and then died.[47] And the mother of a general beat him for even the slightest disobedience.[48] Mothers and grandmothers also had considerable say in arranging marriages.[49]

Mothers encouraged their sons to behave well and garner achievements. The beaten general had a distinguished career, with his success attributed to a stern mother. And the scholar Huangfu Mi, orphaned at an early age and raised by an uncle, looked to his aunt as a surrogate mother. She appealed to the example of Mencius's mother, a famed paragon of maternal duty, to encourage him to study hard. Because of her exhortations, Huangfu applied himself diligently and went on to serve in office and earn a reputation for scholarship. After winning fame and rank, he attributed his success to her exhortations.[50] But with power comes responsibility, so people held mothers to increasingly high standards. A magistrate punished a woman for failing her maternal duty by abandoning her child.[51] And a man's misbehavior could be blamed on his mother's negligence.[52]

Awareness of the potential plight of the elderly further animated discussions of filial piety. Many writings depict old people as poor and vulnerable. The elderly depended on grown children for sustenance and comfort, so a lack of offspring or an irresponsible son could doom an old person to destitution and even starvation. The historian's description of ninety-year-old woman and her seventy-year-old daughter living together, sickly and alone, deliberately evokes pity in the reader.[53] And when society plunged into chaos, the elderly were most vulnerable. Some people simply abandoned their parents and fled.[54] This sort of negligent behavior made the filial son seem all the more praiseworthy.

The stories of filial children became integrated into the historical record in recognition of their moral significance. *Records of Song (Songshu)* was the first dynastic history to include a section of biographies dedicated to the filial and righteous.[55] In reaction to widespread corruption, the author Shen Yue (441–553) emphasized purity (*qing*) as a key moral quality.[56] He believed that instead of seeking profit and fame, the "pure" gentlemen should cultivate his character. The moral exemplar was often a filial son, as this virtue symbolized integrity in general. Readers assumed that the filial man must surely have lesser virtues as well.[57] As a result of this mindset, Shen Yue gave biographies of filial role models a place of honor. This precedent had a major impact on historiography. Although Shen wrote about a minor dynasty, he produced a particularly well-written and erudite history that exerted a significant impact on the genre.[58] Subsequent historians often followed his example and inserted biographies of filial children in accounts of the past.

History, fiction, and the visual arts all celebrated filial children. Even hagiographies of monks and nuns, who left their parents to pursue a cloistered life, nevertheless acclaimed them as exemplars of filial piety when young.[59] In this period, expectations still focused mostly on sons. Significantly, representations of filial sons emphasize their devotion to mother as well as father.[60] Dynastic histories usually depict filiality in realistic terms, describing how a son served his parents while young. In many cases, the father had already died, bringing hardship to his family. The young filial exemplar had to take on heavy responsibilities to ensure his mother's comfort.[61] In later life, some of the men in these narratives became highly successful. One poor man diligently cared for his mother while young, then grew up to be ennobled for his military accomplishments.[62] These happy endings imply that caring for a parent offered not just a moral accomplishment but practical rewards as well.

Filial piety was not just a duty for the young. Adults also exhibited this virtue. Concern for aged parents took many forms. Emperors had a unique lifestyle, giving them the most distinctive ways to display filial regard. A ruler could visit his mother often, preferably every day.[63] He could also provide her with a suitably grand space in the palace or else give her a mansion elsewhere in the capital.[64] For most people, however, devotion to a parent came down to providing sustenance and basic support, even when circumstances became difficult.[65] The devoted son also cared for his mother when she fell ill. If detained by official duties, he might still find a way to secretly visit her and look after her health.[66] In times of war and disorder, the good son managed his mother's security, either sending her off to a peaceful haven or personally escorting her there.[67] Fleeing with an elderly woman, who was only capable of slow travel, could be perilous. One man who insisted on bringing his mother as he fled from danger ended up being killed.[68]

Some depictions of filial piety lauded an offspring who went to extremes in serving a parent. A Northern Wei sarcophagus from the year 524 depicts the classic tale of the filial exemplar Ding Lan, whose story became popular during the Eastern Han dynasty.[69] After Ding's mother died, he commissioned a wooden statue in her likeness, which he served as he would a living mother. In this way he could continue to demonstrate his devotion even after his mother had died. Other filial tales describe similarly superhuman commitment. When one man's elderly grandmother fell ill, he nursed her so diligently that for seventy days he did not even take time to change clothes.[70] And in an unusual case, a man used misogyny to prove that he loved his mother to the exclusion of all other women.[71] He served his mother dutifully, showed no interest in sex, and expressed hatred of womankind and everything associated with them. Vengeance served as another extreme manifestation of filial devotion. As in the Eastern Han, retribution on behalf of kin remained common. Popular opinion considered revenge for a murdered parent not just pardonable but "greater than heaven."[72]

In stories of filial children, food often symbolizes care.[73] During the Han dynasty, feeding a parent became a standard way to show love and concern, and Six Dynasties writings continued to employ this trope. A virtuous son would somehow manage to feed his mother in a time of privation. When one poor man stole pigs and cows to so that he could feed the meat to his elderly mother, virtuous intentions excused his thievery.[74] A sick mother might require special foods, and the exemplary son would somehow manage to procure them. One man dreamed that if he went to a certain mountain, he would obtain a medicinal bamboo shoot that could cure his mother's illness.[75]

A filial son might also refuse to eat as long as his sick mother refused nourishment as a way of sharing her suffering. One man went without food for five days while he devoutly nursed his mother. When she finally became strong enough to eat some congee, he finally broke his fast and ate her leftovers.[76] The Buddhist cleric Huimu would chew food for her toothless mother to make it soft enough to consume.[77] In doing so, Huimu broke the monastic prohibitions against tasting meat and eating after midday, so she could not receive full ordination, a considerable sacrifice for such a pious woman. Other stories describe how a filial son would somehow obtain his mother's favorite food, even if he had to go to great lengths to do so. One woman liked eating scorched rice from the bottom of the pot. Every time her son cooked rice, he would save some scorched rice and collected it in a sack for her to enjoy.[78] Another woman liked fresh fish, so in winter her son would arduously smash through ice so that he could catch fish for her.[79]

Elaborate funerals and burials displayed filial virtue to the community. Following Han dynasty precedent, sons tended to put most emphasis on their mother's funeral. Although the ritual canon emphasized mourning for the father, Han dynasty accounts describe sons mourning for mothers more than twice as often as for fathers. People saw grief for a mother's death as an authentic emotion, not just a duty compelled by the rites, so they admired it more than the necessary mourning required for a father.[80] These views informed early medieval mourning practices, so anguish for a deceased mother could be extravagant.[81]

As before, ethical norms dictated that parents receive a proper funeral and appropriate mourning. Biographies of filial sons often mention that they conducted full funerals for both parents.[82] A representative memorial concerning funerals likewise stresses the importance of conducting proper obsequies for both mother and father.[83] This emphasis on mourning both parents reflected the orthodox ritual position. However, as in the

Han era, historical works mention funerals for mothers far more often than those for fathers. A mother's funeral continued to elicit strong emotions. When someone wanted to curry favor with a powerful man, he could attend his mother's funeral. Similarly, a warlord had the tomb of a potential ally's mother rebuilt to demonstrate his good will.[84]

Lu Tui justified mourning more intensely for a deceased mother. After his mother died, he composed an obituary for her even though he had not done so when his father had passed away. When someone asked him why he treated his parents differently, he explained, "Surely it must be because a man's virtue is displayed in his conduct of affairs, while a woman's excellence, unless it be the subject of an obituary, would never be made public."[85] According to this reasoning, while a woman ought to be reticent in life, a son could use his mother's funeral to publicize her hidden virtues and achievements. The distinct lifestyle of each sex justified different kinds of funerals.

Mourning for mothers became so important that failure to observe the expected obsequies provoked scandal. During the mourning period for the mother of Ruan Ji (210–263), this unconventional litterateur attended a party at which he ate meat and drank alcohol in violation of basic mourning rules.[86] After a fellow guest criticized him for this appalling ethical lapse, the host defended Ruan on philosophical grounds. He interpreted this scandalous behavior as an expression of Daoist naturalness, hence indicative of superior cultivation. Ruan's radical metaphysics justified peculiar actions that otherwise would result in censure.

Because funerals and mourning served to express filial piety, scholars discussed their correct performance in great detail. Han dynasty precedents provided the foundation for medieval funerary customs, which consolidated during the Wei.[87] Generally speaking, northerners observed mourning more strictly than counterparts in the south. Mourners conducted rites prior to burial, during the entombment, and throughout the subsequent mourning period. Deceased men and women were honored with similar rituals. In theory, the rank of a man's father determined the degree of extravagance in mourning his mother. Also, mourning for a mother ought to vary depending on whether she had been a father's wife or concubine.

People sometimes mourned a mother to an exaggerated degree far exceeding ritual standards. After the death of a parent, an official would often temporarily resign to devote the requisite three years to mourning.[88] A proper funeral and mourning not only took considerable time but could also involve considerable expense. A high-born lady was sent off to the netherworld together with the luxuries she had enjoyed in life. The tomb of Madam Pan, who died in 357, included fine garments, jewelry, handkerchiefs, towels, cosmetics, perfumes, toilet articles, sewing items, bedding, food, and money.[89] The expense of such an opulent funeral could become onerous. Authorities sometimes tried to regulate the size of funerals to reduce this burden, but it seems that these decrees had no practical effect.[90]

Ritual authorities sometimes disagreed on the proper ways to conduct funerals and mourn. Some classicists wanted to revive Zhou dynasty norms. For example, they wanted people to use the ancient system of posthumous names for women, which had gone into abeyance.[91] Other ritual experts discussed the burial of palace women. Given the need to calibrate the degree of mourning for consorts of each rank, palace mourning rites were inescapably complex.[92] Authorities also debated how long a man should mourn for a father's former wife.[93] Should she be treated the same as a birth mother, or did he owe her different ritual obligations? And scholars discussed whether or not a man should reduce the degree of mourning for his mother if his father had divorced her.[94] Ritualists also discussed mourning for more distant female kin, such as a grandmother or aunt.[95]

The rhetoric of filial piety emphasized proper mourning because everyone knew how much difficulty this could entail. Funerals and mourning required the expenditure of considerable time, money, and effort. Even under ideal circumstances, orthodox arrangements could be difficult to carry out to the letter. And in this poor and violent age, many people found it impossible to inter their deceased parents in a suitable manner. The histories mention men who could not bury their mothers due to poverty, war, or some other difficulty.[96] One impecunious man had to abandon his wife and children so that he could spend what little money he had on his mother's funeral. Although people today would consider him irresponsible, at the time people lauded him as a paragon of virtue.[97] Another man sold his daughter into slavery to pay for his mother's funeral.[98] Sometimes a man left a deceased mother's body with someone else for safekeeping until he could return and conduct a suitable funeral.[99] One man fleeing to a safe haven brought along his mother's corpse. When bandits approached, he had no choice but to abandon the body. Yet in the end he managed to return, reclaim the body, and eventually give her a proper burial.[100]

Men holding government office were expected to withdraw from worldly affairs for three years while mourning each parent, interrupting their careers. Some dismissed this custom as a nuisance, ignored ritual propriety, and remained at work. Others continued with their job by appointing proxies to carry out their orders.[101] However, these seem to have been unusual cases. When the mother of a government minister died, he would usually resign immediately and devote his full attention to the upcoming ceremonies.[102] Many ethnic Han officials in the north hated their foreign masters, so they gladly used mourning as an excuse to resign an unwanted position. It became very common for northern officials to take a long leave of absence or resign not only when their mother died, but even when she took ill.[103] Some men even renounced their office simply because their mother had become old.[104]

The standard histories include stories of men who mourned intensely for a deceased mother against all odds, making them icons of filial piety.[105] Descriptions of virtuous and successful men often mention that they scrupulously performed mourning obligations.[106] Some people even extended mourning for a parent beyond the mandatory three years. After one woman completed the conventional period of mourning for her deceased father, she continued to abstain from meat and alcohol, which were forbidden during a time of grief.[107] Of course royalty had to be especially punctilious about mourning, and a ruler commemorated a deceased parent in a suitably grand fashion. Many constructed an ancestral shrine or Buddhist temple as an act of remembrance.[108]

Occasionally mourning became so intense that observers considered it strange or excessive. Some people praised intemperate mourning, in spite of its heterodoxy.[109] But others complained about immoderate mourning that exceeded the bounds of propriety.[110] Sometimes intense grief could give rise to bizarre scenes. Two brothers mourned the death of their mother with uncontrolled wailing and leaping.[111] Another man did not drink anything for six days after his mother died.[112] Because Buddhist writers routinely describe miraculous events, religious texts include many instances of exaggerated lamentation. After the father of the nun Sengmeng died, she allegedly wept until she vomited blood, died, and then came back to life.[113] When the mother of another Buddhist devotee died, she cried herself to death. The local magistrate erected a stele in recognition of her filial devotion.[114] These sorts of stories about the outer bounds of filial piety underscore the high place of mothers in early medieval society. When a woman bore children, she took on a highly respected social role, raising her status with the family and making her the focus of intense and conflicted emotions.

3

Politics

Within China's patriarchal system of government, women lacked political power in their own right. Nevertheless, in accordance with Han dynasty precedent, a tie with the emperor could give a woman substantial influence. As a result, the marriages of emperors and their close kin carried political significance, and an ambitious mother, wife, or daughter of a ruler sometimes turned kinship links into clout.[1] A woman's male relations might also benefit from her bond with the ruler. Other than the crown prince, emperors excluded their other sons from participating in government, leaving in-laws as their most useful kin.[2]

Imperial marriage also affected the composition of the elite. As marriage reflected social standing, a union with an emperor connoted power and prestige. When a family married with the imperial clan for the first time, this event often heralded their rising fortunes. Nor was imperial marriage an empty honor. Many rulers rewarded their in-laws with offices and titles.[3] Because marriage with an emperor could bring tangible benefits, many families sought to wed with the imperial line. And by periodically renewing their ties with the throne, some families remained prominent for generations.[4]

After the fall of Han, the strongmen of the Three Kingdoms era (220–280) initially paid little attention to marriage politics. The wife of Cao Cao (155–220) did not come from a powerful family, nor did any of the empresses in this period.[5] In this time of incessant warfare, brute military strength held the key to power, so the Cao did not feel the need to cultivate influential in-laws. Moreover, rulers recognized the problems caused by haughty Eastern Han consort kin and so deliberately chose women from minor backgrounds to diminish their in-laws. Even so, one empress dowager, surnamed Guo, appealed to Han dynasty precedent to dethrone an emperor whom she regarded as unsuitable and replace him with another, who happened to be much younger and more pliable.[6] This incident attested to the continued potential for imperial consorts to seize authority.

Tottering regimes in the north and south sought to construct stable norms and institutions. Some arranged marriages to achieve their goals. Marriage strategies differed by region and dynasty as rulers chose their spouses and minor consorts to address pressing problems or take advantage of opportunities. Marriage policy in the southern dynasties often followed Eastern Han models. Emperors took their primary consorts from prominent families to gain powerful allies and reinforce their connections with the uppermost elite. Southern emperors usually observed other traditional Chinese marriage customs as well, including surname exogamy, concubinage, the ban on elevating a concubine to the status of wife, and taboos on incest and cross-generation marriage.[7]

Southern emperors usually took their wives from families with a history of bureaucratic service. About two-thirds of empresses in the formative Jin dynasty came from official families. Seven out of eight Liu Song empresses came from old clans that predated the dynasty as did six out of seven empresses in the Southern Qi.[8] As these were marriages of convenience, emperors often had little to do with their wives. Few southern empresses bore children, and it seems that some emperors did not have sexual relations with their spouses.[9] Harem women gave birth to most heirs to the throne.

Although marriage with the imperial line raised a family's status, certain unions could also bolster an emperor's reputation.[10] The founders of the Liu Song, Chen, and Liang dynasties all came from embarrassingly modest military backgrounds. If a parvenu emperor allied with in-laws from an old family that had a long history of government service, he strengthened his legitimacy. This strategy carried risks, as powerful consort kin might threaten a weak dynasty. Nevertheless, an insecure emperor sometimes still married a wife from a prestigious family to imbue his reign with greater decorum.

Not all southern imperial marriages fit the standard model. A ruler who feared domineering in-laws might deliberately marry down, so some empresses came from relatively modest backgrounds.[11] Other emperors selected wives from their own circle of relatives. The Liang dynasty emperor Wenxian married his first cousin and her father had been married to the ruler's aunt.[12] Emperors also wed princesses from a previous dynasty, thereby transferring the aura of legitimacy from one ruling house to the next via marriage.[13]

The northern dynasties took a very different approach to imperial marriage. In the preconquest Tuoba system, neither the wives of chieftains nor their kinsmen participated in politics. The Tuoba traditionally did not even have a rank equivalent to queen or empress. Only when they established themselves in China did they feel compelled to adopt this unfamiliar practice. Even so, conquerors from the steppe did not feel obligated to respect Han dynasty precedent or even the most basic principles of Chinese marriage. For example, northern emperors sometimes promoted a concubine to empress in violation of fundamental ritual norms.[14] Rulers in the north also faced very different circumstances from southern counterparts, and they adjusted their marriage policies accordingly.

When the Tuoba adopted the Chinese imperial system, they had to decide how they would select an empress. Tuoba rulers had previously participated in a nonreciprocal marriage system, taking their brides from one of three prominent steppe clans of different ethnicities.[15] The resulting kinship network linked together leading pastoral families and encouraged them to resolve their differences peacefully. Powerful kin also provided useful support. The Tuoba's affines helped them conquer China and establish the Northern Wei dynasty.[16] After the conquest, the invaders initially continued to intermarry with other steppe peoples to maintain ethnic solidarity and avoid assimilation.[17]

After establishing the Northern Wei dynasty, the Tuoba found that they had to deal with the threats posed by strong consort kin. Although they had traditionally cultivated powerful in-laws, they soon realized that within the Chinese context, powerful in-laws might corrode governance and precipitate decline. In response, the Tuoba altered their marriage practices. They established a system centered on agnatic kinship to ensure that emperors ruled as well as reigned.[18]

To reduce threats posed by the empress dowager and her kin, from the beginning of the dynasty the Tuoba chose capable adults to rule. When faced with a succession crisis, outer court ministers handled national affairs, which usually prevented the empress dowager from seizing control. Fear of domination by consort kin led the Tuoba to establish a system of controlled mésalliance, deliberately selecting wives from modest backgrounds.[19] None of the early Wei empresses had politically active kin and none bore children. Most came from families new to government service.[20] During the Eastern Wei and Northern Qi dynasties, about two-thirds of empresses' families had only come to prominence under the Tuoba. Only one-third of empresses' families from the Western Wei and Northern Zhou had been prominent during the Eastern Han or Three Kingdoms. Although the proportion of empresses from official families fluctuated with each era, they tended to have much lower backgrounds

Figure 3.1. Woman on horseback.

than the wives of southern rulers.[21] Some consorts even came from very
lowly circumstances, including captives and slaves.

The most extreme strategy for reducing female political power dates
to the beginning of the Northern Wei. As the Xianbei studied Chinese
history to find prototypes for their own institutions, they discovered an
unusual precedent. The Han dynasty Emperor Wu (156–187 BCE) had
forced the mother of his heir apparent to commit suicide, thus ensuring
that an empress dowager would not dominate his successor.[22] Tuoba Gui
(Emperor Daowu, 371–409) likewise forced the mother of his heir to kill

herself. Thereafter, whenever the ruler appointed one of his sons as heir apparent, the boy's mother was expected to commit suicide.[23] A wet nurse or one of the emperor's concubines then raised the heir. Sometimes the surrogate mother then ended up being declared empress. The Tuoba often chose the heir's substitute mother from a conquered people so that her kinsmen would not threaten their supremacy. This cruel custom proved highly effective, and imperial affines had little influence during the Northern Wei. Eliminating the possibility of a powerful empress dowager also made it safe for the Tuoba to switch from fraternal succession, which had been their traditional practice, to Chinese-style primogeniture.[24] Later in the dynasty, as the Tuoba felt more confident, they began to reconsider the unseemly sight of empresses from humble families. Emperor Wei Gaozu (r. 417–499) felt that marriage with such lowly women disgraced the imperial house. From his reign onward, the emperor and his brothers began to take wives from more important families, and the rulers of subsequent dynasties in the north often chose their empresses from families of civil officials or generals.[25]

As in the south, marriage with the emperor brought a family immense prestige. The male relatives of an empress sometimes even received noble titles.[26] A few northern families managed to marry repeatedly with the imperial line, thus maintaining their high standing for a long period of time. For instance, three daughters of Dugu Xin, an important chieftain, became empresses under the Northern Zhou and Sui dynasties.[27] However, this strategy rarely succeeded. Unlike their counterparts in the south, most northern consort clans did not manage to marry with an emperor more than once. Northern rulers preferred to arrange marriages to construct a wide-ranging network of kinship ties, so they took their consorts from various families.[28] Over time, however, Tuoba marriage strategies began to fail. In spite of the various measures to constrain the power of in-laws, over time the empresses came from increasingly important families well placed to meddle in administration. By the fifth century, consort kinsmen played key roles in the administrative system, and the Tuoba ruling line began to lose control of the government.[29]

Unlike the southern dynasties, northern emperors saw marriage as way to improve relations with neighboring peoples.[30] Given the complex multiethnic composition of north China and the adjoining steppe lands, rulers found it difficult to bind together numerous tribes and clans. Before entering China, the Tuoba and other nomads already used marriage to build bonds between different peoples, and they employed similar measures in their new homeland.[31] After conquering north China, Tuoba interests expanded considerably, so they extended their marriage policies to cover a much larger area. While Han dynasty emperors had also conducted marriage alliances with foreign peoples, the practice had previously been one-sided. Chinese rulers sent out ethnic Han women to marry steppe chieftains, but they would not deign to allow a foreign woman to become empress of China. In contrast, nomadic rulers practiced reciprocal marriage ties. Tuoba rulers could accept foreign empresses and consort kin because their emperors were usually capable adults who could not be easily dominated. Affines had little room to interfere with administration, so marrying a foreign woman posed little threat.[32] When two groups married one another's women, they produced a very tight kinship bond that strengthened their alliance.

The Tuoba also sometimes married into important Han families to gain useful native Chinese allies. Although many native aristocrats looked down on steppe peoples and kept them at arm's length, those willing to cooperate with the conquerors received tangible rewards. As leading Chinese and steppe families intermarried, they produced a new mixed-blood elite.[33] Northern rulers even found marriage politics useful in neutralizing troublesome warlords and potential rebels.[34] However, this strategy empowered potential rivals, so Tuoba marriage strategy gradually shifted.[35] Instead of strengthening potentially hostile foreign forces through intermarriage, Tuoba emperors increasingly married women from defeated clans who posed no threat.

A woman could become empress in various ways. Many wed the heir apparent and received the title of empress when her spouse became emperor.[36] A few emperors elevated a minor consort to the rank of empress. And a concubine who bore the heir could receive the same honors as an empress even though she lacked the title.[37] The status and powers of northern empresses varied immensely.[38] Many were nonentities, while others participated in politics to some degree. The chief responsibilities of an empress were ceremonial, participating in routine court rituals and assisting the emperor in religious sacrifices.[39] An empress might even have a sacrificial temple built for her own ancestors.[40]

Policies for systematically weakening empresses and consort kin came together during the formative Northern Wei dynasty. After the Tuoba conquered China, they had to establish an administrative system acceptable to both Xianbei and Chinese. After the conquest, even though the Wei rulers imitated many established Chinese political customs, they considered the institution of empress inherently dangerous.[41] A few empresses exercised some authority, and their favorites sometimes received wealth and office, proving their potential for destabilizing the dynasty.[42] To prevent these women from endangering the status quo, northern rulers took steps to neutralize them politically. Whereas Han dynasty empresses and their kinsmen had enjoyed immense wealth, even the southern emperors limited the emoluments that they granted their in-laws.[43] Some emperors declared more than one woman empress in violation of ritual norms.[44]

Granting this title to several women weakened the position of each. Northern Zhou Emperor Xuan (559–580) gave the title to five women.[45] Other rulers took the opposite approach and did not officially marry or appoint an empress.[46] Sometimes the ruler deliberately alienated the heir from his mother to prevent her from eventually becoming a powerful empress dowager. Some heirs to the throne did not even know their mothers' identity.[47] A ruler could also refuse to give the title of empress to the mother of the heir. Instead, he could choose a low-ranking woman or even a slave. In this way they observed the Chinese custom that demanded the appointment of an empress while guaranteeing that she would remain politically insignificant.

During the Northern Wei, these preventative measures reached an extreme. Some emperors selected an empress in a deliberately frivolous manner to lower her standing in the eyes of the court. In the late fourth and fifth centuries, craftsmen cast metal images of each candidate for empress. Courtiers then perused these sculptures, and the woman represented by the best image was declared empress.[48] A consort selected in such an arbitrary and humiliating manner would remain a powerless figurehead. Moreover, most Wei empresses remained uneducated, and ignorance further restricted their power.[49] Also, the Tuoba emperors initially practiced fraternal succession, making it virtually impossible for an empress dowager to dominate the state.[50]

In spite of these elaborate precautions, a few empresses in the north and south nevertheless became powerful figures.[51] An ambitious woman could accrue authority in a number of ways depending on her situation and goals. An empress might try to blackmail the ruler into getting her way. Threatening suicide or refusing to feed the emperor's son might persuade a weak-willed monarch give in to her demands.[52] Some empresses possessed qualities that aided their ambitions, such as charm, bravery, or talent.[53] Occasionally a woman found power thrust upon her. The simpleton Emperor Hui of the Jin dynasty could not manage affairs of state, so his wife Empress Jia Nanfeng (257–300) and her family assumed control.[54] However, she ruled with cruelty and arrogance, so the emperor's relatives eventually stepped in, deposed Empress Jia, and forced her to commit suicide.

The revered role of mother provided another avenue to power. The empress dowager was officially considered mother of the heir, even if he had been born to another woman. Filial piety dictated that the emperor should respect and even obey his mother, potentially placing her above the monarch in rank.[55] When an emperor died, an empress dowager might follow Eastern Han conventions and enthrone a child. That way she could rule as regent until the young emperor reached maturity.[56] An empress could even arrogate power by claiming to be mother of the entire realm and demanding filial deference from the entire populace.[57]

However many precautions the northern dynasties took to neutralize female power, certain ideas and customs still favored the empresses.[58] Although Confucianism restrained female behavior, confined women to the home, and discouraged mixing of the sexes, Tuoba society traditionally lacked these restrictions. In fact, the Xianbei were accustomed to assertive women. An ambitious northern empress could readily appear in public, discuss important matters with men, and participate in affairs of state.

Sometimes an empress cultivated an air of mystery to bolster her prestige. During this era, supernatural tales fascinated both the Chinese and pastoralists. Literature and historiography contain many stories describing a person's miraculous conception or birth, presaging a great destiny.[59] Historians sometimes seized on this popular trope and claimed that unusual signs or strange events had accompanied an emperor's birth.[60] Although supernatural birth stories originated in Chinese writings, the Xianbei found this genre particularly useful. The Tuoba's ancestors had lived in felt tents and herded sheep, and their Chinese subjects despised these lowly origins. To bolster their legitimacy, steppe rulers invented supernatural tales that would exalt their heritage. Northern Wei rulers claimed descent from a celestial female divinity.[61] And miraculous omens marked the birth of emperors and empresses in north and south. For example, a pregnant woman might have an unusual dream presaging the greatness of her forthcoming child. Sometimes a visiting shaman, monk, or nun predicted a baby's bright future. Or mysterious red lights signaling a significant event illuminated a pregnant woman's bedroom.

An ambitious empress could also manipulate her lifestyle to craft a positive public image and thereby attract support. Although frequent wars had decimated the economy, the Six Dynasties elite nevertheless reveled in luxury. Some empresses deliberately lived very lavishly, residing in grand abodes and wearing sumptuous clothing.[62] An extravagant way of life flaunted their superior status and implicitly commanded obedience. Other empresses, particularly in the south, took the opposite approach and tried to appear serious. The beautiful Jin dynasty Empress Wu Daoyang (257–291) earned her husband's favor by being "mild mannered with female virtues."[63] An ambitious empress might seek comparison with famed female paragons of antiquity.[64] Or she could affect feminine modesty by wearing unusually simple attire, washing her own clothes, and eating plain food with basic utensils.[65] Empresses could also prove their humility and industry by personally raising silkworms, spinning thread, and weaving cloth, in imitation of virtuous Han dynasty empresses.[66]

Pious devotion to Buddhism could also display an empress' virtue to the world, gaining public approval. Buddhism had many enthusiastic adherents at the time, and patronage by elite women often had sincere motivations. However, piety could also be politically useful. In contrast

with the classical Chinese canon, Buddhist teachings specifically permitted female participation in politics. The sutras even taught that a woman
could become a *chakravartin* (*zhuanlun shengwang*), a universal Buddhist
ruler.[67] Buddhist dogma gave palace women confidence, sanctioned their
participation in affairs of state, and also provided a sophisticated ideology
that could legitimize a woman as virtuous and capable.

Pious empresses read sutras, visited temples, and conducted religious
ceremonies.[68] Empress Dowager Ling (d. 528) sent a monk to the western
regions to search for untranslated scriptures.[69] Most visibly, empresses
financed the construction of numerous temples, statues, and steles.
Empress Ling even reduced official salaries by one-tenth to finance the
construction of an immense temple complex.[70] The size and opulence of
the religious sites erected by empresses awed visitors.[71] These Buddhist
facilities often served as extensions of the palace. Luxurious nunneries
provided a convenient place for harem women to worship and a refuge
for those who lost imperial favor.

As during the Han, empresses dowager were particularly well placed
to gain power.[72] When a ruler died, his widow often served as the figurehead who legitimized the new emperor and ensured an orderly succession. If the previous emperor had not nominated a regent, an empress
dowager might choose an immature monarch, allowing her to exercise
considerable power or perhaps even serve as regent herself.[73] Due to the
dictates of filial piety, even adult rulers had to show deference to the empress dowager by paying her visits and showing concern for her welfare.[74]
Given these advantages, some empresses dowager became key figures
at court. One dismissed an adult emperor on grounds of immorality.[75]
Rebels even used an empress dowager's sanction to justify a change of
dynasty.[76] Given the powers that a dowager could possess, some women
resorted to intrigue and even violence to ensure that they would end up
in this position. Whenever a harem woman gave birth to an imperial heir,
she threatened the position of the current empress. Not surprisingly, some
of these women perished under mysterious circumstances.[77]

Beginning in this era, empresses dowager began using a curtain to modestly shield themselves from the eyes of ministers and generals while conducting official business, a custom that continued to be observed in later
dynasties.[78] Dowagers had various duties and powers. They had to carry
out numerous court rituals in accordance with the elaborate ceremonial
calendar.[79] Although tedious, presiding over these rites emphasized their
power. They also exercised authority within the imperial clan. Dowagers
sometimes chose the emperor's wife and made other important family
decisions.[80] More substantially, a few empresses dowager received memorials and issued edicts, effectively taking control of the state.[81] Under such
circumstances, everyone knew who wielded ultimate power. When one

Wei empress dowager sent her representative to meet with a warlord, he referred to the envoy as coming from the "country of women" (*nüguo*).[82]

The most aggressive and capable empresses dowager could be formidable. If the ruler or ministers challenged them, they might respond by accusing the monarch or his intimates of dissipation and threaten to depose him.[83] Aggressive and ambitious women, such as Empress Dowager Ling, also took control of the military, overseeing campaigns and quelling rebellions.[84] And at court, these women could cow opponents with peremptory decisions. A dowager could instantly elevate anyone who attracted her attention and depose those who displeased her, thereby surrounding herself with a supportive clique. In the north, where men and women interacted more freely, a few empresses dowager became infamous for their partiality toward handsome male favorites. However, they also had to suffer the condescension of jealous adversaries who belittled them for gaining their privileges in such an unseemly manner.[85]

In spite of the potential power of empresses dowager, their authority should not be exaggerated. Unlike the Eastern Han, when women dominated the dynasty for long stretches of time, most empresses dowager in this era had little authority. Their claim to power came obliquely through marriage and kinship, so bureaucratic institutions could usually contain their ambitions. Northerners took elaborate precautions to limit female power. And in the south, the appointment of multiple regents usually shifted power to the officialdom during an emperor's minority. Also, when a ruler died without issue and the empress dowager had to select a new emperor, she was expected to choose an adult, precluding a long regency. Even if an empress dowager managed to seize control of the government, she had few natural allies. When she became enfeebled from sickness or old age, rivals quickly sidelined her.[86] Empresses also knew that ambition courted danger. A handful of them ended up deposed or assassinated.[87]

Consort kinsmen usually had little role in government.[88] During the Eastern Han, a powerful consort usually employed her father, brothers, and nephews to serve as regents, generals, and high civil officials. In this manner, consort kin frequently seized control of the state as a group. In contrast, only one early medieval regent was related to an empress, and consort kin never took over the government. In the north in particular, steppe tradition held that a leader should be a competent adult. Because the Northern Wei and other conquest dynasties tended to follow this dictum even after settling in China, there were few regents, and adult emperors did not have to depend on their in-laws.

Although consort kinsmen did not dominate the government, they enjoyed privileges and sometimes even a degree of power. A marriage with the emperor brought immense prestige, and a consort's family found themselves instantly elevated in rank. Because the ancient classics taught that a man should respect his mother's brothers, rulers often allowed their in-laws unusual privileges.[89] When an imperial affine committed a crime, only the most foolhardy official would judge him guilty.[90] In the south, although consort kinsmen never seized the government outright, they often served in high office.[91] Because southern emperors and their heirs customarily married with important families, distaff relatives routinely served as officials.

In spite of the many safeguards to restrict female power built into northern institutions, two Wei empresses nevertheless took control of the government for a time. Empress Dowager Wenming (surnamed Feng, 442–490) was the first woman to dominate a medieval court.[92] Descended from royalty, she came from an important ethnic Han clan in the northeast, and this lofty background gave her confidence and standing. When Wenming's step-son Emperor Xianzu ascended the throne, the strongman Yi Hun led the government.[93] Wenming convinced an imperial kinsman to execute Yi in 466, declared a regency, and seized power. Within a year, however, she abdicated. Whether or not she made this decision voluntarily remains unclear. After a time the emperor retired, leaving his three-year-old son as titular ruler. Taking advantage of this power vacuum, Wenming had the retired emperor killed and became regent again, remaining in this role until her death. Wenming carefully managed her public image, cultivating a reputation for intelligence, Buddhist piety, and austerity. Her policies had a notable impact. Wenming's Chinese ancestry inspired her to undertake a sinicization campaign that turned the dynasty away from its Xianbei roots.[94] And she carefully arranged the imperial clan's marriages to build support among a range of important families, hoping to eventually call on their support to invade the south and reunite China.[95] Yet in spite of her charisma and achievements, regicide, harshness, and rumors of sexual license tarnished Wenming's posthumous reputation.[96]

Empress Dowager Ling (surnamed Hu, d. 528) likewise ruled the Northern Wei dynasty in all but name.[97] After five-year-old Emperor Xiaoming ascended the throne, two women held the title of empress, and they struggled for supremacy. Empress Gao had been married to the previous ruler, while Empress Ling was the child emperor's mother. The overbearing behavior of Gao's family aroused intense opposition among the elite. Ling took advantage of this enmity to assassinate her rival's key kinsman and declared herself regent. Like Empress Wenming, Ling was also ethnic Chinese, and she encouraged further resinicization. She also enthusiastically patronized Buddhism, financing devotional art and huge temple complexes.[98]

Empress Ling served as regent twice. Historians consider her first regency a success. During her second time in power, however, her immoral and irresponsible behavior hastened the dynasty's downfall. After her son challenged her, she foolishly murdered him, not only undermining her legitimacy but also critically weakening the fragile imperial institution. A Tuoba general advanced on the capital, murdered the hated empress dowager, and brought down the dynasty. Thereafter the northern region split between the unstable Northern Qi and Northern Zhou realms. Historians traditionally evaluated Empress Ling's performance according to standards set down by Sima Qian (ca. 145–186 BCE). According to his model of the rise and fall of dynasties, the appearance of an evil woman marked the final phase of each era. Historians concluded that Ling's immorality had led heaven to withdraw its mandate, hastening the dynasty's collapse. As a result of this interpretation, Empress Ling traditionally received much of the blame for the collapse of Wei.

Beneath the empresses, lesser harem women had a prominent place in palace life. During this era, the harem expanded to unprecedented proportions. Aristocrats considered a large household a tangible sign of status, and this mindset led the emperors to maintain an enormous number of women in the palace. Rulers also kept a huge harem to affirm their potency and cultivate an air of distinction.[99] Early medieval palaces contained thousands of concubines, performers, servants, and slaves. This far exceeded the number of palace women in earlier eras and was rarely matched in subsequent dynasties.[100]

In the north, palace concubines came from both ethnic Chinese and steppe backgrounds. Some were northerners and others were from the south. A few had prominent families, but many more came from the bottom of society. Emperors sometimes brought a woman from an important clan into the palace to build useful ties or accepted women sent in by friendly foreign kingdoms such as the Korean states of Baekje and Goguryo. However, most imperial concubines were chosen for their beauty or talent.[101]

As the Xianbei conquered north China, they captured many women and pressed some into palace service.[102] Whenever the ruler overthrew a rival, he might take the other man's women into his palace to symbolize domination, thereby augmenting the harem even further. When an emperor died, however, the inner palace underwent a major upheaval. Incest taboos prohibited the succeeding emperor from having sexual relations with his predecessor's concubines, so they had no place in harem life.[103] When a new emperor ascended the throne, he was expected to eject the former emperor's sexual companions from the palace. These women might return home to be married off by their family or choose a life of celibacy and become Buddhist nuns.[104] Occasionally rulers forcibly married minor harem women to widowers and poor men to show their concern for the unfortunate.[105]

Given the widespread poverty that blighted the age, entry into an enormous and luxurious palace must have come as a shock. Court poets imagined the reactions of innocent young women as they confronted the opulence of their new surroundings:[106]

> Don't you see at Changan's tavern gate
> A young girl called Peachroot from the house of song?
> So poverty-stricken she spins by night without a lamp or candle—
> What a surprise! She gets to serve His Majesty! . . .
> Up cinnabar rafters and kingfisher pillars flowing storax scent flies.
> Over scented log cassia smoke she cooks wild rice.
> The year was topsy-turvy, there were no set rules.
> "It's a mean life being a woman"—but not to be despised!

The emperor lived apart from the empress and they rarely developed much of a relationship. Favored concubines had a far greater presence in the emperor's life, and the most important assumed a role akin to consorts.[107] Early medieval empresses gave birth to only nine sons as opposed to 247 born to imperial concubines.[108] Only four emperors were the sons of empresses, while concubines gave birth to the remaining twenty-one. Rulers usually did not limit themselves to a single liaison but had relationships with numerous palace ladies. For example, thirteen women bore the Liu Song Emperor Xiaowu his twenty-eight sons.[109] The birth of numerous sons to different mothers inevitably gave rise to succession disputes, periodically threatening the dynasty's stability.[110] Some imperial concubines became extremely close to the ruler. But even in these cases, if the women had no political authority, historians considered them virtual nonentities and often did not even bother to record their names.[111]

Nursemaids also resided in the palace.[112] Mothers from the upper reaches of society did not want to raise babies themselves, so they turned them over to wet nurses and nannies. An anecdote attests to the indispensability of these women. Lady Guo Huai murdered her son's wet nurses out of jealousy, assuming that they were having an affair with her husband.[113] Even so, when she gave birth to another son, she still did not deign to nurse the child herself and instead handed him over to a new wet nurse. Most emperors had been cared for by nannies during their formative years. Some rulers regarded their wet nurses with affection and treated them with filial regard as surrogate mothers.[114] Empresses also showed favor to former nursemaids.[115] Proximity to the imperial heir or a child emperor gave some wet nurses a central role. Once officials of the Northern Wei complained that they were never allowed to see a young emperor, as he spent his days surrounded by nannies and met with no one else.[116]

Ancient ritual texts dictated that a child from a noble family should have a high-born wet nurse. However, elite women regarded childcare as a menial task, so the aristocracy followed Han dynasty custom and employed women of debased status. Many were slaves and lowly servants.[117] Some were even the wives and daughters of convicts, enslaved in the palace following a man's conviction.[118] Yet even the lowliest nursemaid would find her life transformed if her charge became emperor. Some men presented their former wet nurses with gifts and other minor favors.[119] Favored wet nurses might even be granted titles and their sons allowed to enter the officialdom in spite of their humble backgrounds.[120] Occasionally a wet nurse acted as a trusted advisor to the monarch and involved herself in court politics.[121] Northern Wei emperors even gave some of these women the title of nursemaid empress dowager (*bao tai-hou*) or even empress dowager.[122] The shocking contrast between these women's base origins and subsequent high position scandalized an aristocratic society based on strict hierarchy, spurring troubled discussions about what sort of relationship a man ought to have with the lowly woman who nursed him.[123]

The myriad female inhabitants of the palace inevitably came into conflict. Emperors sought to maintain order by organizing the harem systematically and clarifying each woman's relative status. Cosmology, the ritual canon, and Han dynasty precedent all justified the classification of palace ladies into ranks.[124] People took these titles very seriously. In *Records of the Three Kingdoms (Sanguo zhi)*, the historian Chen Shou (233–297) employed different titles for the consorts of each state's ruler to implicitly convey his opinions about the relative legitimacy of each regime.[125] Palace reforms classified harem women into more numerous ranks and gave each a graded title, neatly placing them in a clear hierarchy.[126] Women of each rank wore distinctive clothing and jewelry, rode in particular vehicles, affixed a certain kind of seal to official documents, and received different degrees of ceremony, mourning, and posthumous sacrifice.[127]

Since the Zhou dynasty, the titles of palace women had sometimes been equated with grades of male bureaucratic office. The ancients believed that concubine and official held a similar kind of connection with the ruler, as both relationships were unequal, uncertain, and charged with emotion.[128] However, previously analogies between male and female rank had been purely aesthetic as female ranks did not come with a specific administrative duty. Because large harems served no practical purpose, Han dynasty moralists frequently criticized them as a frivolous drain on the nation's resources.[129]

During the era of division, as harems swelled to an unprecedented size, a new bureaucracy staffed largely by women took shape to manage the situation. Emperor Wei Gaozu not only classified palace women into ranks corresponding to male offices in the civil bureaucracy, in imitation of the Han, but also gave these women specific administrative and scribal duties in the inner palace. Rulers put harem women in charge of managing clothing, provisions, and other practical matters.[130] This female palace bureaucracy became increasingly elaborate and systematic over time. Both the northern and southern dynasties involved women in palace management.[131]

As the harem became increasingly bureaucratized, talented women became especially welcome in the palace as they could serve useful roles in the burgeoning inner palace bureaucracy.[132] The daughter of Li Biao (444–501) (whose name was not recorded) had mastered classical learning and calligraphy, and she entered the palace as a teacher.[133] Likewise, the wife of Yu Zhong (460–518), daughter of a prince, had also studied the ancient classics. She became a female retainer at court and even received an aristocratic title.[134] Rising standards of female education among the elite had the unintended side effect of providing the harem with learned women capable of administering palace matters.

The welcome extended to talented women also allowed educated Buddhist nuns to play a visible role in palace life. Many of them oversaw routine religious rituals.[135] But while most female clerics came from humble origins, a small number had aristocratic or imperial backgrounds. Elite nuns could use their education and connections to attain prominence in the inner palace or even the outer court. They became close to the powerful, dispensing advice, influencing events, and participating in intrigues.[136] Zhi Miaoyin, abbess of the Simple Tranquility Convent in the Jin capital, exemplifies the politically involved nun.[137] She became a trusted confidant of the monarch, who solicited her opinion on affairs of state.

Unmarried princesses also lived in the palace, and they also sometimes affected the political calculus.[138] Marriage to a daughter of the emperor linked the groom's family to the imperial line, raising their status. When a princess could choose her own spouse, she would likely try to find someone handsome and entertaining.[139] However, since antiquity it had been customary for the Son of Heaven to wed his daughters to important subjects, and Six Dynasties rulers continued to observe this custom.[140]

In the south, emperors married their daughters to a range of prominent families.[141] Matters were far more complex in the north, where rulers used the marriages of princesses to bind together an ethnically fragmented society. The Northern Wei pioneered a marriage strategy that later dynasties copied. Emperors carefully chose marriage partners for their daughters to absorb conquered populations and pacify potential enemies.[142] Later the Tuoba began marrying princesses to the Han elite to integrate important native clans into the Wei system. Of the fifty-two recorded princess marriages, 48.1 percent were to ethnic Han, 38.5 percent to Xianbei, and the remainder to other foreign peoples.[143] The resulting mixed-blood elite tended to intermarry with one another and frequently received titles and offices.[144] This closed group of ethnically mixed families ended up dominating the bureaucracy.[145] The Tuoba model of princess marriage had pros and cons. Although the Tuoba used this strategy to attract support from numerous important clans, they alienated traditional marriage partners and produced powerful affines who might potentially threaten the ruling house.[146]

A man who married a princess elevated his family. However, these women had reputations as troublemakers. Elaborate etiquette directed every aspect of the life of a princess. She did not even live in the same building as her husband, instead maintaining a separate residence. A princess had an independent income and came into the marriage with numerous retainers.[147] In spite of their lofty background, some of these women made mild and affectionate spouses.[148] However, others were spoiled and arrogant, earning the hatred of husbands and in-laws.[149] For example, one daughter of Emperor Wei Gaozu appalled her spouse's family with her haughtiness, licentiousness, and loud ugly voice.[150]

There was little that a suffering husband could do in these circumstances. Unlike a conventional marriage, a princess stood above her husband in rank. Insulting her risked execution.[151] Even so, some men managed to extricate themselves from a hated marriage to an emperor's daughter. The students of one educated man declared his princess wife to be immoral, and he used their disinterested criticism as grounds to divorce her.[152] Given the problems that princesses could cause, some men went to great lengths to avoid marrying an emperor's daughter. One prospective bridegroom hurriedly wed someone else.[153] Another simply declined the marriage and resigned his official position. The offended ruler punished him for his temerity.[154] Refusing to marry a princess could even be fatal. When one man snubbed a marriage proposal from the palace, his rivals seized the opportunity to slander him, leading to his execution.[155]

The sight of powerful empresses, dowagers, wet nurses, consorts, and princesses evoked deep feelings of unease among the officialdom. The Six Dynasties inherited misogynistic political rhetoric that condemned female political influence. These ideas grew out of the mandate of heaven ideology of the early Western Zhou era. Ancient thinkers had asserted that a ruler's legitimacy derives from heaven and warned that malfeasance risked the loss of the celestial mandate and would bring down the dynasty. During the Warring States era and Han dynasty, this ideology underwent a major revision.[156] Historians began to aver that a dissolute high-placed woman could incite heaven to withdraw its support for a dynasty, thus hastening its collapse. Western Han historians integrated this belief into the standard narrative of the rise and fall of dynasties. Henceforth this historical model served as the orthodox account of the impact of women on government.[157]

During the Six Dynasties, the mandate of heaven informed portrayals of past women. One historian noted how the mother of Emperor Qin Shihuang and the wife of Han Gaozu "sullied two states."[158] An admonitory memorial to the throne discussing the fall of the Han dynasty emphasized the corrosive role of empresses and their kinsmen.[159] And a postscript to a collection of biographies of empresses noted how evil women had brought down past dynasties.[160] Emperors paid particularly close attention to the failures of the chaotic Eastern Han dynasty, which had been plagued by haughty empresses and their rapacious kinsmen. Their own policies often emerged as a reaction to that dynasty's mistakes.[161]

The excesses of this era's most powerful women seemed to bolster the arguments of those who demanded limits on female power. Empress Dowager Ling issued imperial edicts in her own name, demanded to be addressed as "your majesty" (*bixia*), met with officials in the palace audience hall, received petitions, and acted like an emperor in virtually every respect. Historians accuse her of murdering her son and engaging in depraved sexual acts. Her tumultuous rule brought ruin to the dynasty, resulting in the massacre of thousands of officials and the division of north China.[162] Although Ling represented the most extreme case, a handful of other powerful Six Dynasties women also earned infamy for their arrogance and malfeasance.

In response, historians reasserted the anti-female ideology that had crystalized during the Han. As before, they continued to criticize irresponsible rulers.[163] However, they also emphasized the dangers of an alluring woman, as an evil beauty might entice the emperor to behave immorally and bring down the dynasty. One essay cautions, "A beautiful appearance seeks one to be fond of. This is something that the gentleman hates."[164] As the post-Han era commenced, Emperor Wen of Wei (Cao Pi, 187–226) expressly prohibited women from any role in politics.[165]

Women's involvement in government is the root of chaos. Henceforth officials will not send memorials to the empress dowager. Consort kinsmen will neither serve in office nor receive noble titles. May this edict be transmitted to posterity. Whoever defies it should be punished by the entire world.

Suspicion toward female power permeated literature, diffusing this idea into the marrow of elite culture. Liu Xie, the fifth-century author of the influential *Literary Mind and the Carving of Dragons (Wenxin diaolong)*, criticized female interference in politics, citing examples from the past to prove his point.[166] In his discussion of historiography Liu argued that only the affairs of emperors belong in the central annals (*benji*) section of the standard histories. An empress, however powerful, should have her actions relegated to the less important portions of historical records. This editorial choice implicitly criticized female participation in politics and treated it as illegitimate. Even court poetry absorbed this critical viewpoint. Poets ironically described an attractive woman as a "city destroyer" or "state destroyer."[167] A powerful woman might be able to gain control over the state, but eventually the men who wrote history and poetry would have many opportunities to exact their posthumous revenge.

4

Work

In the impoverished society of early medieval China, most people had to work very hard simply to survive. However, workers did not have equal control over their productive capacity. Social conventions determined how a family's members benefitted from their collective labor. Although the average woman toiled each day, she usually did not own the fruits of her labor as law and custom mostly excluded women from inheritance. Property passed down the male line, thus excluding women from a full share of accumulated family wealth. When a couple died, under most circumstances the family's wealth devolved to their sons.[1]

Historians have long debated the mechanics and principles of Chinese inheritance.[2] Ideas about ownership and inheritance evolved to bolster the established structure of society and economy.[3] It seems that the Chinese never considered women to be part owners of communal family property. Nevertheless, real behavior often diverged from simplistic patrilineal ideology. People may have had strong ideas about how property should be owned and transferred, but the complications of real life often demanded pragmatism. In light of these contradictions, the control of family wealth frequently resulted from a compromise between principle and circumstance.[4] Representatives of the state rarely interfered in inheritance, so elders had great latitude in distributing common wealth. They often ruled on matters of female inheritance in an ad hoc manner that valued expediency over abstract ideals.[5] Female family members belonged to a common budget group that managed and shared the household's income and deployed collective resources. And a widow could often manage her deceased husband's property, including land, until her son reached the age of majority and assumed control of family finances.[6]

A woman normally went into marriage with a dowry. If her parents died before she married, their estate funded her dowry. A wife owned her dowry outright. Even so, a husband sometimes took control of the goods that a wife brought with her from her own family.[7] The rites emphasized the betrothal gift or bridewealth (*pin*), presented by the groom's side to the family of the bride, as the primary transfer of wealth during marriage. In this era, the betrothal gift remained more valuable than dowry. Even so, a bride received a dowry when she married in lieu of inheritance upon the death of her parents, providing her with a share of family property when she left home. Because the ancient rites did not regulate dowry, its value varied considerably. Some brides seem to have received modest dowries while women from wealthy families received a substantial sum.[8] Wealthy merchants dowered their daughters generously to attract a prestigious son-in-law and raise the family's status. On the contrary, some recluses deliberately married off their daughters with minimal dowry to symbolize their otherworldliness.

Princesses entered marriage with an extravagant dowry and continued to receive financial support from the palace.[9] When a princess married, she did not live with her husband but instead maintained a separate residence nearby. The palace treasury paid for her upkeep so that she could afford the lavish clothing, food, and accouterments worthy of an emperor's daughter. As for women who married into the imperial house, they also received a stipend from the treasury as well as periodic gifts from the ruler. Even titled ladies unrelated to the ruler could receive income from a fiscal unit called "food benefice" (*shiyi*). They did not own or administer this land but received the tax income paid by its residents.

Daily life was not all drudgery. Even ordinary women might find time for leisure activities. The curmudgeonly Ge Hong bemoaned the decadence of his era and frequently complained about the behavior of those around him. He grumbled that women no longer spent their time raising silkworms and spinning. They neglected household occupations and instead devoted their days to dancing, traveling, and visiting friends. They would even go out at night and roam around town by torchlight.[10]

Poets entertained an expansive vision of female life that included many matters besides work. The ideal woman described in poetry did not just toil at her loom morning to night. She might enjoy dancing and reading.[11] Nevertheless, for all but the wealthy few, survival required labor. The average woman had to work hard to have a decent life. Like most men, women performed a wide variety of tasks during a typical day. Women's work consisted mainly of domestic chores as these could be performed while looking after children.[12] Biographies mention women weaving, sewing, and cooking.[13] In a time before soap or detergents, cleaning and washing were onerous duties. Women also had the responsibility of cooking, which required hauling fuel and keeping fires burning.[14] Besides preparing each meal, they also cured meats, made pickles and sauces, fermented alcohol, and gathered wild vegetables. Even women from aristocratic families often knew how to cook and spent time in the kitchen helping to prepare meals as they considered cooking a respectable way for any woman to spend her time. Women were also the family's caregivers, looking after both children and elders. This obligation placed them in a position to actualize the ideals of filial piety, and this virtue became increasingly associated with women.[15]

Notably, women undertook most tasks within the recesses of the home. Separation of the sexes and female reclusion did not necessarily require much effort. Gendered labor roles confined women to the house for much of the day, hidden from the eyes of men and detached from public affairs. Even so, necessity could force women to take on stereotypically male tasks. In this martial age, men were often away at war. While they were gone, women had no choice but to cross gender boundaries and take on men's work as well as their own.[16] Some even took up the plow or practiced male professions until their husbands returned.

Although women performed many quotidian tasks, textile production was by far the most economically valuable. People considered raising silkworms, spinning, weaving, and sewing to be women's work. Such was the importance of cloth production that it came to symbolize virtuous womanhood in general. Even though women spent each day performing a variety of tasks, ancient thinkers had described the ideal labor of each sex in simplified terms, stating that men plow and women weave.[17] These stereotypes continued to influence medieval ideas about normative female labor. People expected women to spend part of their time spinning and weaving. The cloth that they made accounted for a large proportion of a household's economic output.

Cloth had a central place in the early medieval economy. Governments minted relatively little coin, so people usually bartered for goods using bundles of cloth. Also, the government received more than half of tax payments in cloth, making it a de facto currency.[18] Due to the importance of this female product, women occupied a central place in the economy and fiscal system.[19] At times government functionaries even oversaw women working in the mulberry groves to ensure sufficient silk output.[20] The centrality of cloth to the economy provided incentives for technological innovation, and this era saw significant advances in the mechanics of textile production.

Cloth making was essential to a family's success and the well-being of society as a whole, so people encouraged women to devote as much time as possible to spinning and weaving. Governments endeavored to raise female output by emphasizing the importance of cloth production and lauding women who excelled at this vital craft.[21] Epitaphs praise a woman devoted to textile work as unusually virtuous.[22] And biographies of model women often mention that they enjoyed making cloth. Readers knew that when a writer described a woman sitting at a loom, this was a shorthand way of expressing her inner virtue.[23]

Even palace ladies made cloth. The emperor and those around him had to be attired in uniquely magnificent garb unobtainable on the open market, so palace workshops produced luxurious fabrics and elaborate finished clothing.[24] Female slaves made up much of the work force in palace workshops. Sometimes free women also served as temporary corvée labor. The manufacture of cloth in the palace further heightened its significance. According to political and cosmological theory, the palace was the center of the entire world, so activities there affected the entire realm. Because people saw textile work as an expression of female morality, sometimes even empresses made a show of making cloth to symbolize their own goodness, the integrity of the current reign, and to exert a transformative influence on society at large.

Cloth production appears as a common trope in biographies of model empresses and other imperial consorts. The virtuous Empress Yang Yan (238–274) stood out not just for beauty but for intelligence and virtue as well. Although she enjoyed reading, she often spent her leisure hours at the loom.[25] Similarly, Empress Chi (468–499) became proficient at calligraphy and read the standard histories and their commentaries.[26] The historian emphasizes that in addition to these cultured accomplishments, she also devoted her time to making cloth, thereby assuring the reader that her intellectual pursuits did not preclude virtue. Even the famed Empress Wenming spent some time at the spindle despite having to attend to numerous matters of state.[27] Descriptions of empresses spinning and weaving served as political ideology, emphasizing the morality of the ruling family and thus attesting to its legitimacy.

Stories of model women from ordinary backgrounds also routinely feature cloth making. In the literary context, this mundane activity became a trope symbolizing a woman's fundamental goodness. As in ancient sources, the virtuous mother often spins and weaves to support her children.[28] In many of these stories, the son eventually becomes successful as a result of his mother's industry. The woman at her loom appears wise and sanguine in the face of difficulty, as if this work somehow imbued her with superhuman faculties.[29] Even the tools of cloth manufacture took on an aura of integrity. When a young woman wanted to fend off the unwanted attentions of an insistent male neighbor, she threw the shuttle of her loom and broke two of his teeth.[30]

Poetry expresses the moralistic implications of textile production. One poem employs this device to directly contrast the suspiciously coy courtesan with the virtuous wife who has nothing to hide. "Singing girls trill, hidden by fans, / Young wives weave behind open blinds."[31] Due to the ethical implications of spinning and weaving, it could be used to evoke uxorial virtue. When a husband was away from home for a long time, his faithful wife spent her time making cloth. "I don't resent the bitter lot of shuttle and reel, / What I mourn is this thousand-league separation."[32]

Abandoned women feature prominently in the ancient *Classic of Poetry* anthology, and these emotional verses inspired medieval authors. As with ancient prototypes, Six Dynasties poets depict the woman who has been divorced, separated, or widowed as sad and adrift. Lacking a man to provide for her, she works hard raising silkworms, spinning, and weaving to support herself.[33] In this setting, textile work suggests emptiness and misery rather than virtue. The widow or divorcée has nothing to look forward to in her life other than an endless succession of lonely days devoted to hard work. The termination of marriage has robbed her life of meaning.[34]

Early medieval women had a prominent role in agriculture. Since antiquity, heavy farm work such as plowing had been considered a male duty. Nevertheless, as farming constituted the backbone of the economy, women had also traditionally participated in some agricultural activities.[35] During the early medieval era, the link between women and agriculture intensified. New land tenure systems demanded that women enter the fields and do agricultural labor on a regular basis.

In the pandemonium that accompanied the collapse of the Eastern Han dynasty, numerous peasants died or fled, and much of the most fertile land in China ended up abandoned. Government ministers who wanted to reconstitute order and achieve a modicum of prosperity had to come up with ways to return fallow land to cultivation. The original landowners could often not be located, making the previous system of private property unworkable. Given these extraordinary circumstances, administrators had no choice but to step in and oversee the distribution and use of farmland.[36] In 280 Western Jin authorities established a novel system that allocated fields to able-bodied members of the community. Faced with an alarming decrease in population, the government declared that men and women residing in rural areas would be granted the right to work a piece of land.

With society still in disarray, it seems that the government never implemented this system on a wide scale. Nevertheless, this administrative precedent inspired the Northern Wei to establish a similar system for allocating farmland. Under that dynasty's equal field (*juntian*) system, a man received forty *mu* of fields and a woman twenty *mu*.[37] In addition to this basic allocation, women could also have the use of land to grow hemp for making cloth and could sometimes receive additional fields as well. These measures succeeded in raising production, and governments continued to allocate fields down through the Tang dynasty. Documents from Dunhuang show that although woman did indeed receive land allotments, the state treated them differently from men. Not only did women receive less land, they also faced higher tax burdens. And from the year 624 onward, only widows received land allotments. Yet in spite of these inequities, the equal field system gave women a vital role in agriculture, society's central economic activity, thereby making them far more productive and elevating their status.

Because women had responsibility for childcare, some made it their profession. Noblewomen disdained breastfeeding and caring for babies and outsourced this burden to women of low birth. Nursemaids and nannies often developed an intimate bond with their charges. When society plunged into chaos, a family might send their child away from danger in the care of a trusted nursemaid.[38] This custom allowed women from humble backgrounds the rare opportunity to gain the attention of those at the apex of society. Some men treated their former nursemaids and nannies as family members. After they had reached adulthood, officials and empresses sometimes felt affection for the women who raised them and rewarded them liberally. At the very least, serving as a nursemaid gave a woman the opportunity to avoid both ordinary domestic routine and stoop labor under the hot sun.

Women's position in the family also led them to take on special types of work. Shamanism included curative techniques, giving women a role in healing since antiquity.[39] And because the medicine of the time consisted largely of herbal decoctions, women's familiarity with kitchen work put them in a position to administer herbal remedies. Moreover, women were traditionally responsible for nursing sick family members. So even though men monopolized the medical profession, women undertook routine healing for their families. Male physicians looked down on female medical practitioners and warned against allowing women to prepare medicines. Moreover, because people regarded menstrual discharges as highly polluting, male physicians feared that female filth might render their medications ineffective.[40]

In spite of this skepticism, women continued to serve as the primary caregivers and healers in the home.[41] Mothers looked after the health and cleanliness of their children while wives ministered to sick husbands and parents-in-law. And although the reputation of shamanistic healing had declined, female shamans still conducted ceremonies to expel demons believed to cause illness.[42] Women also acted as midwives, which required an understanding of gynecology and obstetrics medicine. Regardless of

the type of healing, women usually acquired medical knowledge infor-
mally through practical experience, family lore, and discussions with
other women.[43] In this way their medical knowledge differed from the
textual learning of male physicians, and the healing arts practiced by each
sex diverged considerably.

Women also occasionally worked outside the home. A small number
became involved with commerce. As in later times, both the dangers of
the road and social convention prevented women from traveling freely,
barring them from long-distance trade.[44] Instead they focused on retail,
which allowed them to remain close to their family. An ambitious woman
would take advantage of the possibilities at hand. If she had beautiful
long hair, she might shear off her locks and sell them to a wig maker.[45] After picking and processing tea, a woman could go to the marketplace and
sell her crop.[46] Female hawkers also sold a variety of goods in the marketplace, and women sometimes operated and staffed bars and simple res-
taurants.[47] Even so, relatively few women became involved in commerce
during the era of disunion. The overall impoverishment of society, inter-
necine chaos, and the low rate of urbanization limited economic activity,
affecting the prospects of entrepreneurial women as well as men.

Emperors considered it essential to have large numbers of female
performers in the palace as their opulent lifestyle included music and
dance. Rulers and warlords routinely kept hundreds of these women in
their entourages.[48] Most female performers were slaves.[49] Singers and
dancers performed at court banquets and also entertained the ruler pri-
vately.[50] Some had sexual relations with their masters, making them akin
to palace concubines.[51]

The nobility also kept large numbers of enslaved entertainers in their
mansions.[52] During the Eastern Zhou and Han eras, wealthy men sometimes had a few trained female performers attached to their household.[53]
During the Six Dynasties, the number of domestic entertainers rose to
unprecedented levels. Disappointed with the decayed state of society and
frightened by political violence, many aristocrats sought escape by surrounding themselves with beauty and sensuality. Spending huge sums
on female entertainers also served as conspicuous consumption that be-
tokened high status.[54] A proud noble would want to entertain his guests
with elaborate musical performances featuring numerous women.[55]

The rich sold and swapped slave performers alongside other luxury
goods.[56] These women ranked below concubines in the household hierarchy and had no rights or security. Poetry depicts them living hard lives
and enduring contempt.[57] The master could abuse them according to his
whims. When an entertainer became too old or took ill, she might be simply be cast out onto the street. A master could also use these women sexually. However, developing an intimate relationship with her master might

allow an entertainer to better her lot. And if she gave birth to a son, she might be promoted to concubine, raising her position in the household.[58]

Although this impoverished society could support relatively few commercial entertainment venues, cities had bordellos and bars that attracted patrons by offering entertainment.[59] Most prostitutes had no special skills, but some received extensive training in music and dance. The most talented could even compose and recite poetry. These performers were prototypes of the famed courtesans of the Tang and Ming. Male patrons found themselves charmed by women who combined beauty with skill, and an entertainer occasionally attracted the attentions of an important man.[60] Poetry describes their beauty as alluringly sensual, marking the emergence of a new feminine ideal.[61]

The professionalization of entertainment allowed performers to attain a very high level of skill, raising the quality of music and dance to unprecedented heights. Female musicians frequently performed in large groups, allowing rich harmonies. Tomb figurines depict female musicians seated in rows, each playing a different instrument.[62] Highly emotional song lyrics had a major impact on poetry, encouraging writers to describe their feelings more openly.[63] Dance also became highly refined. Most famously, performers perfected the traditional sleeve dance which used the exaggeratedly long sleeves of special costumes to accentuate the dancer's movements.[64] Many new dances also emerged, treating audiences to a broad variety of styles.[65]

As performance culture flourished, these arts became increasingly popular at all levels of society. Many women could play an instrument, sing, and dance. Mastery of these arts even became a respectful attainment for high-born ladies.[66] One poem depicts the ideal young woman as proficient at a variety of skills. In addition to virtuously working at the loom, she also displays her familiarity with both literature and dance:[67]

> She rushes madly to work at loom and shuttle,
> Calm and composed she loves the Chao dance,
> Stretching out sleeves, image of wings in flight.
> Whenever the string stops are raised or lowered,
> Literature and history books are tucked away.

Even Buddhist nunneries sometimes hosted performances featuring music and dance.[68] Some temples only allowed women to attend, but an open-minded patron would allow a mixed audience to enjoy these religious entertainments.

During centuries of war, many people lost their freedoms. In particular, when brigands and rogue armies roamed the land during the third century, the number of free people declined considerably. Unable to defend themselves, peasants looked to powerful landlords and clan leaders for protection. The rich raised private armies for self-defense that allowed them to safeguard poor neighbors. But in return for security, militarized landlords demanded obedience and a share of their neighbors' produce. Under these conditions, the common people in many areas steadily declined to a status akin to serfs. They became bound to the land, had to hand over a fixed portion of their crop each season, and lost their rights and dignity.

Other people fell even lower, reduced to chattel who could be bought and sold. During times of war or famine, some men sold their wives and children into slavery so that they themselves could survive. Others enslaved family members to pay off a debt, raise money for taxes, or fund a parent's funeral.[69] The wives and daughters of men convicted of a serious crime could be enslaved in the palace or some other state institution.[70] Invading nomads and native warlords captured people as spoils of war along with other valuables such as gold and horses.[71] Sometimes thousands of people ended up enslaved as the result of a single battle. Authorities sometimes tried to prevent the forcible enslavement of free women and men. But in times of weak government, soldiers armed with weapons knew that they could enslave people with impunity.[72]

The institution of slavery differed in the north and the south.[73] In the south, many war captives, convicts, and the kin of convicts became slaves of the state. Private slaves had various backgrounds. Some were war captives while others had been purchased from kinsmen or dealers. Also, the emperor handed out slaves to his supporters, along with other treasures, as a sign of favor. In the north, a large proportion of slaves descended from captives taken during the initial invasions of China. Emperors often rewarded meritorious officials with slaves. In both the south and the north, many female slaves ended up as domestic servants in the mansions of the aristocracy.

Records of the time describe enormous numbers of slaves. They were a common sight in the urban landscape as they went about the city on errands.[74] Visitors to homes of the wealthy commented on the large number of domestic slaves. In the toilet area of one mansion, ten or more beautifully dressed female slaves stood in line, holding combs, lotions, and other amenities for guests.[75] When household slaves became this numerous, they had few practical duties. Crowds of slave women served to produce an ambiance of luxury. Their masters just wanted to flaunt large numbers of slaves as a status symbol, even if they served no purpose.

Slaves essentially had no rights, and masters often treated them callously. A master could use female slaves for sex, and the household's slaves and servants constituted a de facto harem.[76] A master could even kill a slave with impunity as the murder of a slave was essentially legal.

Masters frequently took advantage of this power, and writers recorded numerous examples of masters killing female slaves.[77] In this cruel age, some people killed slaves for trivial reasons. The violent warlord Shi Chong, infamous for his barbarism, had beautiful women serve alcohol at his banquets. If one of his guests failed to drink all of the proffered wine, Shi ordered one of the women to be killed as a penalty.[78]

Despite the low status of slaves, some enjoyed decent treatment. Most slave women in large households had little to do. And the government or masters sometimes emancipated female slaves.[79] Periodic amnesties freed the enslaved kin of convicts. Emperors also sometimes freed palace slaves and gave them to poor men as wives. Masters frequently emancipated female slaves who reached an advanced age or fell seriously ill. Family members could also ransom a slave from her owner.[80] Because of this practice, a pious Buddhist woman would sometimes voluntarily "enslave" herself to a temple, forcing her family to pay an enormous sum to ransom her back.[81]

A few manumitted slaves rose in status. An emancipated female slave might become the concubine of a powerful man.[82] If she then earned her master's favor, her situation could improve considerably. Under the unusual political system of the northern dynasties, emperors deliberately wed women of extremely low status, so a slave could even become empress.[83] And the children of slave women sometimes prospered. In the south, the son of a prominent father born to a slave might even enjoy a distinguished official career.[84] In sum, early medieval slavery should not be seen as a singular institution or unitary status. A slave's circumstances could vary considerably according to her particular situation.

Warfare defined the age of disunion. Women sometimes had a role in war, and they even undertook certain forms of military service. People respected prowess in the martial arts—in women as well as men—and even empresses and noblewomen honed their skills in horseback riding and archery.[85] For a time, it was fashionable for southern ladies to wear ornaments of gold, silver, ivory, and tortoiseshell in the shape of miniature weapons.[86] People from earlier eras had regarded any female participation in warfare as a gross violation of the fundamental distinction between the sexes. But society had become so thoroughly militarized that it became acceptable for women to have a role in war.

During the Zhou dynasty, the military class of minor aristocrats called *shi* had been considered a moral elite, and strict ritual rules enforced high standards of conduct. Given the ancient connections between military service, high rank, and virtue, a female warrior could gain admiration for her moral superiority.[87] Traditionally, women fought for the sake of Confucian virtues such as righteousness (*yi*) and filial piety. Han dynasty writings describe female role models noted for both bravery and virtue. Moral principles sometimes spurred women to violence, as they sought vengeance on behalf of a wronged kinsman or fended off unwanted sexual advances.[88] Six Dynasties authors continued to celebrate virtuous female fighters. A woman who beat her husband's murderer to death received an imperial amnesty due to her righteous behavior.[89] And when one man wanted to force a woman to marry him, she fended him off with a sword, earning praise as a model of female integrity.[90]

Other women took part in military operations. Emperor Wen of Jin and Empress Wenming conducted an important military campaign together, and she received equal credit for managing important military matters.[91] Northern rulers sometimes employed women from the steppe as palace bodyguards.[92] There was also the case of a woman who became a general, albeit under unusual circumstances. Her father, a noted military officer, had been ordered to lead an army while still in mourning for his deceased mother. He did not want to violate his mourning obligations, so he appointed one of his daughters to be general and another daughter as a high-ranking officer so that they could serve in his place.[93] Historical records do not reveal whether these women prosecuted the war themselves or merely acted as figureheads on their father's behalf. Either way, the soldiers consented to taking orders from a female general.

In wartime, large numbers of women found themselves pressed into military roles. During a siege, female inhabitants served alongside men on the city walls, fighting and also repairing the fortifications.[94] And women born into military households lived a martial life. As these families tended to intermarry, their women spent their lives immersed in war. With conflict so frequent, they often accompanied their husbands on campaigns and lived in army camps.[95] When war loomed, entire families would embark on a military campaign.

Even though classical ritual forbade women from participating in war, some nevertheless took on military roles. As the Han dynasty disintegrated, women began to have a more visible presence in military camps.[96] Both the warlord Cao Cao and his foes used female troops on the battlefield, where they brandished spears, halberds, and bows. In that era, soldiers became a distinct social caste. The daughter of a soldier could only marry another soldier, so a woman born into a military family had no choice but to spend her life in a military environment.

The law sentenced men convicted of certain crimes, and their wives, to military service.[97] Under the Northern Qi, both convicts and their female family members became soldiers.[98] Like their husbands, women pressed into military service lived under strict discipline. If a man committed an infraction or absconded, authorities punished his wife as well.[99] As in armies elsewhere in the world, most of these women lacked special skills or fighting ability.[100] Instead they provided support, constructing

Figure 4.1.   A female Xianbei warrior. She wears a "wind hat" with drooping cover, cape, and a military uniform with armor. Editor at Large, Treasures of Ancient China.

fortifications, handling provisions, mending weapons, defending their camp, and doing domestic chores. Only occasionally did they go out on the battlefield.[101]

During the early third century, Cao Cao established a network of self-sustaining military communities (*tuntian*).[102] Just as the demand for soldiers increased, the fiscal system declined and many areas regressed to a subsistence economy, making it difficult to support large numbers of troops. In response, authorities founded military communities to provide soldiers with land that would make them self-supporting. These troops had to both farm and fight. When men went on a campaign, women tended the fields in their absence. The southern dynasties found military communities useful and maintained them along the frontiers. However, this system was unpopular with the residents of these settlements. People feared the harsh and dangerous life in unstable border regions.[103]

Although the north lacked an institutionalized system of military communities, the women of military households often followed their husbands off to war. The Xianbei traditionally expected their women to be strong and to fight when necessary. The militaristic values of nomadic conquerors gave rise to the famed ballad of Hua Mulan, composed by an anonymous northern poet.[104] In this story, when Mulan's father is drafted, she disguises herself as a man to serve in his place. She becomes an exemplary warrior and distinguishes herself with outstanding heroism. Mulan is even offered an official post in recognition of her courage, which she modestly declines. Instead she returns home, dons female attire, and resumes conventional female life.

The tale of Mulan has captured the imaginations of generations of readers, and it continues to be retold in new ways. Although audiences today appreciate this story as an engaging fantasy, it originally seemed much closer to quotidian reality at a time when many women belonged to military households and received martial arts training. Mulan's respect for Confucian propriety helps account for her perennial appeal. She does not dress like a man or become a warrior out of desire or ambition. Instead she sees these unpleasant actions as a way to protect her father from harm. After succeeding on the battlefield, she refuses to continue dressing as a man and bearing arms. Instead she returns home and resumes a stereotypical female life. The original readers could accept Mulan challenging gender norms and taking on a masculine identity only because she undertook it as a temporary sacrifice for the sake of moral duty. By mixing conservative Confucian integrity with startling violations of feminine decorum, Mulan has captured the hearts of numerous readers and remains an object of fascination both in China and abroad.

5

Religion

War, chaos, and impoverishment can make the period of disunity between the Han and Sui dynasties seem like an age of darkness. Yet
even as some aspects of society declined, others burgeoned. When people
turned away from secular ideals and institutions in disappointment, they
cultivated ingenious alternatives, giving rise to compelling new modes of
thought. In particular, metaphysics and religion flourished. Philosophers
turned their attentions to highly abstract speculation, and legions of believers made faith the axis of their lives. Many women became fervent
followers of the major religions, so changes in belief and the rise of new
institutions had a particularly large impact on their lives.

A few female deities held important places in the spiritual pantheon.
The most important goddesses had emerged in earlier eras and remained
popular objects of devotion. The creator deity Nü Wa (Nü Gua) and the
maternal Xiwangmu (Queen Mother of the West) continued to attract
large followings.[1] Cults dedicated to the goddess of the Han River, associated with immortality, and the sensual Jade Lady also endured.[2] Newly
popular female deities included the female immortal Ma Gu, the shamanistic goddess Ding Gu, and a tea goddess named Guangling Cha Lao.[3]

The folk deity Zi Gu (Purple Mother) stands out as probably the most
unusual goddess of the time.[4] This figure was originally a mortal concubine. Her master's wife became jealous of her outstanding beauty and
abused her terribly, forcing her to do the dirtiest and most humiliating
work in the house, including cleaning toilets. This mistreatment became
so brutal that she eventually died. But instead of being forgotten, this
ill-fated concubine unexpectedly became apotheosized into a goddess.

Due to the way she had been abused, worshippers considered her the residential deity of toilets and believed that she could prevent the incursion of ghosts and demons that tended to haunt these unclean places. Zi Gu could also affect the fortunes of female devotees. Although people worshipped her in the toilet, they considered her a goddess of sericulture as well.

Pastoral peoples brought new mythologies into China, including stories about women. The Xiongnu considered themselves descendants of a mortal woman who mated with a divine wolf and used this tale to explain why Xiongnu songs sound like wolf howls.[5] Nomadic peoples invented other stories to disguise their humble origins. In general, the more obscure a group's beginnings, the more extravagant their claims of divine ancestry. The emperors of the Northern Wei asserted that the founder of the ruling line had been born to a magnificent goddess who descended from heaven along with her retinue.[6] This beautiful deity spent one night together with a Xianbei ruler then suddenly disappeared. She unexpectedly reappeared a year later to present her mortal paramour with a son—the future Emperor Shizu.

Fascination with supernatural tales also brought attention to female spirits. The immensely popular genre of anomaly tales, "accounts of the strange" (zhiguai), included numerous ghost stories, often about female spirits. Many tales describe a ghost unexpectedly appearing before a mortal person.[7] Sometimes the ghost simply wants a living being to acknowledge its existence. Others want something from the living, such as food or drink, or else proper care for its corpse. Some ghosts became friends with a living person. These affable spirits might want to perform music, chat, or enjoy a drink with a live friend.

Poetry portrayed women as fundamentally romantic, and this viewpoint influenced the depiction of fictional ghosts. Some female spirits returned to the land of the living in search of love. A man might be approached by the ghost of a deceased spouse or fiancée or even that of a deceased stranger. Malevolent female wraiths endangered an unsuspecting male lover. An evil demon, such as a fox spirit, sometimes took on the guise of a beautiful woman to seduce a man and eventually do him harm.[8] When a man realized his lover's true identity, he would react with horror and try to chase away the deceitful monster.

Even as organized religions increased in importance, some women adhered to age-old beliefs, serving as shamans and diviners.[9] Shamanism also took on new life by influencing newly popular faiths. Buddhism came to China from abroad, and believers initially had a poor understanding of dogma and ritual. Sometimes Buddhist devotees continued to perform traditional shamanistic rituals under the guise of their new religion, emphasizing magic, healing, and fertility as spiritual practices.[10] Other women served as shamans (*wu*) in a traditional manner.[11] They beat drums, danced to coax gods down from heaven, and implored for favors and insights from various deities and immortals. Although these rites had a dubious reputation, in times of crisis people nevertheless looked to these holy women to induce rain or cure disease. Some shamans specialized in fortune telling, which employed a range of divination techniques. A reputation for mastery of these arts could win a woman respect.[12]

Government functionaries had mixed feelings about shamans. The state employed a few of them on a regular basis.[13] Twice a year in the north, female shamans officiated over ceremonies for the god of heaven, which included animal sacrifice.[14] The government used these sorts of rituals to attract divine blessings and thus assure peace, the ruler's health and longevity, and weather conducive to a good harvest. Shamans could also issue terrifying imprecations against enemies of the state.[15] And residents of the palace employed mysterious magical charms and drugs as weapons in dynastic intrigue.[16] Nomadic culture held these religious practices in high regard and government authorities descended from steppe peoples had great faith in shamanistic powers. Nevertheless, for such awesome powers to be wielded by low-status women implicitly threatened the state, so governments periodically repressed shamanistic rites.[17]

The Six Dynasties stand out as the time when organized religion matured into a major force in Chinese society. During the Eastern Han, Daoists had formalized their religion, constructing a consistent framework of religious and philosophical ideas and establishing organized groups with standard liturgy and a clerical hierarchy. These efforts led to the construction of large Daoist temples that became hubs of culture and social life. Erudite thinkers raised Daoist philosophy to a high level of theoretical sophistication, and the religious manifestations of Daoism attracted an enthusiastic following. The flourishing of institutionalized Daoism provided women with new opportunities for participating in spiritual life.[18]

Religious Daoism includes prominent female imagery, motivated by a celebration of the yin element of the yin/yang dichotomy. Believers also looked to the Dao as the primal force that created everything in the universe, making it akin to a mother that devotees would discuss in feminine terms. Given this metaphysical context, some texts even seem to portray women as superior to men in certain respects.[19] Overall, however, Daoism conceptualizes the perfected person as neither stereotypically masculine nor feminine but androgynous, combining traits from both sexes to fashion the consummate human being.[20] While valorizing both feminine and masculine qualities, Daoists tended to emphasize the former because they considered male traits too dominant in society. They highlighted the benefits of feminine attributes as a necessary corrective for excessive masculinization.

Under Daoist influence, some traditional moral concepts underwent comprehensive reappraisal.[21] In antiquity, *da* referred to strict adherence to Confucian righteousness and ritual. But due to Daoist influence, early medieval writers reversed its meaning. Instead of describing people who observed traditional ethics, the term now designated those with sufficient authenticity to courageously abandon conventional values and thus liberate themselves from temporal restrictions. The iconoclastic spirit of Daoism spurred believers to rethink the nature of womanhood.

Given this prominence of female images and ideas, many women eagerly embraced Daoism, and their contributions shaped the religion's development.[22] The openness and flexibility of religious Daoism also appealed to women as they could readily combine it with Buddhism and folk beliefs. Not only did women influence Daoism, but it also affected female behavior. The Daoist quest for liberation gave women new room for self-expression. Freed from conventional expectations, women reacted in a variety of ways. They might perfect a beautiful appearance, devote themselves to cultivating their talents, or startle bystanders with unexpected behavior.

Some Daoist divinities were female, providing women with supernatural role models. The Daoist pantheon absorbed traditional female deities, giving them new powers and identities. Most famously, they integrated the goddess Xiwangmu into their worship and made her a center of devotion.[23] Some goddesses underwent a complicated development before becoming Daoist figures. The Mysterious Woman of the Nine Heavens (Jiutian xuannü) had been popular during the Han dynasty when worshippers associated her with war, sex, and longevity.[24] Daoists then incorporated her into their own pantheon and altered her persona. In her new guise, the Mysterious Woman became a disciple of Xiwangmu and teacher of the Yellow Thearch, who received divine revelations from her on behalf of humanity. She thus served as a key link in the transmission of esoteric wisdom from the highest deities down to humanity. Unique Daoist deities also emerged. The Jade Woman (Yu Nü) could ingest plasmas from the sun and moon and then deliver them from her own mouth to that of a male adept.[25] Immortals also played important roles in medieval Daoism.[26] A believer who achieved a high level of spiritual cultivation could not only avoid death but might also attain an array of magical powers. Women as well as men could reach a state of such perfection. Dogma also held that female immortals had delivered some of the key Daoist scriptures and other revelations to chosen men, making them important figures in the dissemination of Daoist wisdom.[27]

Women embraced Daoism for various reasons and engaged in cultivation practices and worship to different degrees.[28] Some sought immortality or magical powers. Others looked to religion to escape an unpleasant situation, avoid marriage, or seek new opportunities. Female believers had several options. Some practiced their religion at home or joined a lay organization to engage in self-cultivation with a like-minded group while remaining part of the mundane world. The most devoted left secular society, studied under an accomplished master, received formal ordination and became a Daoist nun (*nüguan*).[29] As in Buddhism, an aspiring nun was supposed to notify her family and obtain their consent before taking vows. A nun either lived alone in an isolated hermitage or resided with a female master who trained her in the regimens of self-cultivation. Novices often sought out remote places to avoid distractions, attune themselves with the natural world, and purify their minds. When an aspiring nun attained sufficient understanding of her faith, she usually entered a larger institution. Daoist convents classified clerics into a hierarchy of ranks, and a nun could gain a higher position as she accumulated experience and wisdom.

Daoism stands out for its sexual egalitarianism. Women and men could achieve comparable levels of cultivation and attainment. Male and female clerics even wore similar garb, although women distinguished themselves with a more elaborate hairstyle. However, the spirit of impartiality had limits. Women had to undertake more complicated self-purification before performing holy rites as people believed that menstrual blood made them fundamentally impure. Moreover, men dominated major Daoist rituals and wrote most religious texts.[30]

Wei Huacun (251–334) founded the Shangqing sect, making her by far the most prominent woman in medieval Daoism.[31] She married young and at first lived a secular life. After her children grew up, she became deeply involved in Daoist practice and learned how to commune with the immortals. These sacred figures conveyed lengthy revelations to her. When written down, the resulting thirty-one fascicles served as the core scriptures of the Shangqing school of Daoism. This sect taught elaborate meditative techniques, with the adept visualizing various parts of the body as a way to obtain wisdom. In promoting meditation and visualization, Wei Huacun helped shift the focus of Daoism away from purely physical practices—most notably the ingestion of certain foods and avoidance of others—toward mystical self-cultivation. Female Daoists often favored the Shangqing school, which seems to have been most open to female participation.

Like men, female adepts pursued various regimens intended to transform themselves into perfected beings, including breath control, dietary restrictions, meditation, chanting sacred texts, and engaging in visualizations that sometimes took them on ecstatic journeys to sacred realms.[32] They believed that if they mastered these techniques, they could gain magical powers and even become immortal. A perfected immortal might be able to fly through the heavens, walk through water without getting wet, sit in a fire without being burned, or cause buildings to move from one place to another.

Most Daoist nuns observed celibacy and lived an austere life centered on spiritual cultivation. Nevertheless, Daoists permitted clerics to remain close to the lay realm. Nuns could participate in secular ceremonies such as the ancestral rites, and were free to leave their convent and marry if the opportunity arose. Daoist nuns also interacted with men far more freely than their Buddhist sisters. A few became close to a man while still a member of the clergy. As a result of their freedom, Daoist nuns gained a popular reputation for romance and unconventional behavior.

Buddhism had a miniscule presence in China during the Eastern Han, but in the ensuing age of chaos and cultural mélange it burgeoned into a leading political, economic, and cultural force. During this turbulent era, many people turned away from secular concerns in disappointment. Instead they looked to the Buddha's gentle teachings for solace and meaning. Although Buddhism attracted considerable grassroots support, imperial patronage brought the religion wealth and influence. Several empresses financed the construction of grand Buddhist temples. Empress Dowager Ling gained a reputation for extravagant piety for sponsoring gigantic religious complexes and ambitious programs of religious art.[33] And if an emperor's mother had been a devout supporter of Buddhism, the ruler often continued supporting the religion out of filial duty.[34] Due to imperial patronage, some temples in the capital had close connections with the palace.[35] Empresses financed religious activities, and the clerics of favored institutions participated in court rituals.[36] Harem women visited temples under imperial sponsorship to study Buddhist doctrine, and some became nuns. Large and lavish, the most prestigious temples boasted magnificent workmanship and elegant gardens.

Palace women moved easily between palace and temple. Elite temples served as extensions of the palace where ladies of the harem and aristocracy could take refuge in times of political crisis or when they lost favor. A palace woman who felt endangered could temporarily serve as a nun until factional alignments shifted and they could stage a comeback. Court ladies did not necessarily see monasticism as an escape from the secular world. Sometimes they feigned piety as a pragmatic strategy for advancing their ambitions within the palace.[37]

Because Buddhism originated in India and filtered through Central Asian cultures before reaching China, some core teachings contradicted native values and customs. The embrace of Buddhism forced Chinese to confront a civilization as sophisticated as their own. This encounter brought established verities into question. Buddhists challenged many time-honored beliefs, including ideas regarding gender. Buddhism had a mixed impact on women. Unlike the monotheistic religions, which have only one canonical book, Buddhists venerate thousands of scriptures with extremely diverse contents that sometimes appear contradictory. Religious teachings ameliorated some prejudices but denigrated women in other ways.[38] Some sutras portray women in a negative light, describing

Figure 5.1. Devout woman with a lotus.

them as morally weak, licentious, hateful, jealous, foolish, and a potential source of disaster.

Mahayana Buddhism encourages sexual equality, and many female characters in the scriptures display outstanding virtue.[39] Sutras mostly describe literary creations embodying religious ideals, not real women. These paragons appear virtuous, wise, and competent. Buddhists also considered women capable of high spiritual attainment. Bodhisattvas could be female, and these perfected beings stood above mortal men. Buddhism also explicitly condoned female participation in politics.

The Buddhist spirit of sexual egalitarianism sometimes awoke female ambitions and desires and gave women the confidence to actively engage with the wider world. Moreover, although men's monasteries were often located in remote scenic places, most convents were in the cities, allowing nuns to remain in contact with the lay world.[40] Due to the open mindset cultivated by Buddhism and the urban orientation of female practice, nuns and their lay associates actively participated in mainstream society, giving them a significant influence on medieval gender relations.

The Buddhist faithful frequently adhered to a variety of religions and philosophies and blithely mixed these beliefs together. Confucianism had the most obvious impact. Sinicized Buddhism absorbed many Confucian teachings and reinterpreted them to conform with religious dogma. Buddhism also amalgamated with both religious and philosophical Daoism, receiving considerable influence from the Dark Learning and Pure Conversation movements. This intellectual mingling injected Buddhist concepts into important scholarly debates but also distorted some Indian concepts by couching them in Daoist terminology.[41] Early Chinese Buddhism also absorbed magic, miracles, healing, divination, and other folk practices, making it less orthodox but more relevant to the lives of ordinary people.

In China, Buddhism evolved under harsh criticism from critics conversant in ancient classics. Erudite detractors such as Xun Ji (early sixth century) lambasted this foreign religion for undermining the pillars of social order and the authority of the state.[42] He considered Indian-style monasticism cruel and barbaric. Xun complained that nuns and monks do not marry or bear children and betray their parents by leaving home and ignoring filial responsibilities. To rebut these denunciations, Buddhists embraced the chief native Chinese virtues and integrated them into religious dogma.[43] In doing so, they came to represent Buddhist practice as an extension of traditional Chinese ethics.[44]

Apologists put particular stress on filial piety, which Mencius had singled out as the fountainhead of all virtue.[45] Biographies and epitaphs of pious Buddhist women often mention their devotion to filiality.[46] Some pious women dutifully served their parents before taking the tonsure, faithfully carrying out the obligations of lay ethics as long as they remained in the secular world.[47] The nun Miaoxiang even divorced her husband because she considered him insufficiently filial. She became a nun so that she could cast off the lax moral standards of lay society and hold herself to the highest standards of virtue.[48]

As Buddhists incorporated filial piety into their religion, they expressed it in novel ways. In particular, Buddhism encouraged believers to generate merit on behalf of parents to keep them from being reborn in hell, portraying this as the most important form of filial service.[49] Female believers who commissioned sacred images or the copying of sutras frequently sought to transfer the resulting merit to their parents to earn them a higher rebirth. In this way, they portrayed Buddhist practice as a form of filial devotion.

The biography of the nun An Lingshou exemplifies the Buddhist reinterpretation of filial piety.[50] The daughter of an official, her family expected her to marry a man from an equally prestigious family and lead a conventional lay life. Unexpectedly, Lingshou declared that she would devote her life to religion. When her father accused her of selfishness and lacking filial obedience, Lingshou replied that her religious practice would gain merit for all living things, her parents in particular. According to this line of reasoning, Lingshou could remain a filial daughter even as she disobeyed her parents.

Most female believers remained in the secular world even as they pursued religious practice. Many ordinary women mentioned in Dunhuang documents have Buddhist-inspired names, highlighting the centrality of religion to their lives.[51] Laywomen engaged in various types of spiritual practice. Like their male counterparts, devout women venerated the images of buddhas and bodhisattvas such as Guanyin and Maitreya.[52] They visited temples where they worshipped alongside men.[53] Many laywomen took vows to observe basic religious precepts. Since Buddhism forbids killing, believers often became vegetarian.[54] The faithful could also attend religious performances that featured women performing music and dance.[55]

Like male counterparts, laywomen expressed their devotion through patronage. Early Chinese Buddhism put great stress on the abstinence ceremony (*zhai*) held twice monthly.[56] At that time, male and female laypeople invited clerics to chant sutras, preach, and accept a vegetarian meal from the faithful. Women from a sufficiently prosperous family would donate money to temples. One old woman from a prominent family even made herself the slave of a Buddhist temple, forcing her sons to pay a huge ransom to "free" her from this fictive bondage.[57]

A woman with sufficient means could commission religious images to generate karmic merit for themselves or others. About 28 percent of inscriptions in Guyang cave at Longmen, south of Luoyang, accompany images donated by women.[58] For example, a woman named Lady Yuchi (454–519) built a shrine containing a sculpture of Maitreya on behalf of her deceased son. The accompanying inscription states that she intended the merit generated by her pious act to help release her son from the cycle of rebirth, or at the very least allow his rebirth in a realm of buddhas. She further dedicated the image to help release all sentient beings from suffering. Lady Yuchi came from the Xianbei elite and had the financial resources to pay for a relatively large shrine. Images commissioned by ordinary laywomen and nuns tended to be more humble. Overall, the niches containing images donated by women usually occupied relatively marginal locations in the grotto, suggesting that female believers held a lower status than male counterparts.

Aside from individual acts of devotion, Buddhists also came together in groups for collective worship. Religious societies sponsored the creation of steles and images, sutra copying, and rituals.[59] They arranged weddings and funerals, cared for the sick, provided relief for members who had fallen on hard times, and organized entertainments. Documents from Dunhuang contain many references to religious coalitions. Most groups consisted entirely of men, although some admitted female members. The Shuiyusi group in Hebei, organized around the year 571, consisted of five monks, two laymen, and thirty-five laywomen.[60] In this case, a largely female group seems to have submitted to male leadership. Other groups consisted entirely of women, implying that the members had access to some financial resources. These self-help organizations allowed women to build bonds with one another and even with pious men. People of lower status could develop relationships with those on the higher rungs of society and overcome their economic limits. In a marginal area like Dunhuang, which had insufficient farmland and large numbers of broken families, coalitions could help women ameliorate the harsh conditions that they faced.

The most committed female believers became nuns. *Biographies of Nuns (Biqiuni zhuan)*, attributed to the monk Baochang, describes the earliest female clerics.[61] This collection focuses on exemplary women and extraordinary activities, and the contents often cross over into ideological fiction. However, it also contains a great deal of factual material as well. This work describes how women established the first order of nuns long after China had male monastics. Many Buddhists initially resisted the ordination of women. Patriarchy partly accounts for this stance as men did not want women to become untethered from male control.[62] Moreover, no *vinaya* texts of monastic rules for women had yet been translated into Chinese, so aspiring nuns did not know how to undergo ordination or what guidelines they ought to follow. In spite of resistance from native

Buddhists, foreign monks eventually stepped in and ordained women. The first recorded Chinese nun, Zhu Jingjian (ca. 292–ca. 361), took her novice vows in 317.[63] She then acted as teacher to a group of women in Luoyang who wanted to organize female clergy. Finally a monk brought a book from Central Asia that outlined orthodox monastic rules for nuns. After a Chinese translation appeared in 357, Jingjian and her group immediately took full vows and used these tenets to regulate their community.[64]

Women joined the clergy at various times in life, from childhood to old age.[65] To become a nun, a woman had to receive permission from the head of household, usually her father. If a girl entered a convent, she would usually serve as a novice until the age of twenty or so, at which time she would take full vows. The women described in *Biographies of Nuns* had diverse backgrounds: members of the imperial clan, palace ladies, nobles, and commoners. They lived in every region of China.[66] Some came from the landed elite, and their privileged upbringing made them prominent among fellow clerics after they took the tonsure.

Women joined the clergy for various reasons.[67] Many seem to have had straightforward spiritual motivations and sought to live a holy life devoted to religious practice. Sometimes a woman became a nun to seek blessings for her parents or another family member. Others took the tonsure to requite a blessing from the Buddha such as surviving a serious illness. Pragmatic factors also led women to join the clergy. Temple life provided a safe refuge from an unruly world. And because major nunneries owned land and received support from the devout, a religious life also promised financial security. Authorities exempted nuns from taxation, giving them additional pecuniary benefits. Convent life also presented women with a chance to escape a failed relationship, eschew marriage altogether, or avoid the dangers of childbirth. In addition, the Buddhist path offered women rare opportunities to obtain an extensive education, travel, and interact with men.

Like religious Daoism, early Chinese Buddhism stressed miracles, and both biographies and religious fiction describe nuns performing amazing feats of magic.[68] Zhu Daorong could make images of monks suddenly appear and fill an entire room. Flowers placed on her mat did not wither. The nun Tanhui could stop breathing when she meditated.[69] The most extreme miraculous attainments could be shocking. One nun could slice open her belly, cut off her head and limbs, slice off the flesh, and then return to normal.[70]

Although readers enjoyed stories about weird events and amazing powers, the average nun lived an extremely undramatic life. Medieval Chinese Buddhism included numerous sects and inclinations. Like their male counterparts, nuns venerated various holy figures, especially the buddhas Amitabha and Maitreya, the bodhisattva Guanyin, and the arhat

Pindola Bharadvaja.[71] Many devout women took the *Lotus Sutra* (*Miaofa lianhua jing*, the Chinese translation of *Saddharma Puṇḍarīka Sūtra*) as the scriptural focal point of their worship.[72] Groups of nuns recited this sutra, studied its contents, and disseminated it, giving the *Lotus Sutra* a strong impact on female beliefs and behavior. This text stressed the importance of refraining from killing living things and even encouraged believers to become vegetarian to avoid having animals slaughtered on their behalf. It also contains the famous story of the eight-year-old daughter of a dragon king who became a buddha by reciting the sutra, thus emphasizing the possibility of women reaching the highest level of enlightenment.

Although today Chinese Buddhists rarely meditate, the earliest sutras portray this spiritual exercise as essential for attaining the highest wisdom. Accordingly, many early nuns and monks devoted a great deal of time to meditation.[73] Both biographies and miracle tales describe the meditation of nuns, a keystone of female religious regimen. According to hagiography, some nuns garnered respect for having become especially proficient at meditation.

Nuns occasionally took their religious passion to an extreme. Chinese had traditionally considered mutilation and tattooing shameful, yet some sutras describe people who mutilated or killed themselves to prove their disregard for the material realm.[74] The *Lotus Sutra* even promoted suicide as the ultimate sacrifice for the Buddha.[75] Biographies of early monks include approving stories of holy men who killed themselves in a spectacular fashion, usually through self-immolation. A few women also engaged in violent religious practice. Of the sixty-five lives detailed in *Biographies of Nuns*, six end in autocremation. According to these stories, the community condoned religious suicide. Some nuns killed themselves in front of a large number of witnesses. Unlike monks, who committed suicide individually, nuns sometimes immolated themselves as a group, attesting to the strength of female coalitions. A few women used the threat of suicide to blackmail family members into allowing them to forego marriage and join the clergy.

Overall, nuns had a level of education. Of the women portrayed in *Biographies of Nuns*, the author describes 80 percent as literate.[76] Of course this work consists of role models, not a cross section of typical nuns. Most educated nuns seem to have come from privileged families. And because a spiritual vocation offered women unique educational opportunities, it appealed to the intelligent and curious. Some biographies note that nuns began their education in childhood, usually by studying the standard secular canon.[77] A woman known simply as the daughter of Li Biao received an extensive education from her father, who taught her the classics and commentaries as well as calligraphy. Due to her reputation for erudition, she became a teacher of women in the palace. Eventually she entered a nunnery where she shifted her focus to Buddhist learning. She mastered the sutras and their rich commentarial tradition and lectured on the dharma, earning the respect of learned monks.[78]

Once a nun took the tonsure and entered a temple, she studied the Buddhist scriptures. The quotidian routine set aside time for reading and memorizing key texts. The recital of sutras constituted a central religious practice, and nuns spent much of their time chanting scriptures, which familiarized them with the contents of a holy work. In addition, people looked upon chanting as akin to magic. Buddhists believed that the words in holy texts had an apotropaic power akin to charms.[79]

Beyond the mastery of basic scriptures, some nuns traveled to receive advanced instruction. Some temples specialized in a certain academic discipline, so a curious nun might have to spend time at several temples to receive a comprehensive religious education.[80] At the time, few women had an opportunity to travel, so the pursuit of learning provided them with an excuse to see the wider world. Talented nuns mastered Buddhist scriptures and some even excelled at secular learning, earning the attention of cultivated men. The fourth-century nun Zhi Miaoyin composed literary essays. She often met with the emperor and court scholars to share their writings and converse about intellectual topics.[81]

In one important respect, educated nuns differed from cultivated laywomen. At the time, people considered poetry the premier form of literature. However, even the most erudite and capable female clerics refrained from writing verse.[82] Nuns seem to have avoided poetry because of its emotional content. Not only did religious women demur from exposing private passions in public, the emotionalism of poetry also contravened the fundamental Buddhist goal of extinguishing desire.

Elite nuns also interacted with political and cultural leaders. Female clerics from aristocratic families had not only received an education but could also leverage their family background to gain entrée into the highest reaches of society. The most important nuns had dealings with rulers, empresses, government ministers, wealthy aristocrats, and famous monks. Influential people sometimes sought out famous nuns to receive blessings or learn about the dharma. In addition, the organs of the state officially recognized the status of top nuns. The southern dynasties organized nuns and monks into a religious bureaucracy and gave the heads of temples official rank.[83] From the fifth century onward, Confucian influence diminished the place of nuns within the government hierarchy. Even so, abbesses still held official rank, which made it easier to meet with powerful men. And influential southern nuns such as the erudite Miaoyin routinely issued advice and participated in factional battles.[84] The activities of these women exemplify how Buddhist nuns seized the opportunities offered by their religion to attain knowledge, power, and respect.

6

Learning

Several important Han dynasty thinkers pondered the question of what place learning ought to have in a woman's life, making it a topic of intellectual discourse. Thereafter this contested issue sparked debate throughout imperial history. In later eras, some thinkers openly declared that women should only receive a limited education. They believed that while learning is an unalloyed good to men, having too much knowledge tends to make a woman less moral. As a seventeenth-century saying put it, "A woman is virtuous only if she is untalented."[1] In contrast, people in earlier times tended to have fewer qualms about the propriety of female learning.

The erudite Western Han scholar Liu Xiang (77–6 BCE) took a Confucian approach to women's education that influenced medieval thinkers. His highly influential *Biographies of Women (Lienü zhuan)* lauds female role models of prior times, depicting women who exhibited both talent and virtue. However, the final section of the text describes evil women who deployed their abilities to destructive ends. Taken together, these opposing narratives give an ambiguous view of female learning. If an inherently worthy woman becomes familiar with ancient classics, she might hold herself to higher standards of conduct. But if she has a weak moral compass, learnedness might exert a corrupting influence.[2] In sum, Liu Xiang saw female education as neither inherently good nor bad. He believed that learning had uncertain effects determined by the character of individual women.

Classical Confucianism promotes self-cultivation for women as well as men, a position that informed Liu's views. In spite of the decline of this school of thought after the fall of Han, this ideal continued to influence medieval attitudes. Artists still painted female moral exemplars.[3] And people also lauded women for innate intelligence or exceptional educational attainment. Early medieval dynastic histories portray many women as quick witted, wise, or learned.[4] The section on women's biographies in *Records of Jin (Jinshu)* depicts the diversity of female talent, with attainments ranging from education to the arts.[5] Some of these women had read widely and exhibited unusual erudition. Others showed talent at oral discourse, entertaining listeners with glib bon mots. The types of sources available in each phase of the early medieval era affected the portrayal of women.[6] Earlier biographies focus on women from the highest backgrounds who were most likely to receive a formal education and interact with learned men. But when historians began to write about women from a wider range of circumstances, they more often placed them in domestic settings.

A heady atmosphere of spirited individualism fostered admiration of female talent. In contrast with the Han dynasty, whose intellectual leaders revered the rites and classical ethics, the female subjects of early medieval biography often deported themselves very freely. As Confucian propriety declined in influence, individual ability and accomplishment became increasingly appreciated. Writers praised men and women who possessed a quality called *da*, which referred to the mastery of one or more skills.[7] This priority can be seen in the biographies of women in *Records of Jin*, which stress both talent and virtue. *A New Account of Tales of the World (Shishuo xinyu)*, a compendium of noteworthy words and actions compiled by Liu Yiqing (403–44), takes this viewpoint even further, placing female ability above moral qualities in importance.[8] Even the meaning of the term "talent" (*cai*) underwent a striking change. While Han Confucians had understood talent largely as a facility for moral cultivation, Six Dynasties writers defined the concept much more broadly, encompassing a variety of skills that included writing, argumentation, artistry, and technical mastery.[9] The uses of female talent also widened. Whereas Han authorities had believed that the intelligent woman should deploy her abilities to improve household management and raise the moral tone of family life, some outstanding medieval women pursued purely personal goals.[10]

Some writers continued to promote ideals that restrained female autonomy in the name of virtue. Zhang Hua (232–300) wrote a piece consisting of rhymed aphorisms entitled *Admonitions of a Female Scribe (Nüshi zhen)*, using the voice of a fictional woman to describe model female conduct and outlook.[11] Zhang seems to have intended this work for the eyes of the empress and other palace ladies with the intention of convincing them to moderate their behavior. He appeals to the ritual canon and the metaphysical system of the *Classic of Changes (Yijing)* to convince women to conform to the prevailing social order. As these exhortations allegedly come from the brush of an erudite woman, his book follows the example of Ban Zhao and uses the prestige of female learning to counsel women to be meek and obedient.

Male education had clear goals. Aristocrats cultivated a reputation for learning as a way to maintain the prestige of their families, win respect from other elite men, and perhaps pursue careers in the bureaucracy. In contrast, female education lacked a well-defined practical purpose, so women's studies tended to be diverse and unsystematic. Most female students focused on religion and literature. Those with the greatest intellectual ambition tackled works of philosophy, history, and the classics.[12] Women in the north and south tended to study different curricula.[13] More southern women studied high-level subjects such as history and ancient texts while northern women were more likely to focus on practical skills.

The ways that women learned varied according to their abilities and circumstances. In an age before printing, when books were few and literacy rare, visual props provided an easy way to acquire knowledge.[14] At least eight artists from the period depicted female paragons, most famously the renowned painter Gu Kaizhi (348–405). Most artists did more than one work in this genre, for a total of thirty-three known paintings.[15] Both women and men enjoyed scrutinizing paintings of model women, which rendered the characters of didactic biography in visual form. An educated person could provide oral commentary to the painting or an accompanying written text might explain the meaning of each image. A woman viewing these paintings seems to have used them as a kind of mirror, imagining herself embodying the moral qualities depicted in each female persona.[16]

Some women pursued a literate education. Epitaphs often brag about a woman's mastery of weighty canonical works, with one noting that the deceased had studied the nine major philosophical schools of antiquity.[17] Other inscriptions describe proficiency in the ritual canon.[18] An unusually learned woman might study history or classical exegesis.[19] Most commonly, however, female learning concentrated on the appreciation and composition of poetry. Encomia to talented women often mentioned that they had studied the *Classic of Poetry*, *Songs of Chu*, and other major collections of verse.[20] Xu Ling (507–583), editor of *New Songs from a Jade Terrace* (*Yutai xinyong*), explains in the work's introduction that he intended this famed poetry collection for a female readership. He recounts the accomplishments of past women who excelled as both authors and connoisseurs of poetry, thus proving that women have the ability to excel in the realm of literature. Xu explains that because he considers Confucian and Daoist texts too difficult for most women to appreciate, he put together a collection of literature to provide them with suitable reading material.[21]

As education had traditionally been strongly linked to moral cultivation, some people fretted that emphasizing literature instead of ethics might degrade female character. The dubious content of some poetry heightened these fears. Many poems, both old and new, had morally ambiguous themes. And some Southern Dynasties poetry was blatantly erotic, leading critics to classify it as decadent literature. Not surprisingly, a woman who immersed herself in poetry might ignore social convention. The daughter of Jia Chong (217–282), a powerful official, secretly fell in love with one of her father's aides and expressed her infatuation by chanting romantic poems.[22]

With women seeking a literate education, authors wrote didactic books about matters likely to interest them. Some of these works found an enthusiastic readership, including *A Mirror for Women (Nü jian)*, *Admonitions for Women (Nü xun)*, *Collected Admonitions for Women (Furen xunjie ji)*, *Instructions for Sisters-in-Law (Disi xun)*, and *An Account of Chastity and Obedience (Zhenshun zhi)*.[23] These books have been lost, but surviving fragments show that the contents varied considerably. Some related interesting narratives and gossip, while serious works taught female ethics in a textbook format.[24]

Medieval writers also continued to compose didactic biographies of women in imitation of Liu Xiang. The classicist Huangfu Mi (215–282) compiled a collection that he called *Biographies of Women (Lienü zhuan)*, even copying the title of Liu's famous work.[25] Although most of the narratives in this collection have been lost, it seems to have been a sizeable volume consisting of six fascicles.[26] By combining together the surviving fragments, perhaps one-third of the original work can be reconstructed.[27] Huangfu's motivations for collating this collection remain unclear. Maybe he just considered moral biography a respectable scholarly undertaking. Or perhaps Huangfu shared Liu's political motivations. Huangfu may have intended to warn his sovereign about the need for powerful ladies to adhere to Confucian ethics, lest an evil woman bring down a shaky dynasty. In addition to Huangfu Mi's freestanding collection, some dynastic histories also include a section devoted to women's biography. Classical ideas about historiography informed biographical narratives about women.[28] Readers expected the historian to subject figures from the past to praise and blame, thereby using their example to instruct the present generation in ethics.

Although most ethical writings about women have been lost, an influential text on family matters preserves one man's views on the rightful place of women in the family. During the Han dynasty, some patriarchs wrote short admonitions for the benefit of their sons, passing down useful wisdom on how to manage the family.[29] Over time these texts became increasingly comprehensive, giving rise to the genre of "family instruction" (*jiaxun*) texts. The scholar Yan Zhitui (531–591) wrote the most famous of these works, entitled *Yan Family Instructions (Yanshi jiaxun).*[30] Yan came from a gentry family that moved south in the early fourth century. They managed to reestablish themselves in their new homeland and served as officials under the southern dynasties. Because the Yan family scrupulously guarded their collective reputation and the recruitment system favored the established aristocracy, they remained important for twenty generations. Yan Zhitui lived during a chaotic time and served under four consecutive dynasties in various roles—as secretary, librarian, and court scholar. At the time, everyone suffered from constant upheaval, even the officialdom and landed elite, and the Yan endured periods of relative poverty. Regardless of the family's circumstances, however, they maintained high standards of education and propriety. Yan Zhitui set down the principles behind his family's enduring success in *Yan Family Instructions.*

Yan directed this book toward the family's men, informing them of the best ways to maintain a stable and harmonious household. In doing so, he discusses how women ought to behave.[31] Yan considers women capable of learning and developing their abilities. Nevertheless, he emphasizes the need to distinguish between the sexes, cautioning that women and men ought to deploy their talents differently.[32] While men should participate in the outside world of politics, women ought to devote themselves to household management and safeguarding the moral tenor of the family. Yan sees a family's reputation as its prime asset. Both women and men have a solemn responsibility to uphold their collective reputation by behaving cautiously and maintaining a high standard of conduct.[33] To this end, the family's women should be virtuous, submissive, and chaste. They need to refrain from jealousy and serve as model wives and mothers.

Although Yan sees women as capable of learning and integrity, he nevertheless regards them as an implicit threat to the patrilineal order. Father and sons share a close bond based on blood. In contrast, their wives come in from the outside, so they might have conflicting interests. Wives tend to encourage their husbands to prioritize the nuclear family over extended kin, thereby threatening the bonds between male family members.[34] Yan also discusses the problems that can arise when a man remarries after a wife's death. Although interactions between step-mothers and step-sons had generally become more amicable than before, this relationship nevertheless remained inherently awkward and potentially destabilizing. Yan warns that step-mothers can threaten family harmony by fomenting discord between father and son.[35]

The most learned women of the time were what Virginia Woolf described as "daughters of educated men." Women who came of age in

learned and sophisticated families had ample opportunities to cultivate their minds. Even so, not all elite women received an education.
Families with nomadic roots usually kept their daughters illiterate and
expected women to devote themselves to domestic tasks, worship, and
practical skills such as riding.[36] In contrast, many prominent ethnic Han
families held themselves to high standards of education, and this cultured atmosphere often benefitted girls as well as boys.[37] For example,
all of the daughters of the literary luminary Liu Hui (458–502) became
competent writers.[38]

The challenges faced by prominent old families led them to place enormous value on education.[39] As north China suffered war and invasion,
many important people fled south. Some northern émigrés prospered
in their new homeland while others descended into poverty. For an elite
northern family to prosper in the south, they had to find a way to claim
high status, even though they had neither large landholdings nor military
power. In the end, northern émigrés promoted themselves as guardians
of orthodox culture, stressing the superiority of their learning and refined
behavior. They studied the ritual canon and classical ethics and upheld
some of these dictates, thereby fashioning an image of archaic propriety.
Due to their uncommon values, they sometimes behaved very differently
from the people around them. But instead of dismissing these émigrés as
peculiar, southerners admired them. A combination of cultural orthodoxy,
ritual propriety, erudition, taste, and training in the polite arts won them
esteem in their new homeland. Emperors respected the cultural legacy
of the northern émigrés and used them to legitimize the rump southern
dynasties as the heirs of Chinese civilization.

Women from elite families not only grew up in a refined domestic
atmosphere, but due to the nature of medieval education, also had considerable educational opportunities. Under the Han dynasty, government
schools had trained young men to prepare them for service in the bureaucracy. However, these schools disappeared along with the dynasty.
Afterward, family members and private tutors educated the children of
the aristocracy. Because boys usually studied at home, the family's daughters could learn alongside their brothers, sometimes even studying the
ancient classics in depth. Educated families assimilated cultured activities
into their lives in informal ways as well. The family of Xie An (320–385)
passed snowy days by playing a literary composition game in which they
took turns composing lines in a communal poem. Once Xie laughed with
pleasure at a clever verse contributed by his niece.[40] Talented women from
elite families also gained proficiency in arts such as calligraphy, painting,
music, and dance. Although very few paintings survive from that distant
era, records attest that some women distinguished themselves as accomplished artists.[41]

Figure 6.1. Apsara playing a lute.

The Wang family of Langya exemplifies how a family's cultural heritage could benefit daughters as well as sons. The Wang remained prominent for centuries by systematically pursuing two strategies: repeatedly marrying their children to the scions of other high-ranking families and maintaining a reputation for outstanding cultural achievement.[42] Generation after generation, family members exhibited a proficient grasp of Confucian thought and Daoist metaphysics. Most famously, the Wang gained renown for their calligraphy. Critics rank the works of Wang Xizhi

(303–361) as among the greatest masterpieces of calligraphic art.[43] And the family produced other noted calligraphers as well, including daughters and wives. Wang Mengjiang, the only daughter of Wang Xizhi, emulated her father to become a talented calligrapher.[44]

Since antiquity, Chinese had seen literature as the pinnacle of refinement, and some women became authors.[45] Most often, they wrote poetry. Not only did the educated elite hold verse in high esteem, leading women to pursue this art, but the emotional quality of poetry and its removal from worldly affairs made this type of writing seem particularly appropriate for women. Some model women featured in medieval biography, such as the Eastern Jin exemplar Xie Daowen, not only read the ancient *Classic of Poetry* and other canonical collections but also composed their own works.[46] A Madame Zhong, great-granddaughter of a court tutor, wrote poems and other literary works in a variety of genres.[47] And aristocratic ladies circulated collections of their verse among small circles of connoisseurs.[48]

Men often treated a woman who displayed an aptitude for literature with considerable respect. Even though Zuo Fen (c. 255–300), a concubine of the Emperor Wu of Jin (r. 265–290), stood out for her ugliness, the ruler nevertheless favored her above other women in the palace because of her literary ability.[49] Other respected poets included Liu Lingxian and Shen Manyuan. And later generations looked back on the fourth-century poet Su Hui with a degree of admiration approaching awe for her virtuosic mastery of the torturously difficult art of palindromes.[50] Once she wrote an unbelievably long 840-character palindrome to send to her husband, far away on an official posting, to express her sadness at their forced separation.

Literary critics point out that female authors of the Wei and Jin wrote differently than both women and men in prior eras.[51] Earlier writers had usually emphasized morality, prioritizing orthodoxy over authenticity. Although Chinese rarely viewed literature as art for art's sake, female writers had become much more willing to express their genuine feelings, even if this meant flouting social expectations. Audiences in subsequent eras felt drawn to their fresh and honest writing, and female authors also repeatedly looked back to the innovative discourse of this era for inspiration.[52]

Although female writers usually concentrated on poetry, they wrote other types of literature as well. The beautiful and talented Madame Li, wife of Jia Chong, composed a textbook called *Admonitions for Women (Nü xun)*, apparently in imitation of an Eastern Han work of the same name. Although this book has not survived, contemporary readers held it in high regard, attesting to the author's high educational level and literary capacity.[53] Even so, women rarely wrote this kind of serious work. More commonly, female prose took the form of letters. Although the polymath Tang Jin (d. ca. 556) wrote mostly on topics of male interest, he also composed a book called *Letter Writing Etiquette for Women (Furen shuyi)* that taught women the conventions of correspondence appropriate to their sex.[54] The fact that Tang felt inspired to write this sort of textbook implies that women frequently wrote letters and tried to adhere to standard epistolary guidelines. As couples sometimes found themselves separated by business or calamity, distant wives and husbands routinely exchanged letters to pass on news and express their feelings.[55]

The cultural elite also held oral fluency in high regard. This concern dated back to antiquity, when the Eastern Zhou nobility raised spoken discourse to a refined art.[56] Ancient education stressed techniques of oral argumentation, and people expected the educated person to quote poetry and other canonical texts during formal discussions. Although the famed speakers of antiquity were almost all male, a few women also garnered attention for mastering these skills.[57] During the Western Han, the rise of bureaucratic institutions decisively tilted attention toward the written word, and spoken rhetoric went into eclipse for several centuries.[58] But as the unified imperial system declined, spoken discourse regained prominence. During the late Eastern Han, educated men once again embraced formal conversational activities. Discussions often took place before an audience as a kind of competitive performance. Some speakers gained fame for oral proficiency by discussing profound philosophical matters, while others became known for glib comments. Listeners considered a witty bon mot issued with perfect timing akin to hitting the target in archery.[59] Within this oral milieu, a clever woman could attract attention for exceptional conversational skill. *A New Account of Tales of the World* admiringly records the comments of smooth-talking women.[60] Men sometimes allowed cultured ladies to participate in their intellectual salons and engaged them in debates. Sometimes a woman won the upper hand in a competitive conversation, earning a delighted response from the male audience.

Educated women became teachers and passed their learning on to others. Some entered this profession to earn money in a respectable manner. Zhu Jingjian came from an educated family of officials who fell into poverty after her father's untimely death, so she supported herself by teaching music and calligraphy to the children of noble families.[61] Ladies of the harem invited some of the most educated women in the realm to serve as their teachers. Some held the status of imperial concubines, while others entered the palace simply as tutors.[62] Palace residents took a particular interest in the appreciation and composition of poetry, and female tutors often taught the literary arts. Sometimes imperial concubines and their literature tutors would amuse guests at an imperial banquet by chanting poetry and extemporizing new verses.[63]

Although a small number of women mastered classical learning and felt comfortable discussing and composing poetry, the scope of female learning in the early medieval era should not be exaggerated. Very few women had the opportunity to attain a high-level education or even basic literacy. In an age rocked by chaos, long before the invention of printing, it was rare for a home to have even a single book, so most people did not prioritize reading and writing. Given the limitations of textual learning, female education also encompassed a range of nonliterate knowledge and skills, such as art and music. As a result, many women were capable dancers. Most importantly, people expected a woman to spend part of each day weaving cloth. Since antiquity, diligently manufacturing cloth had been taken as proof of not just female industriousness but of inner goodness.[64] A woman who wanted to display her virtue to the world might flaunt her devotion to spinning and weaving. The Empress Wenming combined a familiarity with poetry and philosophy with textile manufacture.[65]

A story about a man named Xu Xun illustrates these attitudes.[66] In the year 254 officials punished Xu for an infraction that he had committed. When his servants went to inform his wife about his troubles, they found her seated at her loom hard at work. When told her about her husband's predicament, her expression did not change. She merely remarked that she had long known that her husband would eventually find himself in this sort of quandary. This vignette portrays the weaving woman as not just virtuous but also as wise and prescient.

Associating female wisdom with prognostication echoes a larger theme. In Six Dynasties literature, wise women not only dispense sage advice but can also predict future events. For example, a man who intended to marry off his daughter asked his mother for her opinion of the prospective groom.[67] After observing the behavior of the man's family, she issued her assessment, urging her son to marry her granddaughter to someone else. A few years later, the would-be groom died, proving her prescience.

More commonly, women used dreams to apprehend the present and divine the future.[68] Authors often employed dreams as a standard literary device.[69] The mid-fourth-century collection *In Search of the Supernatural (Soushen ji)* contains many stories that feature a woman's revelatory dream. The characters in these stories take women's dreams seriously and treat them as omens.[70] The standard histories also include many accounts of dreaming women. Sometimes a woman had an auspicious dream while pregnant, presaging her child's eventual importance.[71] For men with dubious family background, such as warlords and early nomadic leaders, stories about a mother's mysterious dream bolstered their uncertain legitimacy. Other women used dreams to communicate with deities or foretell the future.[72]

An educated woman had a responsibility to teach her children, and aristocratic families educated their daughters for this purpose. Education began at home, usually under the guidance of parents and other family members. Only after a boy had mastered the basic curriculum would he study more advanced subjects with private tutors. Given the importance of home schooling, elite men hoped to marry a knowledgeable woman who could help teach their sons.[73] A mother who imparted primary knowledge to her son gave him a valuable head start in life and helped set him on the path to professional success.

The parents of prospective grooms appreciated an educated daughter-in-law, as a well-read mother could oversee her sons' education, even if her husband spent time away from home on an official posting. In response, many elite families educated their daughters to attract good marriage partners. This strategy had long proven successful. The famed Cui family gave their daughters a comprehensive education, putting them in high demand as wives and allowing them to intermarry with the best families for generations.[74]

The importance of maternal instruction to a son's success led people to laud it as a virtue. About 10 percent of Liu Xiang's biographies of model women feature a virtuous mother who overcame difficulties to educate her sons, thereby ensuring their success. This theme reemerged in the section on female biographies in *Records of the Wei (Weishu)*.[75] Success at teaching sons also became a standard accomplishment of virtuous widows, an achievement that writers of subsequent eras would increasingly emphasize.[76]

Disunity and chaos often affected the quality of education. Moreover, young students as yet lacked a standard curriculum. Mothers taught their children in various ways, according to their particular knowledge and inclinations. As before, in spite of the general decline of Confucianism, the classics remained central to the education of boys training for an official career. Mothers taught young children about filial piety, ritual propriety, and basic Confucian virtues such as loyalty, integrity, and righteousness.[77] At a more advanced level, a mother with more extensive education might guide her children through the *Classic of Poetry*, ritual canon, and other ancient classical texts.[78]

Maternal responsibility did not end when a son reached adulthood. Some women continued to teach and guide their sons throughout their lives. Due to the obligations of filial piety, even men who achieved high positions often felt obligated to defer to maternal advice and supervision. The shrewd mother might arrange matters so that her son could forge connections with important people.[79] Most commonly, a mother guided her grown son by handing down worthwhile advice. In one case, a prince

threatened to arrest the sons of man he had just punished.[80] Their mother
advised them on how to behave so that they might escape retribution. In
another instance, the mother of a high official advised her son to quit his
position before he got into trouble.[81] He refused to take her advice and
ended up being arrested for an alleged crime.

One-third of the narratives in Liu Xiang's collection describe a woman
giving a man important advice. Medieval depictions of model women
continued to employ this theme.[82] Most commonly, writers described a
sagacious wife dispensing good advice to her husband.[83] The wife of one
official counseled him on how to deal with the emperor.[84] Another woman
offered guidance to her younger brother, who was serving as a general.[85]
The official Li Zhong had so much respect for his daughter's intelligence
that he sought her opinion on every important matter. When she finally
declared that his situation had become completely hopeless, he committed suicide.[86] For a woman to advise or remonstrate with a man did not
necessarily imply that she held superior status. Han dynasty writers often
described a low-status man such as a chariot driver or fisherman dispensing wise advice to a ruler. Good advice earned admiration but did not
elevate social position. Similarly, a prudent woman's good advice did not
free her from the confines of conventional social roles.

The reputation of some women extended beyond their immediate circle.
Men sought the advice of wise women on various matters. In particular,
they solicited women's opinions about the character of prominent people.
Character appraisal became a popular pastime during the mid-second
century and remained common throughout the era of division.[87] The
political situation accounts for the emergence of this practice. As society
frayed and the state struggled to restore order, many critics blamed the
low quality of government functionaries. Some leaders sought officials
with exemplary character, hoping that their moral authority and integrity
could reconstitute a stable system. To this end, authorities encouraged
people to publicly assess leading candidates for office in the hope that
extensive critiques would uncover men of exemplary character.

The range of personal qualities under discussion gradually broadened,
giving rise to a competitive rhetorical game called Pure Conversation
(*qingtan*). In the wake of the declining reputations of Confucianism and
imperial institutions, many educated people no longer wanted to discuss
ethics or policy. Instead, they shifted their attentions to notable personal
characteristics. Participants vied to come up with the most memorable or
amusing observations about each person under discussion, commenting
on appearance, psychology, talent, accomplishments, and so on. Women
not only became subjects of critique but also evaluated men. Women's
distance from the most important political and cultural activities made

them ideal judges of male character. Although refined women could not participate in these undertakings, they often understood them well. Such women could act as independent critics and evaluate male achievement with an air of objectivity.[88] The participation of women in character assessment helped turn it away from practical ends, turning it into entertaining discursive game with little relevance important matters.

Character evaluation constitutes a central theme of *A New Account of Tales of the World (Shishuo xinyu)*, attesting to the importance of this activity.[89] This work describes women judging the characteristics of prominent men and male listeners respecting their verdicts. Women participated with men on an equal footing and could gain attention for insightful comments. The sight of women critiquing men implicitly contested masculine authority.[90] But rather than resist this challenge, men utilized women's character appraisals to work out their own competitive relationships, thereby ordering and reinforcing male hierarchies.

Women not only participated in oral salon games but also helped change the rules. When a man assessed a peer's character, he often emphasized conventional attributes such as Confucian orthodoxy and worldly success. In contrast, female critics tended to stress the sorts of artistic and literary achievements that they themselves might potentially attain. By shifting the standards of character appraisal away from conformity, women challenged the prevailing social order and helped shift it to favor female self-expression and spiritual liberation.[91]

A New Account of Tales of the World includes many examples of women judging men. Madame Han, wife of the Daoist thinker Shan Tao (205–283), secretly observed her husband's interactions with the famed eccentrics Ji Kang and Ruan Ji.[92] The next day she rendered judgment on the three men's relative talent, candidly informing her husband that he was no match for his friends. This incident illustrates how character assessment empowered women. In this exchange, the traditional marital roles have been reversed. Instead of submitting meekly to her husband's authority, the wife places herself in the authoritative role of impartial judge. Having assumed this lofty standpoint, she then declares her husband inferior to the men around him.

Female engagement with character assessment and related oral discourse had a major effect on the ways people portrayed women and the modes that women used to express themselves. Han authors such as Ban Zhao (ca. 45–ca. 117) encouraged women to constrain themselves in accordance with restrictive virtues. In contrast, *Records of Jin (Jinshu)* describes highly individualistic women who express themselves freely.[93] These narratives also stress the importance of female accomplishment, with some women displaying knowledge or eloquence. Critiquing and ranking individuals also affected female discourse, as women increasingly commented on other people.[94] For example, some women wrote eulogies that described the virtues of the deceased. They also critiqued the output of other writers. By taking on the role of judge, women found a way to elevate their rhetorical position, demanding respect for their pronouncements. Female learning did not just imitate that of men. Inventive women used their knowledge to push at the boundaries of social convention. In seeking admiration and autonomy, they made Chinese culture more inclusive and dynamic.

7

Virtue

During the Han dynasty, when writers began to address female concerns in detail, they sought to position them within the intellectual framework of classical scholarship and Confucian ethics. Frustratingly, ancient writings had little to say about women. To fill this lacuna, Liu Xiang, Ban Zhao, and others applied conventional moral principles to discuss matters of particular interest to women, such as a wife's proper place within her husband's family, providing a Confucianized moral framework applicable to women. However, the eventual fall of Han evoked widespread skepticism about the moral verities that had underpinned the dynasty's failed imperial order, including Confucianized gender constructs. In the ensuing age of skepticism, many people reassessed, rejected, or simply ignored earlier ideas about proper female behavior.

Female virtue encompassed many aspects, and people had different opinions on the matter. Overall, the Six Dynasties stand out as a critical phase in the evolution of female ethics. Moral values underwent immense shifts in this era, spurred by the decline of Confucian learning, influx of steppe culture, and the rise of Buddhism and Daoism. Given the complexity of this fragmented society, beliefs and practices increasingly varied considerably according to region and social background. Most significantly, the collapse of a unified imperial state undermined ritual norms, including strict rules against the free mixing of women and men. These standards did not vanish completely. The educated elite remained cognizant of the tenets of Confucianism and continued to revere these principles. In a remonstration to the emperor, one official emphasized the importance of separating the sexes, attesting to the endurance of the old value system amid new circumstances.[1]

Despite these calls to maintain ritual propriety, far fewer people took the old injunctions seriously. The social critic Ge Hong complained that men and women associated freely, a situation that he considered extremely disturbing.[2] He grumbled that instead of modestly hiding themselves from the gaze of strange men and devoting themselves to domestic tasks, women spent their days traveling around to different places and visiting friends, even going out at night by torchlight. High officials mingled with lowly slave women in the marketplace without shame.

Ge Hong does not seem to have been exaggerating. Records of the time confirm that both men and women visited temples, watched performances, participated in religious ceremonies, and engaged in various other activities without any effort to separate them.[3] A few Daoist eccentrics even deliberately befriended the opposite sex to prove their liberation from arbitrary social bonds. The unconventional Ruan Ji justified his unusually close rapport with his sister-in-law by asking, "Were the rites established for people like me?"[4] When drunk he would even sleep next to a barmaid, with her husband's consent.[5] Lax interactions between the sexes sometimes led to the sorts of problems that ritual regulations sought to avoid. When young people had opportunities to meet and become acquainted, some fell in love, bringing them into conflict with parents who wanted their children to marry with the best possible family.[6]

Numerous cases of adultery suggest a lenient view of conjugal fidelity. Records from the early phase of the Six Dynasties mention high-ranking ethnic Han women committing adultery.[7] Women of Xianbei extraction also expressed their romantic feelings freely, as recorded in folk song lyrics, and some had extramarital affairs.[8] Even married officials and their wives had paramours.[9] A husband might even forgive an adulterous wife and continue living with her in harmony.[10]

Nevertheless, tolerance for adultery had limits. In the later part of this era, people discouraged infidelity among the uppermost elite to prevent political problems. And the old story of Qiu Hu, who mistook his wife for a stranger and propositioned her, remained popular. This entertaining story summed up that widespread view that adultery brought misfortune to the family.[11] Indeed, some people paid a high price for an extramarital affair. An official who committed adultery with the wife of a commoner was sued by her husband and lost his position as a result.[12] Another official was dismissed from his post because his son had relationships with married women.[13] A man who suspected his wife of adultery murdered both her and her lover. Afraid that he would not receive a pardon for his crime, he then committed suicide.[14]

Widowhood had not yet acquired an aura of unsullied virtue, and many widows interacted casually with men. Sometimes a widow formed a stable relationship with a man akin to common law marriage. A widow surnamed Li had a sexual relationship with a man and bore him three children.[15] Other widows simply sought sexual release and became a man's sexual companion without any intention of marrying him.[16] The sources include numerous examples of people who held fidelity in scant regard.[17] Even emperors allowed widows to enter their harems. Empress Wenxuan, wife of Emperor Jianwen (r. 372), had previously been married to another man and born him a son.[18]

Parents did not expect daughters to remain chaste if widowed or divorced. Some parents even arranged a second marriage for their offspring. Because men used a daughter's marriage to build connections with useful affines, a son-in-law's death represented an opportunity. Remarrying a daughter expanded the family's allies.[19] Because a woman's remarriage could benefit her family, parents might even bully an unwilling widow to wed. When the husband of Zhuge Ling's daughter died in 328, she declared that she would never marry again.[20] Even so, her father forced her to wed a new husband of his choosing, a union that benefited him. Although she resisted this unwanted marriage and initially rejected her new spouse, over time she came to accept her fate. This woman's desire to remain unmarried seems unusual. Divorced or abandoned women usually remarried if possible.[21] Of the fifty-two princesses whose marriages are recorded in *Records of Wei*, two wed another man after the death of a husband.[22] The fact that even princesses remarried suggests that a second union held no stigma among the uppermost elite.[23]

Government functionaries sometimes even forced women to remarry. The Northern Qi government arranged for 2,600 women, allegedly widows, to marry soldiers. They hoped to repopulate the northeast, which had suffered severe population decline after centuries of chaos.[24] In fact, some of these women were already married. Officials forcibly divorced them from their husbands so that they could wed a bachelor soldier. The northern dynasties also had a custom called "bestowing a wife" (*ci qi*) whereby the state awarded the wives of captured enemies and other low-status women to meritorious officials or soldiers as a reward for their loyal service.[25] Emperor Taizu, founder of the Northern Wei, set a precedent when he presented a key supporter with wife and concubines as well as slaves, houses, and sheep.[26] Subsequent rulers followed his example. Emperor Shizu also rewarded an important backer with a wife, concubines, and assorted valuables.[27]

As "bestowing a wife" became common, rulers needed a steady source of women to present as gifts. The wives of executed criminals could readily be forced into marriage.[28] And generals would execute male captives and distribute their wives and daughters to their troops as booty. When an army looted the Northern Qi palace, they seized masses of gold, silver, pearls, and silk—as well as two thousand women. The ruler of the newly instituted Latter Zhou dynasty distributed these captives to his officers and troops.[29] Even the nuns of a vanquished city might be ravished and forced to marry the victors.[30]

Powerful men often showed little regard for the marriage bond. They could seize a woman from an ordinary family, annul her marriage, and compel her to wed again.[31] The youthful Cao Cao set the tone when he and a friend kidnapped the bride at a wedding party just for fun.[32] They were pretending to be knights errant, although the bride probably saw their behavior very differently. As strongmen considered it their prerogative to seize women and dispose of them according to whim, even ladies from respectable families were sometimes forced into a harem or given to an underling.[33] The slaves of one corrupt and oppressive official, scion of the Wei imperial clan, forced free women of good families to become their wives.[34] Forced marriage had the unintended side effect of driving the ethnic mixing that characterized the age. In particular, the Tuoba custom of marrying off captured ethnic Han women to their soldiers facilitated extensive cultural exchange at the grassroots level.[35]

In later ages, when widow chastity became tightly associated with female virtue, people looked back on this easy acceptance of remarriage with distaste. At the time, however, it was often necessary for a widow to find a new husband simply to survive. Moreover, dire conditions made remarriage seem desirable from the perspective of the state. War, invasion, and the flight of refugees had depopulated many regions, particularly in the north. According to the census of 280, the population had declined by two-thirds in little more than a century.[36] In reaction, authorities strongly encouraged marriage and even remarriage to restore the population level.[37] In 574 Emperor Wu of the Northern Zhou dynasty issued a decree encouraging everyone of marriageable age to wed. He specifically included widows and widowers in this command.[38]

Cultural shifts also expedited remarriage.[39] The eclipse of Confucianism and the classical rites increased female autonomy, making it easier for a woman to leave a detested union. The newly vibrant religions of Daoism and Buddhism did not consider remarriage problematic. To the contrary, Buddhism encouraged women to look after their own interests. Nor did steppe culture deter remarriage. It seems that the Tuoba originally practiced levirate, whereby a man would marry the wife of a deceased family member, such as a brother, to keep her within the family. China had a similar custom in antiquity, but it had gone into abeyance prior to the imperial era, so medieval Chinese regarded levirate as an alien custom of dubious morality.[40] Even so, the open-minded attitude toward remarriage among the conquering elite had an impact.

In most cases, a woman's decision to remarry or remain chaste depended largely on her resources, region, and particular situation. The varying circumstances faced by widows helps explain why they acted differently. If a deceased husband left behind sufficient property, his widow might be able to sustain herself without remarrying. Not surprisingly, most chaste widows seem to have belonged to the landed elite. Whether or not a widow had children also influenced her decision on whether or not to find a second husband.[41] If she did not have any offspring, remarriage had few repercussions. And she could easily take a daughter into a new husband's home. But if she had a son, she would have to leave him behind with her deceased husband's relatives if she remarried. Many chaste widows seem to have refused remarriage not due to fidelity for a dead spouse but because they could not bear to abandon a son.

For most widows, refusing remarriage invited hardship. Without a husband to plow the land, a woman could find it difficult to survive. People imagined widows eating the fodder of pigs and dogs and huddling under livestock rugs to protect themselves against the cold.[42] A woman could theoretically support herself by weaving cloth for sale, but such a life would be extremely difficult.[43] An edict of 575 stated that a lone widow could not survive on her own, even if she was in her prime and capable of hard work.[44] And when a woman without husband or son became too old to work, she lacked any means of support.[45]

Poets used their art to discuss the widow's heartrending plight. At least four early medieval writers wrote poems with the identical title "Widow Rhapsody" (*Guafu fu*).[46] The male poets Cao Pi, Wang Can, and Pan Yue wrote three of these works using a ventriloquistic female voice, and the wife of Ding Yi wrote the other.[47] They seem to have been inspired by ancient poems about the plight of abandoned women from the *Classic of Poetry*. All four poems describe the harsh difficulties faced by widows, each with a slightly different focus. For example, Cao Pi writes in general terms about the widow's sorrow and solitude, while Wang Can provides a more detailed portrait of daily hardships and psychological challenges. These depictions of widows can be read in direct contrast with contemporary poems about goddesses.[48] When writing about a female deity, poets conveyed her beauty by describing each part of her body. But poetic descriptions of the widow did not mention physical attributes, as appearance lacked relevance to her predicament. Instead the poet explores her emotions and actions. The gorgeous femininity of the goddess and the pathetic suffering of the widow, embodying outward appearance and inner turmoil, expressed contrasting aspects of Six Dynasties womanhood.

In spite of the daunting challenges that most widows faced, some people still valued wifely fidelity. Early medieval biographies emphasized chastity more than Han dynasty prototypes.[49] The massive *Complete Collection of Illustrations and Writings from the Earliest to Current Times (Gujin tushu jicheng)*, completed in 1725, contains more chastity narratives from the Six Dynasties than the Han and about the same number as the Sui and Tang dynasties. Nevertheless, these still constitute only 0.08 percent of the chaste women in the collection. Writing about chastity, and indeed every kind of female behavior, increased exponentially in subsequent periods.[50] Of the eleven standard histories covering the early medieval era, three have sections devoted to virtuous women. Female biographies in *Records of Jin* consist of 45.9 percent chaste women and martyrs compared with 42 percent in *History of the Northern Dynasties (Beishi)*.[51] Most chaste widow stories describe southern women.[52] And many portrayals of women disregarded chastity entirely. *New Account of Tales of the World* ignores this virtue and concentrates on female talent instead.

A poem sums up the ideal wife as a virgin on the wedding day and absolutely faithful to her husband thereafter, modestly hiding herself from the gaze of strange men.[53]

> Lovely the girl in her hidden room
> When she became wife in her lord's home.
> Strict her virtue, taught with autumn frost,
> Radiant with beauty, like the morning sun.

Some widows accepted these moral standards and refused to enter a second marriage, regardless of potential hardship.[54] It seems that widow chastity initially emerged as an extension of monogamy. Society had great respect for monogamy, seeing it as both norm and virtue. Writers always cast adultery and other forms of extramarital sex as deviant behavior, even when they tolerated it. China was not unusual in this regard. Throughout the world, most societies practice monogamous marriage, and it had been the standard custom in China since the Zhou dynasty.[55] Although sufficiently wealthy men could take one or more concubines, they did not consider them wives. Moreover, the Tuoba were traditionally monogamous as well, so northern cultural influence did not disrupt the traditional emphasis on conjugal fidelity.[56] Avoiding remarriage also had practical benefits. Step-mothers traditionally had a reputation for cruelty toward their husband's children, complicating even male remarriage.[57] And a widow entering a new household could never be completely certain what sort of situation she would face, making her think twice about a second marriage. Respect for monogamy eventually inspired women to remain committed to their spouses even after they had died.

Figure 7.1. Apsara playing a lute.

With monogamy and female fidelity held in such esteem, some woman began to assume that a husband ought to be as committed to a marriage as his wife. When a man failed to live up to these expectations, his spouse might unleash complaints or even physical violence. Although previous writings mentioned wifely jealousy, it had never been a major topic of concern. During the Six Dynasties, however, jealousy emerged as an important and controversial theme in literature and historiography, and men discussed it in detail.[58] The problems raised by female jealousy and the male infidelity that sparked these feelings would continue to fascinate authors and readers for the remainder imperial history.

Female jealousy grew out of the gross inequities of the Chinese marriage system.[59] The historian Ban Gu (32–92) recognized female jealousy as a legitimate grievance arising from the unbalanced nature of marital arrangements.[60] Ban noted that while men expected their wives to remain faithful, husbands had sexual outlets with concubines, slaves, and prostitutes. Some women burned with anger at this gross inequity, and rising female self-assurance exacerbated their feelings. The early medieval custom of wealthy men keeping large numbers of concubines and female slaves further aggravated the problem.[61]

A wife felt threated by her husband's dalliances.[62] At the top of society, a palace concubine who bore an heir might sideline a barren empress. And even ordinary men cast aside their wives in favor of someone younger and prettier.[63] Poetry captures the feelings of the apprehensive wife as she contemplates her rivals, contrasting their youthful beauty with her own homely looks:[64]

> Mansions in the capital are full of pretty charms,
> Brilliant, brilliant are the city people.
> Elegant they step with soft, slim waists,
> Bewitching smiles show white teeth.
> Their loveliness is so enviable,
> This ugly wretch is hardly worth a mention.

Numerous poems juxtapose the very different lives of men and women. Husbands are mobile and wives stationary. Husbands control family wealth and wives depend on them financially. Moreover, writers portrayed the life of a lone woman as sterile and incomplete. As a result of this inequity, a wife dreaded abandonment, and her uncertain hold over her husband made her even more fearful.[65]

Several trends intensified jealous feelings. The decline of ritual standards and Confucian ethics allowed women to express their feelings far more freely. *A New Account of Tales of the World* depicts spouses speaking to one another forthrightly. As women dared to vent their true feelings, they expressed insecurity and jealousy.[66] Also, many women now expected connubial life to include some romance, so humdrum reality disappointed them. Xianbei influence also stoked jealousy. The Tuoba and other steppe peoples observed strict monogamy and lacked concubinage. Although Chinese historians have conventionally portrayed pastoral society as relatively "open," some nomadic kinship customs were in fact more restrictive than those in China. Confronted with the values of northern peoples, some women began to question looser Chinese norms, leading them to demand greater fidelity from husbands.[67]

Also, marriages arranged for financial gain could also produce jealousy. Sometimes a woman from a higher-status family married a wealthy spouse from a lower background. In such a situation, she would likely look down on her husband as a social inferior and feel little compunction about criticizing his conduct. Princesses were infamously haughty and jealous. When a man married a princess, even if the couple did not have sexual relations he was still forbidden from taking a concubine. Due to this rule, some family lines died out because their heir married a princess.[68]

Women expressed their jealousy through a wide spectrum of behavior, ranging from muttered complaints to violence. Sometimes a wife targeted her husband, berating him ferociously.[69] As jealousy arose from the desire to enforce marital loyalty and fidelity, even female paragons of virtue showed possessiveness.[70] Princesses had a degree of power over their husbands as they could appeal to the throne to punish an errant husband.[71] However, a wife could almost never attack her husband physically, limiting the bodily damage she could inflict on him. More commonly, a wife lashed out at other women. A wife's female rivals were usually her social inferiors, so they could easily be crushed. In this unequal society, an aristocrat could kill a lowly woman with impunity, so high-ranking wives murdered or abused their husbands' concubines and female slaves.[72] When one man died, his irate widow took revenge on his beloved slave by having her buried alive in his tomb.[73] Another woman had her child's nursemaid murdered, as she suspected that the woman had caught her husband's eye. Her own baby starved to death as a result.[74] Jealousy also drove women to kill a husband's children born to another woman. Lady Xu, a minor consort of Emperor Yuan (r. 552–555), infuriated the ruler with her drunkenness and slovenly appearance. She even flaunted her affair with a Daoist cleric. Yet in spite of her own faults, she felt so insanely jealous that she personally ripped the fetuses out of his pregnant concubines.[75]

Princess Lanling stands out as perhaps the most notorious woman of the Six Dynasties, as she embodied female jealousy. Lanling married Liu Hui, a royal scion whose grandfather had surrendered to the Wei. As a descendant of royalty and member of the high aristocracy, Liu Hui was accustomed to having his way. Even after marrying a princess, he still had numerous affairs. When Liu impregnated one of his female slaves, Lanling went berserk. She beat her rival to death, ripped out the fetus, filled the corpse with straw, and displayed the naked stuffed body to her horrified husband. However, rather than frightening him into fidelity, Lanling's viciousness appalled him. Thereafter he shunned his wife's company. The princess then appealed to her sister-in-law, the domineering Empress Dowager Ling, who rescinded Liu Hui's noble title and arranged for the couple to divorce. However, Lanling later had second thoughts and the couple remarried. Once again, Liu Hui had dalliances with other women. When the pregnant Lanling confronted him, their violent altercation ended in her miscarriage and death. A furious Empress Dowager Ling ordered Liu's mistresses enslaved in the palace and their brothers exiled to the frontier. Authorities charged Liu Hui with murder, but he eventually received a pardon during an imperial amnesty.[76]

Southern men particularly detested demanding wives, but husbands throughout China found uxorial possessiveness extremely unsettling and struggled to cope with it.[77] Writers debated the root causes of jealousy. Some argued that jealous women failed to properly carry out the wifely role, with one described as garrulous, obstinate, and mean.[78] Others analyzed conjugal dynamics to understand why a wife would cause trouble for her husband. Some took a Confucian perspective, stressing the importance of moral education. They considered aggressive female behavior an outgrowth of ignorance and argued that a woman who had studied the classical rites would meekly accept her husband's extramarital affairs. Alternatively, others saw jealousy as a character flaw. According to this viewpoint, women who unleashed such extreme emotions simply lacked emotional maturity and basic self-control.[79]

Writers praised wives who lacked jealousy as female role models, hoping that other women would emulate them. The example of Princess Changshan, noteworthy for her lack of jealousy, provided a temperate alternative to Princess Lanling. Because Changshan did not bear a son, she generously arranged for her husband to take a concubine who could provide him with an heir.[80] Epitaphs also praised a deceased woman who avoided jealousy and encouraged her female descendants to imitate this ancestral virtue.[81]

Powerful men sometimes made recourse to the law to moderate female behavior. The husbands of jealous wives may have envied men in the Mongol kingdom of Shiwei, where a husband would simply kill a jealous wife and abandon her corpse on a mountaintop to rot. If her family wanted her corpse, they had to ransom it with a payment of horses and cattle.[82] In China, however, the law did not sanction the murder of a jealous wife. Even so, a husband could appeal to authorities to chastise an excessively demanding spouse. Officials punished a few prominent women for undue possessiveness, and a woman could even be executed for extreme jealousy.[83] Other men saw jealousy as a medical problem and recommended that a fierce wife should receive treatments to moderate her emotions. Because the extensive Chinese pharmacopoeia included ingredients believed to regulate potency and other sexual issues, it seemed reasonable to use herbal medicine to cure jealousy as well.[84]

Perhaps most often, men shamed jealous women by demonizing them. After the death of the cruel and jealous Empress Xi (468–499), wife of Emperor Wende, she supposedly transformed into a dragon that inhabited in a well in the rear of the palace and communicated with the ruler through dreams.[85] By portraying the jealous wife as a serpentine monster, historians made it clear that women should avoid this sort of behavior. Religion also embraced this theme. The soul of a concubine victimized by a jealous wife transformed into the goddess Zi Gu, guardian deity of toilets, and people sacrificed to her out of pity or fear.[86] The apotheosis of a murdered concubine into a goddess implied that violent jealousy offends the fundamental order of the cosmos.

Given the importance of a supportive husband to his wife's well-being, a man's death presented his spouse with tough decisions. Many women had to confront the challenges of widowhood and the possibility of remarriage. Grooms tended to be older than brides. And given the dangers that men faced in that violent age, husbands suffered a high rate of unnatural death. As a result, husbands generally predeceased wives, sometimes by many years. According to one study, the husband of the average widow commemorated with an epitaph died when she was 39.8 years of age, and she went on to live another 17.9 years.[87] Occasionally even young widows refused remarriage. One woman's husband died when she was just seventeen years old and their son died a few years later. In spite of her youth, she refused to enter a second marriage and remained chaste for the rest of her life.[88]

Widows who rejected remarriage had various motivations. Some may have simply disliked conjugal life. For others, a devotion to lifelong fidelity spurred them to remain chaste after the death of a husband. One young widow mourned her deceased husband excessively and remained devoted to his memory. She not only rejected remarriage but also remained in a permanent state of mourning, refusing to bathe or eat meat for the rest of her life.[89] For a childless young widow to forego remarriage involved considerable sacrifice.[90] She marginalized herself from family life, which constituted the central organizing institution of society. Moreover, she would not bear children to care for her in her old age. Even more ominously, no one would sacrifice to her spirit after she died, condemning her to an uncertain posthumous fate.

In later eras, when widow chastity had become more common, women frequently rejected remarriage to continue caring for their parents-in-law. Some early medieval women already had this sense of duty, which arose as an extension of filial piety and the wifely duties described in the ritual canon. A woman officially joined her husband's family on her wedding day, and some wives felt strongly committed to this bond.[91] Occasionally widows remained in their deceased husbands' homes so that they could look after their parents-in-law.[92] *Records of Wei* tentatively linked widow chastity to caregiving for parents-in-laws.

In spite of these cases, relatively few Six Dynasties accounts describe women devotedly serving their in-laws, as this behavior had yet to become intimately associated with widow chastity.[93] Rejecting remarriage for the sake of in-laws did not become commonplace until the eleventh century, when Neo-Confucianism demanded that women conform to stringent ethical dictates.[94] During the era of division, a widow's in-laws did not yet expect her to remain chaste for their sake. One widow who decided to remain with her deceased husband's family did so even though her two brothers-in-law urged her to return home.[95] They believed that a widow should return to her blood relatives. The father-in-law of another widow said to her father, "Your worthy daughter is still young, and of course it is proper for her to remarry."[96]

In this age of intense faith, religious doctrines also affected ideas about chastity. Daoist scriptures describe spiritual utopia as a place where everyone adheres to virtue, and so the women there comport themselves chastely. In contrast, in an evil country to the west ruled by a menacing fox spirit, the ruler and his son seduce women and force them to behave licentiously.[97] Through this sort of rhetoric, Daoists took female purity as emblematic of society's overall moral tone.

Buddhism had an even greater impact on ideas about female virtue. Thousands of sutras and other religious works conveyed many messages, sometimes contradictory, about how women ought to behave. In some respects, Mahayana Buddhism encouraged sexual equality. Overall, the sutras tend to portray women positively and emphasize their capacity for spiritual attainment. Some scriptures encouraged women to seek equality and autonomy.[98] Yet other texts had more conservative content, emphasizing the importance of physical purity, sexual chastity, and modest separation of sexes.[99]

In spite of teachings about spirituality and transcendence, Buddhism also emphasized a woman's physicality, associating female virtue more closely with the condition of her body. Prior to the entry of Buddhism into China, moralists had emphasized correct behavior as central to female virtue. Buddhists shifted attention toward physical purity, making the integrity of the body central to female virtue.[100] According to this viewpoint, it was insufficient for a woman to merely behave well. To be considered truly virtuous, she also had to safeguard the purity of her body by forgoing sex entirely or at least remaining faithfully committed to her husband. Translations from Sanskrit employed secular Chinese jargon associated with chastity, thereby introducing Buddhist ideas about physical purity and sexual integrity into chastity discourse.[101]

This intermingling of secular chastity rhetoric and Buddhism inspired some widows to become nuns so that they could avoid remarriage and guard their chastity within a safe and respectable environment. A woman could serve as a nun for a period of time and eventually reenter lay life, sometimes to marry.[102] Usually, however, they treated monastic vows as a lifelong commitment. Numerous widows entered a temple in order to remain chaste.[103] Some aristocratic families had unusually stringent family ethics that included widow chastity, and their widows sometimes became nuns in grand temple complexes. A wealthy family might even build a nunnery so that their widows would have a place to live.[104] Some nuns took the idea of chastity to an extreme, believing that they should avoid all marriage and sexual relations.[105] For them, the nunnery represented a place of refuge from the physical pollution caused by sexual intercourse.

A few believers took radical measures to maintain the integrity of their bodies. Some nuns martyred themselves rather than give in to sexual advances. When an evil official made advances on Zhixian (ca. 300–ca. 370), she steadfastly rebuffed him. In a rage he stabbed her twenty times with his dagger. She fell unconscious but later miraculously recovered.[106] Others threatened suicide simply to avoid marriage. Sengri (ca. 330–397) refused her mother's demands to get married and fasted until she was on the brink of death.[107] Her bridegroom, also a devout Buddhist, did not want her to marry against her will, so her mother finally relented and allowed her to become a nun.

Chinese Buddhism imported the extreme practice of self-immolation from India. Some clerics, usually monks, burned themselves to death to cast off their physical form and attain a higher state of being.[108] Women occasionally followed their example and threatened fiery suicide if their parents did not allow them to become nuns. A few actually immolated themselves.[109] Although only a handful of women went to such an extreme, these dramatic cases nevertheless had a significant impact on the way people thought about chastity as justifying self-destructive behavior.

The early medieval era marks a turning point for chastity. Rhetoric became increasingly extreme as authors emphasized mutilation and death.[110] Some widows killed themselves to avoid being forced into an unwanted second marriage.[111] One account describes a warlord who murdered the husband of a young woman and then tried to take her as a concubine. When she refused, he killed her as well.[112] Women who rebuffed the advances of bandits were murdered or committed suicide.[113] One story from the north had a woman slashing her cheeks to make herself unmarriageable. Her behavior seems to have been inspired by the pastoral custom of cheek slashing during mourning, which widows appropriated for their own purposes.[114] Of the thirty-six early medieval biographies featuring chastity, two describe a woman shearing off her hair to make herself unmarriageable, in three the martyr cuts off an ear, two describe facial mutilation, five of the women are killed, and seventeen stories end in suicide. Only seven of these narratives lack violence.[115] The standard histories of the southern dynasties relate most of these episodes, so readers encountered chastity tales in as an authoritative genre that presented extreme behavior as morally orthodox.

Violent chastity episodes in the standard histories take the female body as a symbol of Chinese nationhood.[116] Some ethnic Han aristocrats in the north seem to have encouraged their women to remain chaste as a way of flaunting their commitment to Chinese culture, thereby

distinguishing themselves from conquering nomads who had no com-
punctions about remarriage.[117] Stories about mutilation and suicide
imbued sexual passions with an ideological dimension, positioning
them within the period's complex cultural politics. In an era of widespread dislocation and carnage, people readily identified with women
who made extreme sacrifices. Although few Chinese wanted to die for
the sake of their nation and culture, violent chastity stories served as
fantasy material in which they could imagine their own moral predica-
ments played out by someone else. To some extent, stories of suicidal
widows represented the wishful thinking of male readers who liked to
imagine themselves forcefully resisting China's enemies, even if they
never really dared to take such risky actions.

As widow chastity accrued political connotations, governments revived the Han dynasty commendation system, presenting chaste role
models with prestigious symbolic rewards and practical prizes such as
bolts of cloth and tax exemptions.[118] Even northern conquest dynasties
handed out these awards, despite the fact that their rulers came from
cultures that did not value chastity. Northern rulers recognized that embracing chastity lent them legitimacy and moral authority. So as chastity
became increasingly valued, different groups used it for their own ends.
While the native elite took chastity as an instrument of cultural solidarity,
resisting China's invaders by reasserting their traditional values, foreign
conquerors used it to prove themselves moral and civilized.

In spite of all the discussion of chastity, most women could still remarry
freely. Although no one considered a second marriage praiseworthy,
neither did they regard it as unacceptable. Even so, a number of factors
pushed the rhetoric of female virtue toward extremes.[119] Many societies
react to prolonged crisis by redefining sexual norms.[120] Centuries earlier, the fin-de-siècle atmosphere of the decayed Western Han court had
inspired Liu Xiang to take on female integrity as a major moral theme.
Likewise, amid the bewildering chaos of the Six Dynasties, some people
tried to police the female body as a way of restoring order and certainty
to their world.

Moreover, in this highly stratified society, some of the elite adopted
stringent ethical standards to claim superiority. Keeping the family's
widows chaste, in contravention of the standard customs of the day,
demonstrated the social supremacy of the high aristocracy. Over time, the
lower gentry and commoners imitated this behavior, seeking to elevate
their status by imitating their superiors.[121]

Masculine honor also became identified with the behavior and physical
integrity of female kin.[122] As female purity increasingly redounded on the
reputations of husbands, brothers, fathers, and sons, it became important
for men to restrain the women around them. People despised the man

who allowed the women's quarters of his home to sink into disorder.[123] And a woman's misconduct, even behind closed doors, could potentially ruin the reputation of a husband, father, and brothers. For this reason, a man could disgrace a woman to humiliate a male enemy. One malevolent official forced his rival's wife to sit naked in front of her children, then raped his younger sister as her mother watched.[124] Men were willing to go to extremes to shield their womenfolk from this sort of disgrace. When one man's enemies were about to capture his family, he threw his young daughter off the top of a building, killing her for the sake of righteousness.[125] In doing so, he not only saved her from humiliation but also safeguarded his own posthumous honor.

Although widow chastity served various political and social functions, for most women practical concerns determined whether or not they would remain chaste. Did they have enough resources to live comfortably in permanent widowhood? Would they lose their children if they remarried? They also had to consider the potential humiliation of entering a family that would likely look down on them.[126] And a remarried woman would have to face a lifetime of guilt for failing to live up to the most stringent ideals of female integrity.

A horror story uses fiction to convey the unease felt by remarried women.[127] In this tale, a thoughtless widow fails to observe the full mourning period for her deceased husband. Instead she immediately remarries, and her new husband moves into the dead man's house. Furious at this betrayal, the deceased man turns into a ghost and terrorizes the couple. They end up fleeing the haunted house, which subsequently became a temple. This ghost story can be read as a metaphor for the emotions evoked by remarriage, with the malevolent ghost embodying the widow's intense guilt. This story resonated with readers of the time because they knew that every remarried woman had to confront similar feelings of remorse. Even so, despite the psychological pressures that widows faced, most of them remarried, putting aside their misgivings so that they could enjoy the benefits of conjugal life.

8

Ideals

Han dynasty writers and artists portrayed the ideal woman as a moral paragon, a belief that endured even after that dynasty ended. This image can be seen in a series of wall paintings in the tomb of Sima Jinlong (d. 484) that depicts male and female role models. Alongside pictures of rulers, generals, high ministers, and other great men, the artist painted virtuous ancient queens and women renowned for wisdom or self-sacrifice.[1] This cycle of didactic portraits replicates the traditional view of women, seeing them through the lens of ethics and politics, even though the world that produced these stereotypes had crumbled long before.

Newer images of women had more relevance to the changed circumstances marking the age of disunion. The disorienting chaos of this era stimulated people to question basic verities, including assumptions about gender, giving rise to new, original, and sometimes contentious images of womanhood. Some of these ideas had currency for a short time while others endured to affect subsequent eras. The surge in religious faith led some believers to imagine the model woman as a goddess. One epitaph compares a deceased woman to the goddesses of the Xiang and Luo rivers.[2] Overall, however, female role models were rarely so simplistic. Society had become extremely diverse, and the creative class had to come to grips with contradictory influences. Pastoral cultures introduced images of lively and brave women. Yet Confucian influence lingered, perpetuating the belief that women should be submissive and passive. Presented with conflicting gender norms, it was hard for men to know what they wanted from women, and even harder for women to understand how to be themselves.[3]

This era also saw the growth of a darker view of femininity. Men regarded menstrual blood with horror. They believed that the periodic discharge of menses renders a woman permanently unclean, however beautiful she might appear.[4] Medical texts increasingly stressed the inherent pollution of the female body, portraying women as physically inferior to men in consequence. However, the female physique also harbored innate curative powers. Physicians used menstrual fluid as an ingredient in certain healing concoctions, apparently assuming that such a loathsome material could expel disease. Menses also allowed women to become powerful shamans and sorcerers. Ready access to potent menstrual blood allowed them to brew potions that could harm others. In sum, people saw the female body in contradictory ways, as beautiful yet dangerously polluting.

The mechanics of early medieval scholarship and intellectual discourse differed fundamentally from prior practices. The Han dynasty elite looked to ancient texts to understand and order their world, imposing intellectual and cultural conformity. Moreover, they assumed that the writers have a duty to serve the state.[5] Working under the influence of Confucianism, Han authors made literature a tool of politics. As propriety discouraged the criticism of corruption or malfeasance, poets often ended up indiscriminately praising the flawed status quo.[6]

During the age of disunion, modes of writing changed in significant ways.[7] Poets still wrote rhapsodies (*fu*), but they redirected their output to new ends.[8] Poetry became more critical and self-conscious. And poets increasingly wrote about intimate subjects, including female matters.[9] The women in these poems seem very different from the taut female subjects of Han dynasty literature. They no longer appear as one-dimensional moral paragons or metaphors for government ministers. Instead, poets rendered women as individuals driven by strong emotions and desires.[10] These poems treat women with a new sense of interest and respect. Poets began to take the inner psychological world of their subjects seriously, seeing female emotions as an important theme that deserves contemplation.

Six Dynasties poets reacted against the traditional view that their writings should teach, cultivate, and provide moral guidance. Instead, versification became an independent realm of discourse with principles and values detached from the interests of the state.[11] When taken to an extreme, this deliberately disinterested attitude turned poetry into little more than a clever word game. Many writers produced works in deliberately complex and affected styles to make their pastime more challenging.[12] Even so, the poetry of this era cannot be dismissed as mere decadence. The new air of freedom and creativity also allowed poets to express more authentic ideas and feelings, examine other people in detail, and explore the world around them with candor.[13]

As poets unleashed their creativity, they pioneered new ways of looking at women. The ancient *Classic of Poetry* contains the earliest feminine tropes, and it had an immense influence on medieval literature. This canonical collection portrayed many types of women, from suffering widows to idealized queens. Notably, many of them speak with strong voices. In contrast, few Han dynasty poems even mention women. Rather than exploring individual experience, Han poets composed bombastic rhapsodies (*fu*) in praise of the state and orthodox order. When writers bothered to describe female matters, Confucian moralism took precedence, so they conventionally portrayed women as gentle and submissive.[14]

During the brief but culturally fecund Jian'an era (196–220), an atmosphere of despair enveloped the enfeebled Eastern Han dynasty. Poets felt themselves to be standing on a precipice and gazing into an abyss. They knew that impending dynastic collapse would soon bring dislocation and terrible suffering. As they contemplated their melancholy fate, educated men became disenchanted with orthodox poetry. They felt no desire to praise the deteriorating Han system. Dissatisfied with traditional subject matter, they turned their backs on politics and directed their attentions to emotional and individualistic subjects. As they searched for interesting new themes, poets once again started to write about women.[15]

Only eleven poems about women survive from the four centuries prior to the Jian'an era. In contrast, this brief period of giddy cultural effervescence produced twenty-eight poems on female matters. Some poets portrayed women realistically, describing prosaic female matters. Others explored female emotions and psychology. For example, a poet might describe the frustration of a woman who felt compelled to repress her desires for the sake of propriety. Writers also composed verses about goddesses, positioning the essence of femininity within a framework of transcendent metaphysics.

New Songs from a Jade Terrace (Yutai xinyong) stands out as the most important extant collection of Six Dynasties poetry. Notably, the editor Xu Ling (507–583) states in his preface that he assembled these poems specifically for a female readership. Some scholars now believe that Xu hid his true intentions. This revisionist reading argues that he claimed to target women as a way to justify ignoring traditional political and moral themes.[16] Whatever his intentions, the collection contains numerous poems of interest to women. In recent years, many critics have come to believe that Xu Ling did indeed assemble this collection for female readers. At the very least, by stating that he intended women to read these poems, Xu encouraged them to enjoy southern palace poetry. By attracting a diverse readership, the groundbreaking female images in these poems had a significant impact on educated people of both sexes.

Many thinkers considered themselves to be living in an age of decay, and this belief informed their view of the individual. Thinkers had long assumed that a society's particular characteristics largely determined the limits of personal agency. Mencius famously declared that the world passes through a series of ages, alternately light and dark, and these changes largely determine what sort of life people in each period can lead.[17] The Six Dynasties cultural elite confronted dim prospects, so they considered themselves to be living in a time of decline. This attitude affected how they viewed the participation of women in high culture.

Southern palace-style poetry of the sixth century unapologetically embraced this glum mindset by taking a blatantly decadent tone. Writers employed delicate diction and affected sensibilities to describe an elegant world of artificial luxury. Critics often describe this overly polished language as feminine, even though the poets were men. Male writers crafted a feminized literary persona as a kind of shield that could insulate them from the frustrations of cruel reality.[18] This womanly style of poetry exerted a major impact on literature and culture. For example, a circle of Tang poets revived the style of Liang palace poetry and wrote about women in an exaggeratedly delicate style.[19]

The earlier genre of rhapsodies (*fu*) written to "celebrate objects" (*yongwu*) guided the evolution of Liang dynasty writings about women.[20] Although the most famous rhapsodies acclaimed the ruler and state, some Han poets employed a similarly orotund tone to describe trees, clouds, animals, and other features of the natural world. The intensity of description gave this style of poetry its impact. Extravagant and repetitive language not only conveyed the outer appearance of a thing but also sought to expose its inner essence. As literature detached from politics, poets writing in other genres introduced flamboyant rhapsodic techniques into their own verses. But instead of confining their attentions to the natural world, they explored novel themes that they found interesting. Widespread impoverishment had fostered an obsession with extravagant wealth, so poets described luxury items such as bronze mirrors, finely crafted musical instruments, and so on. And given the wide interest in character judgment, they applied this type of grandiloquent writing to describe people.

When poets wrote about women in the style of "celebrating things," they produced a literary hybrid. Because this genre conventionally described beautiful and luxurious objects, poets portrayed women in the same manner. Writers applied the technique of intensive description to represent female subjects, describing an individual or group of women in exhaustive detail.[21] These portrayals often include critical appraisals

Figure 8.1. Apsara carrying an offering.

of beauty, with the poet taking on the role of judge. Rhapsodies that depicted a subject at length and in fine detail often directed the reader's attention to specific parts of a female subject's body. Literary critics refer to the practice of praising a woman piece by piece as "the blazon."[22] Although the rhapsody pioneered these sorts of detailed verbal sketches of female anatomy, writers introduced it into other genres.[23]

> Moth eyebrows part in kingfisher wings,
> Bright eyes illumine her clear brow.
> Cinnabar lips screen white teeth,
> Delicate her face like scepter jade.

Describing a woman piece by piece was more than just an exercise in anatomical classification. Naming and describing each part implicitly claimed ownership of a woman's body and control over her public image. When men wrote about women in this manner, poetry became a gendered mechanism of control.

During this era, men wrote a great deal of poetry in a first-person female voice that critics refer to as the literati-feminine voice.[24] Men continued to write this sort of ventriloquistic poetry in large quantities all the way down to the modern era, exerting a strong influence on images of women. In Liang dynasty palace poetry, a man impersonates the speech of a highborn woman surrounded by accouterments of wealth, thereby associating femininity with luxury. An invisible man, both poet and reader, secretly peeks through the bedroom curtains to gaze at her. Because of this artificial voyeuristic perspective, even as the poet takes on a female voice, the woman he constructs does not seem real. She talks and acts in ways conducive to erotic male fantasy. An actual woman would regard her boudoir as a mundane space for quotidian activities. In contrast, the poet turns a woman's bedroom into a sexually charged zone, with the goal of titillating male readers. The rise of the literati-feminine voice influenced notions about ideal female appearance. The term *yan* originally simply referred to a woman's beauty, but critics used the term to categorize poetry that uses lush language to make women seem both lovely and erotic.[25]

In palace poetry, the writer usually situates the female subject in the innermost recesses of a mansion. Her surroundings might seem grand, but they confine her, evoking an unsettling sense of claustrophobia. In spite of this woman's beauty and privilege, she feels miserable. Like the melancholy female prototypes in ancient poetry, she pines for an absent lover. Her life seems incomplete without the man of her dreams. She languishes in her boudoir, increasingly pathetic and weak. The luxurious but hollow surroundings of her lonely chamber intensify her feelings of insecurity. Even though the beauty knows that her lover will probably never return, she nevertheless broods on her hopeless passions, as these emotions are all that she has left. The outsider might regard her as pathetic, yet she savors the intensity of her thwarted love.

Some of these poems create a melancholy mood by emphasizing the interminable succession of empty hours rendered meaningless by the absence of her loved one:[26]

> In her room still the water-clock drips and drips,
> Time's infinity, the hush of hushed night.
> Grass insects flit though the night door,
> Spiders entwine autumn walls.
> She faintly smiles, but she is not happy,
> She softly sighs, but it turns to sorrow.
> Gold pins droop down her hair,
> Jade chopsticks trickle on her dress.

However much anguish she feels, her lover never returns. As the passage of time wears her down, the increasingly depressed woman falls apart.

Her sumptuous beauty, the quality that initially attracted the poetry's attention, begins to decay:[27]

> The winter dawn sun shines on rafters,
> Morosely she gets down from her bed,
> Lifts from the curtains her bamboo-leaf sash.
> Turns to the mirror her caltrop-bloom radiance.
> Certain there's no one to see her like this,
> What's the use of early-morning rouge?

Chinese poets deal with feelings of frustration differently from European counterparts. Western authors traditionally employed a "double bind" situation in which neither option seems acceptable as the starting point for tragedy.[28] Elevating a character's suffering to tragic proportions makes it seem important and meaningful. In contrast, the women in Liang dynasty poems seem merely pathetic. As with the character of Western tragedy, they loom above the average person. Their wealth and beauty makes them larger than life. However, unlike the protagonists of Greek tragedy, they do not suffer through any fault of their own, so they lack a tragic flaw. Nor does the poet celebrate female suffering as an act of defiance or source of wisdom. Instead of ending in catharsis, the protagonist's misery lingers as an inescapable fact of life. This sort of futile despair seems little different from the suffering of animals in the natural world.

In palace-style poetry, the poet regards the female character not as a fully developed human subject but as a physical object. One poem describes a beautiful woman looking at a painting of another beauty. By juxtaposing them in this manner, the poet reduces both the real woman and painted image to analogous objects that exist solely for the appreciation of the male reader.[29] In objectifying the woman at the center of the poem, the writer demotes her from a complete human being to an emotionally charged symbol.[30] Her appearance matters far more than what she does. Immobile and confined to her bedroom, her actions lack importance. Instead, appearance becomes the focus of attention. In contrast to the Han dynasty image of a virtuous woman whose attractive exterior reflects a virtuous core, this woman's form has nothing to do with integrity. The poet describes her loveliness simply to attract and hold the male gaze.[31] Misery at her lover's absence suggests that the reader might potentially replace him and become the recipient of this beautiful woman's intense affection.

By objectifying women and using them to construct erotic male fantasies, southern dynasties poets created a new and extremely different image of the ideal woman. As an object, a woman's suffering lacks meaning. Her melancholy mood is simply a static characteristic that defines her. The poet does not expect the reader to show this miserable woman much empathy. Instead, he is invited to appreciate her aesthetically as a beautiful but empty shell with sexual potential.

The particular ways that writers understood beauty informed the objectification and aestheticization of women in poetry. The Chinese idea of beauty differed somewhat from Western analogues. Plato considered beauty to have ontological presence beyond the human realm. In contrast, Chinese understood beauty (*mei*) as the pleasurable sensation that people feel when viewing something orderly and harmonious.[32] Being subjective, beauty can mean different things to different people. During this era in particular, the standards of female beauty provoked intense debate, giving rise to contradictory viewpoints.

Previously a woman's beauty had often been equated with virtue more than appearance, and this idea still had considerable resonance.[33] The *Classic of Poetry* emphasized the importance of good character to a woman's beauty, and Han dynasty literature and painting adhered to this position. According to this viewpoint, if a woman appears beautiful, it was likely due to her fundamental moral qualities. In ancient poetry, the male reader views a female subject and judges her beauty. There are no descriptions of women observing women. Instead poets and artists depicted beautiful women in situations, costumes, and poses calculated to appeal to the men who would observe and judge them. Due to the prominence of ethical values, they often stressed noble character above physical attributes.

Some writers in the early medieval period maintained these standards, likewise associating beauty with goodness. Descriptions of a woman often tell the reader little about her looks. *A New Account of Tales of the World* describes a woman's appearance only once.[34] Even in this instance, her beauty embodies good character. Conversely, the author condemns licentiousness, even when couched in physical beauty. Overall, this book turns the reader's attention away from the female body and toward personality. This more comprehensive view of beauty encompasses traits such as integrity and emotion. Charm and elegant bearing reveal inner cultivation.[35] Virtue still serves as the foundation of beauty, in line with traditional portrayals of women.[36]

> Lovely the girl in her hidden room
> When she became wife in her lord's home.
> Strict her virtue, taught with autumn frost,
> Radiant with beauty, like the morning sun.

If a woman moves and behaves too freely, she cannot be beautiful. Instead, she must act in accordance with the ancient rites. By abiding by these regulations that control her body, she can become truly beautiful.[37]

Writers frequently emphasized the connection between character and beauty. A representative vignette relates the predicament of a man married to an ugly woman. He did not even want to visit her because of her repulsive appearance. However, after she chided him for putting good looks before virtue, he felt ashamed of his shallowness and thereafter held her in high regard.[38] And for some men, virtue alone remained insufficient. They sought a woman who combined beauty with refinement. The woman that Cao Pi chose for his wife combined good looks with a gentle demeanor.[39] Another husband similarly respected his wife because she possessed two key female qualities: virtue and beauty.[40]

After the fall of Han, many writers challenged the traditional view of beauty as the physical embodiment of morality. Instead of female character, they turned their attentions outward and focused on the body. To some extent, this emphasis on the physical arose in reaction to the dangers that women faced in a time of upheaval.[41] As society disintegrated into civil war, banditry, and warlordism, many women suffered sexual abuse. It became more difficult for a woman to maintain control over her body, making the preservation of physical purity seem more important. This focus on physical integrity encouraged people to appreciate the female body in its own right, rather than regarding it largely as a manifestation of hidden inner qualities.

Developments in painting exhibit these changing points of view.[42] Han dynasty painters had little interest in the beautiful body in its own right. Confucianism taught that attraction to physical appearance easily devolved into licentiousness. So instead of stressing the beauty of the female body, Han painters usually portrayed women to illustrate Confucian virtues. After the fall of Han, however, painters turned their attentions to the exploration of aspects of physical beauty. The Southern Qi painter Liu Zhen (460–501) specialized in female figures, and his influential works inspired other artists to take beauty as a primary theme. Some painters still continued to portray female models of Confucian propriety. Yet the modern critic cannot help but wonder if this moral project had devolved into an excuse to paint a gallery of beautiful women. In Han dynasty painting, virtuous women have a ponderous bearing. But early medieval artists began to portray them as elegant, light, and serene. Some undulate and even float in the air.[43]

> Slim of waist, but not a Chu lady,
> Light of body, but not a Zhao girl.

As people took increasing interest in the female body, they began to discuss beauty casually, making it a common topic of conversation. During the Han it would have been considered scandalous for a man to comment

on the appearance of another man's wife or daughters. But in the succeeding age it became acceptable to look critically at a man's daughter and
declare her beautiful or ugly.[44]

Southern palace-style poetry had an immense influence on shifting
standards of beauty.[45] Even when people viewed paintings of beautiful
women, they interpreted what they saw through conventions that had
been established and popularized by poetry. When an artist portrayed
a woman seated in her boudoir, the viewer knew from poetry that she
felt anguished by a lover's absence. By reading painting through poetry,
viewers imputed strong emotions to images of women in static poses. As
in literature, even certain plants became associated with female beauty,
plum blossoms in particular.[46] Painters portrayed women together with
meaningful flowers to provide the viewer with subtle guidance on how
to perceive them.

Some people held beautiful women in such high regard that they assumed that they could not possibly exist in the mortal realm. As a result,
they elevated beauty to a supernatural state.[47] Writers and painters often
rendered the beautiful woman as a goddess or immortal who had descended from the heavens. Other kinds of female spirits and even ghosts
could also be beautiful, in spite of their danger. With prettiness elevated
to an otherworldly quality, many beauties in medieval literature are not
really mortal women but divine beings.

Some anomaly stories describe relationships between a mortal man and
a paranormal woman.[48] The goddess, immortal, or ghost personifies ideal
femininity: beautiful, gentle, and kind, yet also erotic and passionate.
When their relationship ends, the man bears no responsibility to his former beloved. These narratives of romance and sex without consequence
served as fantasy material for male readers. In contrast, because a woman
could not decently have an affair outside of marriage, writers portrayed
relationships between women and supernatural beings as negative. The
supernatural male is often a malevolent demon who possesses a woman
and sickens her until she can have him exorcised.

Beauty did not rely on physical appearance alone. Just as importantly,
a woman's clothes, jewelry, and luxurious surroundings constituted important aspects of her beauty. In an age of widespread destitution, the
elite flaunted their luxuries with unembarrassed enthusiasm. Ensconc-
ing themselves in sybaritic surroundings, they kept society's unpleasant
truths at arm's length. For this reason, palace poetry inevitably describes
the beautiful woman as living in a gorgeous environment. The poet rel-
ishes describing architecture, interior design, and accouterments, evoking
an atmosphere of flamboyant luxury.

With such a high value placed on luxury, ornamentation became a
crucial aspect of female beauty. As in every era, fashion served as a

mode of nonverbal communication. A woman's unadorned body represented a blank surface that could be inscribed with meaningful symbols. Decorating her body with clothes and jewels displayed high station and materialized elite taste.[49] When a woman dressed according to orthodox standards, she produced an image that people regarded as beautiful. Then she and others would judge the effect of her embodied performance according to common standards.[50] In this way, the body became a metaphor for the person.[51]

Elaborate fashion created an artificial look intended to convey wealth and leisure. Impractical garments and ornaments revealed that a wealthy woman consumed without producing, expressing high status in symbolic form.[52] At the time, leisure was not just enjoyable but also a sign of high status. Even if a woman lacked interest in fashion, it behooved her to use it to her advantage as she could raise her status by presenting her body in a certain way. And many women clearly enjoyed ornamenting themselves. Not only did they like wearing pretty clothes, they also liked playing the game of fashion.[53] These activities fascinated poets, who portrayed a woman's accouterments as integral to her beauty. Moreover, describing clothes and jewels seemed more elegant than focusing attention on the body itself.[54] Associating body with ornament made people perceive female beauty more obliquely, elevating it above pure physicality.

The most important principle of high fashion is conspicuous waste. To be seen as fashionable, clothing styles must constantly change.[55] Early medieval attire underwent many shifts.[56] Women and men still wore long robes, but sometimes they donned a jacket tucked into a skirt or trousers. As before, clothing remained very loose, and the apparel of both sexes looked similar. Hairstyle became an important sexual marker, and women wore their hair in many ways, often adorned with elaborate pins and caps.[57]

Fashion absorbed many influences from the clothing of steppe peoples.[58] Because pastoral women rode horses and helped to herd animals, their clothes differed considerably from female attire in agricultural regions. Loose flowing garments would have been completely impractical for a woman on horseback. Instead they wore tunics, trousers, and boots. Chinese perceptions of foreign garments evolved over time. In the fifth century, this type of clothing seemed extremely alien. But just a century later, Chinese had accepted it as native garb. Women sometimes even wore the clothing of male nomads. The practicality of steppe styles of clothing made cross-dressing acceptable.

Because the clothing of woman and men looked so similar, jewelry became an important sign of gender identity. Poets describe the beautiful woman bejeweled with jade, pearls, coral, and gold.[59] Copious jewelry marked her sex, and the costliness of these baubles defined her as beautiful and desirable. The poet describes the beautiful woman as a luxurious object of male desire, one with her jewelry. At the apex of society, jewels took on extremely specific meanings. Palace officials classified the jewelry of harem women into grades based on their cost and formality. Regulations dictated the occasions when palace ladies could wear different types of clothing and ornaments.[60] Women also applied heavy cosmetics.[61] Blatantly artificial makeup became so intimately associated with attractive appearance that stylish men also used it to accentuate their looks.[62]

Elements of stylish dress usually originate at the top of society and gradually affect women further down the social scale.[63] Such was the case with Six Dynasties fashion as well. And yet this dauntingly elaborate vision of female beauty began to seem superficial.[64] Detailed poetic descriptions of luxurious clothing, hair, and jewels lacked relevance to deeper concerns and lost significance over time. Palace-style poetry repeated standard tropes of female beauty so often that they eventually devolved into stale clichés, devoid of genuine emotions or ideas.

Beauty may have been hotly contested, but people always regarded it as an important female quality. Some men even married a woman of low birth simply because of her beauty.[65] However, the experiences of the erudite thinker Xun Can (212–240) reveal the limits of this attitude.[66] Xun declared, "A woman's virtue is not worth praising; her beauty should be considered the most important thing." Yet in spite of his flippant bon mot, Xun felt strong devoted to his spouse. One winter when she became sick and developed a high fever, he stood outside in the cold and then joined her in bed, pressing his chilled body against hers to try to bring down her fever. In the end, despite his loving ministrations, his wife died. Xun felt devastated and went into deep mourning. A visiting friend reminded Xun of his previous remark, reasoning that if only beauty matters, his dead wife should be easy to replace. Xun then reversed himself and admitted that it would be difficult to find another woman so good. Instead of remarrying, he pined away from sadness and died a year later. Xun Can's example shows that however much men appreciated appearance, female personality and character would always remain important.

Conclusion

An Awakening of Female Consciousness

Catastrophe can bring unexpected opportunity. During the early third century, people universally regarded the collapse of the Eastern Han dynasty and ensuing bedlam as unmitigated disaster. Given the failure of the previous dynasty and society's altered circumstances, they had no choice but to begin to reconstruct their world along different lines than before, trying to make the best of a bad situation. As a result, life changed in fundamental ways. Daoist metaphysics, Buddhist thought, and alien steppe customs all brought unprecedented changes that affected women as much as men.

In reaction to these transformations, a new and radically different mode of female thought emerged in this era. In their actions, values, and ideas, women of the Wei and Jin manifested a keen sense of self-consciousness. They became much more aware of the implicit possibilities in their lives and were increasingly willing to exercise agency and experiment with alternative ways of thinking and behaving. The appearance of this new mindset marks the age of disunion as a key juncture in women's history.

Scholars have long regarded the Six Dynasties as a major turning point in Chinese history. In the 1920s the Chinese literature specialist Torao Suzuki (1878–1963) argued that the early medieval period saw a major rupture in underlying modes of thought. Comparing poetry from this period with previous works, Suzuki noted the advent of a new and very different attitude. Han dynasty literature had been highly conformist and writers gained esteem by carefully conforming to orthodoxy. But because Confucianism became so politicized, it decayed along with the Han dynasty system that it buttressed. In the early fourth century the pessimistic social critic Ge Hong complained about the resulting decline in ritual propriety: "When friends drink together, some squat and others crouch. In summer, they bare their heads and strip to the waist. All they care about are board games, and they mostly talk about music and sex."[1] As the hold of the Confucian ethical canon and ritual rules weakened, people gained more psychological freedom and began to think in new ways. Literature became highly emotive, creative, and even eccentric. Chinese have always regarded literary works as encapsulating the author's worldview, including values, concerns, attitudes, and feelings. So a shift in the style and content of literature reveals a basic change in the way people understood themselves. The new mindset showed a high degree of self-consciousness and gave rise to unforeseen ideas and behavior.[2]

Heightened awareness had a particularly large impact on women. As self-consciousness blossomed, female matters rose in visibility and importance. Women thought about their lives in new and sometimes very different ways.[3] Of course female self-awareness was not entirely new. Ancient poetry describes women expressing themselves straightforwardly. Sometimes these early characters proclaim sentiments that run contrary to Confucian propriety, publicly discussing their desires or venting grievances. But during the Han dynasty, Confucian orthodoxy suppressed authentic female voices. Women either became mute or else parroted moral platitudes.

The subsequent explosion of female self-consciousness during the Six Dynasties cannot be explained away as merely a revival of ancient modes

Figure 9.1. Pottery female singer and musicians from the Northern Wei Dynasty. Unearthed at Caochangpo, Xi'an, Shaanxi Province, 1953. BabelStone.

of thought. Women transcended previous standards of expression to explore their minds with unprecedented freedom.[4] Innovative and supple literary genres provided new tools for self-expression, allowing women to articulate their feelings more candidly and men to write about women in new and diverse ways.

A new sense of personal space also emerged, revealing a growing sense of what might be termed "individualism." Men increasingly distinguished between their public and private personas, altering their behavior in each sphere. Men behaved far more authentically in private and cultivated relationships with people unrelated to their professional lives. These new kinds of relationships were founded on the novel assumption that the individual ought to have a zone of authentic personal space apart from the contrived façade presented in public.[5] Individualism allowed people to behave in increasingly dissimilar ways. As new types of conduct proliferated, society had to understand and evaluate these unfamiliar actions. In reaction, it became popular to discuss people's capabilities and achievements and rank them accordingly. This emphasis on personal attainment gave individuals increasing incentive to distinguish themselves, even if this meant departing from convention and behaving in a contrary manner.

Women embraced the new spirit of individualism.[6] Whereas Ban Zhao had insisted on strict adherence to the rites, the female role models described in *Records of Jin* often express themselves very freely. These biographies also stress the importance of talent, education, and artistic accomplishment. Some archetypal women display considerable learning or eloquence. And many of the women in *A New Account of Tales of the World* violate ritual norms, ignore rules separating the sexes, or refuse to obey men.[7] Heightened female autonomy was not unprecedented. Liu Xiang described women disobeying men. Nor were women of the time entirely liberated. Most continued to politely obey the social conventions that restrained them. Nevertheless, rising self-consciousness made women far more aware of the possibilities in their lives, giving them far greater leeway as they navigated their world.

Women behaved differently from before. As spouses embraced love and empathy, the dynamics of marriage took on new forms.[8] To some women, a loveless arranged marriage now seemed inadequate. Instead they dreamed of romance. A few women demanded to choose their own husbands, putting personal happiness above family duty.[9] The dynamics of marriage also changed. Spouses spoke to one another more forthrightly, and wives felt emboldened to challenge their husbands. If a self-assured wife went too far, her husband would regard her as a termagant, earning his fear and hatred. Shrews became stereotypical literary characters embodying the negative side of female assertiveness.

Changing narratives about model women show how the new female spirit challenged many earlier beliefs. At the end of the Western Han dynasty, Liu Xiang established female biography as a respectable literary genre, treating women as an independent topic of inquiry. Following Liu's example, subsequent writers tended to discuss men and women very differently.[10] They classified men into different types according to their achievements and qualities, putting their stories in various parts of a historical work. In contrast, historians placed narratives about very different kinds of women together in the same chapter or collection, showing that they still considered a woman's gender more important than her personal qualities.

In contrast to the Confucian orientation of female biographies and the standard histories, *A New Account of Tales of the World* established very different criteria for judging women. A chapter devoted to the "worthy and attractive" (*xianyuan*) had a major impact on views of female behavior and inspired numerous epigones.[11] Private scholars unconnected to politics wrote most *xianyuan* works, so they had little interest in conventional propriety. Even though they employed some Confucian terminology, they redefined these terms to accord with Daoist ideals that they found far more compelling. For example, Confucianism narrowly defines the term *xian* as virtuous obedience to an external code of ethics. But these writers imbued the term with far broader connotations, expanding it to convey a woman's overall worthiness. Rather than demanding that women adhere to an external body of rules, *xianyuan* focused on the inner psychological realm, commending authentic ideas and behavior.

In these works, the praiseworthy woman acts in accord with the Way (*dao*) and exhibits a depth of character grounded in philosophical awareness. Instead meekly adhering to restrictive Confucian norms, she yearns to be educated, talented, independent, capable, and strong willed. The ideal woman shows composure, quick wit, and moral courage. The *xianyuan* genre also redefined the related term *yuan*, a quality that might be translated simply as beauty. However, *New Account of Tales of the World* has little to say about female appearance.[12] Instead, the beautiful woman unleashes her inner qualities, making her seem charming and alluring. The beautiful woman is one who has actualized her potential.

Medieval authors enjoyed appraising people's character, and *xianyuan* similarly judges women. "Worthy and attractive" women who attracted attention had varied personas. Some were accomplished writers or elegant conversationalists known for their witty repartee. But a woman did not have to rebel to earn respect. She could also earn praise by being a good wife or mother, which required a kind of commonsensical talent. So regardless of a woman's roles in life, ability could elicit praise.

The new mentality gave rise to a freer and more active female life-style.[13] Not only did women continue to participate in family gatherings at home, but they also ventured outside to interact with unrelated men. A cultivated woman could discuss poetry and philosophy with men in a salon setting, earning praise for erudition and wit. Women attended parties hosted by people of both sexes. They went on excursions to view temples, gardens, and scenic landscapes. Female devotees attended varied religious ceremonies. And they also enjoyed the special events that accompanied various holidays.

Overall, the emancipation of female consciousness had mixed consequences. This era's model women often displayed extremely strong feelings. Some treated a man with great affection.[14] Others, however, suffered from prickly pride and sensitivity. The fragile egos of talented women complicated their interactions with those around them. Many felt dissatisfied with their marriages and relationships. Unleashing women's consciousness in a society that still bound them with so many restraints did not necessarily make them happy. Instead the ultimate outcome was often frustration.

Burgeoning female self-awareness, and the strikingly different kinds of behavior it inspired, signaled a major transition in the history of Chinese women. In later eras, when Neo-Confucianism imposed heavy restrictions on female behavior, people of both sexes looked back on the openness of gender relations in the Six Dynasties with mixed feelings. Many men found the writings from this era extremely unsettling. They felt disconcerted by descriptions of women roaming about freely and engaging in witty repartee with strange men. In contrast, women looked back to this era for inspiration. Inspired by popular early medieval songs, Tang courtesans wrote candid poetry, sometimes even adopting a mischievous tone.[15] Song dynasty women similarly looked to the Wei and Jin for inspiring role models.[16] And so it was in every subsequent era. About thirty imitations of *A New Account of Tales of the World* appeared from the Tang down to the early twentieth century.[17] This genre kept the spirit of female self-consciousness alive, inviting each generation to confront the disturbing and exciting mentality of early medieval women and assess its significance for their own time.

Glossary

An Lingshou	安令首
Ban Zhao	班昭
Baekje	百濟 (백제)
bao taihou	保太后
Baopuzi	抱朴子
Beishi	北史
benji	本紀
Biqiuni zhuan	比丘尼傳
bixia	陛下
cai	才
Cao Cao	曹操
Cao Pi	曹丕
Chang (empress)	常
chang (entertainer)	娼
Changshan	常山
Chen Shou	陳壽
Chi	郗
Chu ci	楚辭
Chunqiu	春秋
ci qi	賜妻
da	達
dao	道

Daowu	道武
Ding Gu	丁姑
Ding Lan	丁蘭
Ding Yi	丁廙
Disi xun	娣姒訓
Dou	竇
Du ji	妒記
Du Yu	杜預
Dufu ji	妒婦記
Dugu Xin	獨孤信
Feng	馮
fu	賦
furen	夫人
Furen ji	婦人集
Furen shuyi	婦人書儀
Furen xunjie ji	婦人訓誡集
furu	腐儒
Gaozu	高祖
Ge Hong	葛洪
Goguryo	高句麗, 高麗 (고구려)
Guafu fu	寡婦賦
Guangling Cha Lao	廣陵茶姥
Gujin tushu jicheng	古今圖書集成
Guo Huai	郭槐
Guyang	古陽
Han (lady)	韓
Han Gaozu	漢高祖
Hou Hanshu	後漢書
Hu	胡
Hua Mulan	花木蘭
Huangfu Mi	皇甫謐
Hui	惠
Huimu	慧木
ji (hair pin)	笄
ji (performer)	妓, 伎
Ji Kang	嵇康
Jia Chong	賈充
Jia Nanfeng	賈南風
jiaji	家妓

Jianwen	簡文
jiao	教
jiqie	妓妾
jiaxun	家訓
jian	賤
Jian'an	建安
Jin Wudi	晉武帝
Jinshu	晉書
jiupin	九品
Jiutian xuannü	九天玄女
jun	君
junjun	郡君
juntian	均田
Langya	琅琊
Lanling	蘭陵
Laozi	老子
li (rites)	禮
Li (madame, widow)	李
Li Biao	李彪
Li Chong	李沖
Li Hongzhi	李洪之
Li Zhong	李重
Lienü zhuan	列女傳
Ling	靈
Liu Fang	劉芳
Liu Hui (literary critic)	劉繪
Liu Hui (husband of Lanling)	劉輝
Liu Lingxian	劉令嫻
Liu Xiang	劉向
Liu Xie	劉勰
Liu Yiqing	劉義慶
Liu Zhen	劉瑱
Longmen	龍門
Lü	呂
Lu Tui	陸退
Luo	洛
Ma Gu	麻姑
mei	美
Miaofa lianhua jing	妙法蓮華經

Miaoxiang	妙相
Ming	明
mu	畝
mude	母德
Mulan	木蘭
Mulian	目連
muyi	母儀
Naitō Konan	内藤湖南
Nü jian	女鑑
Nü Wa	女媧
Nü xun	女訓
nüguan	女冠，女官
nüguo	女國
Nüren zan	女人讚
nüshi	女師
Nüshi zhen	女史箴
Pan	潘
Pan Yue	潘岳
pin	聘
qi	棄
qie	妾
Qin Shihuang	秦始皇
qing	清
qingtan	清談
qingyi	清議
Qiu Hu	秋胡
Ruan Ji	阮籍
Sanguo zhi	三國志
Sengji	僧基
Sengmeng	僧猛
Shan Tao	山濤
Shangqing	上清
Shen Manyuan	沈滿願
Shen Yue	沈約
shi	士
Shi Chong	石崇
Shijing	詩經
Shishuo xinyu	世說新語
Shiwei	失韋

shiyi	食邑
Shizu	始祖
shuixian	水仙
Shuiyusi	水浴寺
Sima Jinlong	司馬金龍
Sima Qian	司馬遷
Song shu	宋書
Soushen ji	搜神記
Su Hui	蘇蕙
sui	歲
Suzuki, Torao	鈴木虎雄
Taiping jing	太平經
Taizu	太祖
Tanbei	曇備
Tang Jin	唐瑾
tangmuyi	湯沐邑
Tanigawa Michio	谷川道雄
Tujue	突厥
tuntian	屯田
Tuoba	拓拔
Tuoba Gui	拓拔珪
Wang Can	王粲
Wang Mengjiang	王孟姜
Wang Xizhi	王羲之
Wei (empress)	魏
Wei Huacun	魏畫存
Weishu	魏書
Wen	文
Wencheng Wenming	文成文明
Wenchengzhao	文成昭
Wending	文定
Wenming	文明
Wenxian	文獻
Wenxuan	文宣
Wu (emperor)	武
wu (shaman)	巫
Wu Daoyang	武悼楊
xi (female shaman)	覡
Xi (empress)	郗

Xianbei	鮮卑
Xiang	湘
Xianming	獻明
Xianwen	獻文
xianyuan	賢媛
Xiao jing	孝經
Xiaoming	孝明
Xiaowu	孝武
Xie An	謝安
Xie Daowen	謝道韞
Xiwangmu	西王母
Xu	徐
Xu Ling	徐陵
Xu Mian	徐勉
Xu Xun	許詢
Xuan	宣
Xuanwuling	宣武靈
xuanxue	玄學
Xun Can	荀粲
Xun Ji	荀濟
yan	豔
Yan Shigu	顏師古
Yan Zhitui	顏之推
Yang Yan	楊艷
Yang Zhi	楊芷
Yanshi jiaxun	顏氏家訓
Yaoguang	瑤光
yi	義
Yi Hun	乙渾
Yifu Hun	乙弗渾
Yijing	易經
Yin Chun	殷淳
yinghu yueji	營戶樂籍
yingji	營妓
Yongning	永寧
Yu Nü	玉女
Yu Tongzhi	虞通之
Yu Zhong	于忠
Yuan	元

Yuanyang	元楊
Yuchi	尉遲
yuehu	樂戶
Yutai xinyong	玉臺新詠
Yuye nüjing	玉耶女經
Zawen	雜文
zhai	齋
Zhang	張
Zhang Hua	張華
Zhuang Shuai	張率
Zhao Dingchen	趙鼎臣
Zhao Ji	趙姬
Zheng Xuan	鄭玄
Zhenshun zhi	貞順志
Zhi Miaoyin	支妙音
zhiguai	志怪
Zhixian	智賢
Zhong	鐘
Zhou li	周禮
Zhu Daoxing	竺道馨
Zhu Jingjian	竺淨檢
Zhuge Ling	諸葛令
Zhuangzi	莊子
zhuanlun shengwang	轉輪聖王
Zi Gu	紫姑
Zuo Fen	左芬

Notes

INTRODUCTION

1. For an overview of the political history of the era, see Hans Bielenstein, "The Six Dynasties, Vol. 1," *Museum of Far Eastern Antiquities Bulletin* 68 (1996): 5–324; Hans Bielenstein, "The Six Dynasties, Vol. 2," *Museum of Far Eastern Antiquities Bulletin* 69 (1997): 11–191.

2. Fang Xuanling et al., *Jinshu*, annotated by Wu Zeyu (Beijing: Zhonghua shuju, 1974), 4:108.

3. Thomas J. Barfield, *The Perilous Frontier: Nomadic Empires and China, 221 BC to AD 1757* (Cambridge, MA: Blackwell Publishers, 1989), 90, 99.

4. William G. Crowell, "Social Unrest and Rebellion in Jiangnan during the Six Dynasties," *Modern China* 9, no. 3 (1983): 319–54.

5. Tanigawa Michio and Joshua A. Fogel, "Problems Concerning the Japanese Periodization of Chinese History," *Journal of Asian History* 21, no. 2 (1987): 150–68; Dennis Grafflin, "The Great Family in Medieval South China," *Harvard Journal of Asiatic Studies* 41, no. 1 (1981): 65. Chinese Marxists view medieval China as "feudal," like most of their nation's history. Nevertheless, they attribute some innovations to the period to rescue China from an image of timeless stagnation. C. P. Fitzgerald, "The Chinese Middle Ages in Communist Historiography," *The China Quarterly* 23 (1965): 106–21.

6. Fang, *Jinshu*, 42:1208.

7. François Guizot, *The History of Civilization in Europe*, trans. William Hazlitt (London: Penguin, 1997), xxxvii.

8. Wendy Swartz, Robert Ford Campany, Yang Lu, and Jessey J. C. Choo, "Introduction," in *Early Medieval China: A Sourcebook*, ed. Swartz et al. (New York: Columbia University Press, 2014), 3.

9. Albert E. Dien, "The Bestowal of Surnames under the Western Wei/Northern Chou: A Case of Counter-Acculturation," *T'oung Pao* 63, nos. 2 and 3 (1977): 139–40.

10. Jennifer Holmgren, "Family, Marriage and Political Power in 6th Century China: A Study of the Kao Family of Northern Ch'i, c. 520–550," *Journal of Asian History* 16, no. 1 (1982): 11.

11. Richard Miles, *Carthage Must Be Destroyed: The Rise and Fall of an Ancient Civilization* (London: Penguin Books, 2010), 324.

12. Ping Wang, "Literary Imagination of the North and South," in *Early Medieval China: A Sourcebook*, ed. Wendy Swartz, Robert Ford Campany, Yang Lu, and Jessey J. C. Choo (New York: Columbia University Press, 2014), 79.

13. Wang Yitong and Cao Hong, trans., *A Record of Buddhist Monasteries in Luoyang* (Beijing: Zhonghua Book Company, 2007), 145.

14. Charles Holcombe, "Re-Imagining China: The Chinese Identity Crisis at the Start of the Southern Dynasties Period," *Journal of the American Oriental Society* 115, no. 1 (1995): 14.

15. Wang, "Literary Imagination of the North and South," 77.

16. Jessey J. C. Choo, "Between Imitation and Mockery: The Southern Treatments of Northern Cultures," in *Early Medieval China: A Sourcebook*, ed. Wendy Swartz, Robert Ford Campany, Yang Lu, and Jessey J. C. Choo (New York: Columbia University Press, 2014), 63, 68. Matthew Wells, "*Baopuzi*," in *Early Medieval Chinese Texts: A Bibliographical Guide*, ed. Cynthia L. Chennault et al. (Berkeley: Institute of East Asian Studies, University of California, 2015), 6–12, introduces this complicated text.

17. Patricia Buckley Ebrey, *The Aristocratic Families of Early Imperial China: A Case Study of the Po-Ling Ts'ui Family* (Cambridge: Cambridge University Press, 1978), 17–21; Grafflin, "The Great Family in Medieval South China," 65, 67.

18. Yen Chih-t'ui, *Family Instructions for the Yen Clan: Yen-shih Chia-hsün*, trans. Ssu-yü Teng (Leiden: E. J. Brill, 1966), xviii–xxv.

19. Tanigawa Michio, *Medieval Chinese Society and the Local "Community,"* trans. Joshua A. Fogel (Berkeley: University of California Press, 1985), xxii.

20. Charles Holcombe, "The Exemplar State: Ideology, Self-Cultivation, and Power in Fourth-Century China," *Harvard Journal of Asiatic Studies* 49, no. 1 (1989): 99–100, 118.

21. Timothy M. Davis, "Ranking Men and Assessing Talent: Xiahou Xuan's Response to an Inquiry by Sima Yi," in *Early Medieval China: A Sourcebook*, ed. Wendy Swartz, Robert Ford Campany, Yang Lu, and Jessey J. C. Choo (New York: Columbia University Press, 2014), 128–29.

22. Zhao Hui, *Liu chao shehui wenhua xintai* (Taipei: Wenjin, 1996), 10–11.

23. Li Yanshou, *Beishi* (Beijing: Zhonghua shuju, 1974), 10:359.

24. Zhao, *Liu chao shehui wenhua xintai*, 12.

25. Ban Gu, *Hanshu*, annotated by Yan Shigu (Beijing: Zhonghua, 1962), 1A:1, note 4; 2:90, note 1.

26. Zhao Dingchen, *Zhuyin jishi ji*, in *Siku jiben bieji shiyi*, ed. Luan Guiming (Beijing: Zhonghua shuju, 1983), 20:189.

27. Scott Pearce, "Form and Matter: Archaizing Reform in Sixth-Century China," in *Culture and Power in the Reconstitution of the Chinese Realm, 200–600*, ed.

Scott Pearce, Audrey Spiro, and Patricia Ebrey (Cambridge, MA: Harvard University Asia Center, 2001), 161.

28. Yi Jo-lan, "Social Status, Gender Division and Institutions: Sources Relating to Women in Chinese Standard Histories," in *Overt and Covert Treasures: Essays on the Sources for Chinese Women's History*, ed. Clara Wing-Chung Ho (Hong Kong: The City University Press, 2012), 132–33, provides convenient tables that show which standard histories have sections devoted to empresses and other imperial consorts, princesses, consort kin, and exemplary women.

29. Zong-qi Cai, "A Historical Overview of Six Dynasties Aesthetics," in *Chinese Aesthetics: The Ordering of Literature, the Arts, and the Universe in the Six Dynasties*, ed. Zong-qi Cai (Honolulu: University of Hawaii Press, 2004), 1–3.

30. A. Leo Oppenheim, *Ancient Mesopotamia: Portrait of a Dead Civilization*, rev. ed. compl. Erica Reiner (Chicago: University of Chicago Press, 1964), 232.

31. Timothy M. Davis, *Entombed Epigraphy and Commemorative Culture in Early Medieval China: A History of Early Muzhiming* (Leiden: Brill, 2015), introduces this genre of writing.

32. Liu I-ching, *Shih-shuo Hsin-yü: A New Account of Tales of the World*, commentary by Liu Chün, trans. Richard B. Mather (Minneapolis: University of Minnesota Press, 1976), 135 (4.82); Liu Yiqing, *Shishuo xinyu huijiao jizhu*, annotated by Liu Xiaobiao and Zhu Zhuyu (Shanghai: Shanghai Guji Chubanshe, 2002), 4:133.

33. Yan Yaozhong, "Muzhi jiwen zhong de Tangdai funü fojiao xinyang," in *Tang Song nüxing yu shehui*, ed. Deng Xiaonan (Shanghai: Shanghai cishu, 2003), 2:469–71.

34. All ages in this book are given in *sui*. The Western reckoning of a person's age is usually one year younger than the age in *sui*. Ping Yao, "Women in Portraits: An Overview of Epitaphs from Early and Medieval China," in *Overt and Covert Treasures: Essays on the Sources for Chinese Women's History*, ed. Clara Wing-Chung Ho (Hong Kong: The City University Press, 2012), 164–66. Jen-der Lee, "Women and Marriage in China during the Period of Disunion" (PhD diss., University of Washington, 1992), 143, provides a relatively high estimate of 52.7 as the average life expectancy of elite women recorded in epitaphs. Sanping Chen, "'Age Inflation and Deflation' in Medieval China," *Journal of the American Oriental Society* 133, no. 3 (2013): 527–33, explains how and why ages were often recorded inaccurately.

35. Anne Birrell, *Chinese Love Poetry: New Songs From a Jade Terrace, A Medieval Anthology* (London: Penguin Books, 1986), 87–88; Xu Ling, *Jianzhu yutai xinyong*, annotated by Wu Zhaoyi (Taipei: Guangwen shuju, 1966), 2:10b–11a.

36. Lee, "Women and Marriage," 229.

37. Wei Shou, *Weishu* (Beijing: Zhonghua, 1974), 96:2108.

38. Wei, *Weishu*, 98:2187.

39. Yao Silian, *Liangshu* (Beijing: Zhonghua, 1973), 39:557; Liu, *Shih-shuo Hsin-yü*, 15 (1:28); Liu, *Shishuo xinyu huijiao jizhu*, 1:26.

40. Shen Yue, *Songshu* (Beijing: Zhonghua shuju, 1974), 91:2247

41. Yang Mingzhao, *Baopuzi waipian jiaojian* (Beijing: Xinhua shudian, 1991), 1:25:618; Zhang Chengzong, *Liuchao funü* (Nanjing: Nanjing chubanshe, 2012), 373–78.

42. Zhao, *Liu chao shehui wenhua xintai*, 148–51, gives examples from various social strata.

43. Barfield, *The Perilous Frontier*, 25–26; Arthur F. Wright, *The Sui Dynasty* (New York: Alfred A. Knopf, 1978), 64.

44. Albert E. Dien, "Everyday Life," in *Early Medieval China: A Sourcebook*, ed. Wendy Swartz, Robert Ford Campany, Yang Lu, and Jessey J. C. Choo (New York: Columbia University Press, 2014), 443.

45. Beatrice Spade, "The Education of Women in China during the Southern Dynasties," *Journal of Asian History* 13, no. 1 (1979): 33; Jen-der Lee, "The Life of Women in the Six Dynasties," *Funü yu liangxing xuekan* 4 (1993): 50–51.

46. Charlotte Furth, *A Flourishing Yin: Gender in China's Medical History, 960–1665* (Berkeley: University of California Press, 1999), 46; Robin D. S. Yates, "Medicine for Women in Early China: A Preliminary Survey," *Nan Nü* 7, no. 2 (2005): 141, 173–74.

CHAPTER 1

1. Shiga Shūzō, *Chūgoku kazokuhō no genri* (Tokyo: Sōbunsha, 1967), 50–58.

2. Shiga, *Chūgoku kazokuhō no genri*, 459–66. Gan Huaizhen, *Tangdai jiamiao lizhi yanjiu* (Taipei: Taiwan shanwu yinshuguan, 1991), 16–30, explains early medieval ancestral sacrificial rites.

3. Yen, *Family Instructions for the Yen Clan*, 9–10; Mark Edward Lewis, "Writing the World in the Family Instructions of the Yan Clan," *Early Medieval China* 13–14, no. 1 (2007): 38, 41.

4. Xu Zhuoyun, "Handai jiating de daxiao," in *Qingzhu Li Ji xiansheng qishi sui lunwenji*, ed. Li Fanggui et al. (Taipei: Qinghua xuebaoshe, 1967), 789–806.

5. Keith N. Knapp, *Selfless Offspring: Filial Children and Social Order in Early Medieval China* (Honolulu: University of Hawaii Press, 2005), 14.

6. Wei, *Weishu*, 58:1302.

7. Xue Ruize, "Wei Jin beichao hunyinzhong de erqi xianxiang," *Baoji Lixue Xueyuan xuebao* 1 (2000): 77–81.

8. Wei, *Weishu*, 53:1189.

9. Wei, *Weishu*, 89:1919.

10. Shao Zhengkun, *Beichao jiating xingtai yanjiu* (Beijing: Kexue chubanshe, 2008), 25, 31–32, 34–35; Zhang Guogang, *Jiating shihua* (Beijing: Shehui kexue wenxian, 2012), 38.

11. Zhang, *Jiating shihua*, 46.

12. Liu, *Shih-shuo Hsin-yü*, 349 (19.14); Liu, *Shishuo xinyu huijiao jizhu*, 19:577.

13. Naomi Quinn, "Anthropological Studies on Women's Status," *Annual Review of Anthropology* 6 (1977): 211.

14. Rebecca L. Warner, Gary R. Lee and Janet Lee, "Social Organization, Spousal Resources, and Marital Power: A Cross-Cultural Study," *Journal of Marriage and Family* 48, no. 1 (1986): 121–28.

15. Zhao Chao, *Han Wei nanbeichao muzhi huibian* (Tianjin: Tianjin guji chubanshe, 1992), 374; James L. Watson, "Anthropological Overview: The Development of Chinese Descent Groups," in *Kinship Organization in Late Imperial China, 1000–1940*, ed. Patricia Buckey Ebrey and James L. Watson (Berkeley: University of California Press, 1986), 283.

16. Jennifer Holmgren, "The Making of an Elite: Local Politics and Social Relations in Northeastern China during the Fifth Century A.D.," *Papers on Far Eastern History* 30 (1984): 16–17.

17. Wei, *Weishu*, 15:383, 32:758, 32:763, 42:950, 70:1561.

18. Fang, *Jinshu*, 109:2822; Wei, *Weishu*, 50:1117, 50:1119, 51:1130; Li, *Beishi*, 37:1353.

19. Yao Silian, *Chenshu* (Beijing: Zhonghua, 1972), 9:154.

20. Zhang, *Jiating shihua*, 41–42; Lee, "Women and Marriage," 175–76.

21. Liu, *Shih-shuo Hsin-yü*, 445 (27.9); Liu, *Shishuo xinyu huijiao jizhu*, 27:710–11.

22. Holmgren, "The Making of an Elite," 35.

23. Wei, *Weishu*, 20:527–28; Li, *Beishi*, 19:685.

24. Zhang Bangwei, *Hunyin yu shehui (Songdai)* (Chengdu: Sichuan renmin, 1989), 46–47, 97; Lee, "Women and Marriage," 54–58. Nevertheless, cross-cousin marriages still occurred in the north. Li, *Beishi*, 56:2032.

25. Li Mingren, "Tuoba shi zaoqi de hunyin zhengce," *Shiyuan* 20 (1997): 107. Lu Yaodong, "Tuoba shi yu zhongyuan shizu de hunyin guanxi," in *Cong Pingcheng dao Luoyang* (Taipei: Dongda tutu, 2001), 315–38, provides a long series of tables giving information about specific Tuoba marriages.

26. Jennifer Holmgren, "Imperial Marriage in the Native Chinese and Non-Han State, Han to Ming," in *Marriage and Inequality in Chinese Society*, ed. Rubie S. Watson and Patricia Buckley Ebrey (Berkeley: University of California Press, 1991), 77.

27. Among some peoples, endogamy was the standard custom. Li, *Beishi*, 22:828.

28. Shao, *Beichao jiating xingtai yanjiu*, 69–70.

29. Lu, "Tuoba shi yu zhongyuan shizu de hunyin guanxi," 230, 252–53. The lyrics of northern folksongs describe this practice. Zhang Zongyuan, "Lun beichao minjian 'hunlian' geci," *Fudan xuebao* 2 (2003): 116–17.

30. Lu, "Tuoba shi yu zhongyuan shizu de hunyin guanxi," 231. For the general attributes of bride service, see Alice Schlegel and Rohn Eloul, "Marriage Transactions: Labor, Property, Status," *American Anthropologist* 90, no. 2 (1988): 299, 304–5.

31. Wei, *Weishu*, 101:2242.

32. For example, an edict of 544 CE forbade levirate marriage. Li, *Beishi*, 5:158.

33. Knapp, *Selfless Offspring*, 24.

34. Fang, *Jinshu*, 19:579; Wei, *Weishu*, 21A:534, 48:1074; Li, *Beishi*, 2:72; Li Yanshou, *Nanshi* (Beijing: Zhonghua shuju, 1975), 12:349. In contrast, rather than viewing marriage through the lens of morality, poetry celebrated the wedding simply as a happy occasion. Guo Jianxun, "Liang Han Wei Jin cifu zhong de xianshi nüxing ticai yu xingbie biaoda," *Zhongguo wenxue yanjiu* 4 (2003): 33.

35. Yang, *Baopuzi waipian jiaojian*, 25:628.

36. Wu Chengguo, "Lun Dong Jin nanchao hunyin lizhi de diyu chayi," *Hubei Daxue xuebao* 3 (1996): 54–58. Chen Yun, "Wei Jin Hunli yanjiu" (MA thesis, Guoli Taiwan Shifan Daxue, 1980), 51–75; Lee, "Women and Marriage," 90–98; Liang Mancang, *Wei Jin nanbeichao wuli zhidu kaolun* (Beijing: Shehui kexue wenxian, 2009), 286–300.

37. Zhuang Lixia, "Huhua secai de beichao hunli xisu," *Zhaotong Shifan Gaodeng Zhuangke Xuexiao xueyuan* 4 (2006): 36–38.

38. Zhang, *Jiating shihua*, 39.

39. Lily Xiao Hong Lee, "Language and Self-Estimation: The Case of Wei-Jin Women," *Journal of the Oriental Society of Australia* 25–26 (1993–1994): 150–64.

40. Li Guie and Gao Jianxin, "Cong *Shishuo xinyu* kan Wei Jin shiren jinbu de funüguan," *Nei Menggu Daxue xuebao* 35, no. 4 (2003): 50.

41. Liu, *Shih-shuo Hsin-yü*, 406 (25.8); Liu, *Shishuo xinyu huijiao jizhu*, 25:657.

42. Zhang, *Jiating shihua*, 40–41.

43. Zhang Chengzong, "Wei Jin nanbeichao shiqi yu funü xiangguan de falü wenti ji sifa anjian," *Nanjing Ligong Daxue xuebao* 22, no. 2 (2009): 25.

44. Jen-der Lee, "The Death of a Princess: Codifying Classical Family Ethics in Early Medieval China," in *Presence and Presentation: Women in the Chinese Literati Tradition*, ed. Sherry J. Mou (New York: St. Martin's Press, 1999), 23.

45. Lee, "Women and Marriage," 243.

46. Linghu Defen, *Zhoushu* (Beijing: Zhonghua shuju, 1995), 7:116.

47. Zhang, "Wei Jin nanbeichao shiqi yu funü xiangguan de falü wenti ji sifa anjian," 28–30. Nevertheless, a man would not necessarily be punished for assaulting his wife. Lee, "The Death of a Princess," 12–13.

48. Yano Chikara, *Monbatsu shakai seiritsu shi* (Tokyo: Kokusho kankōkai, 1976).

49. Li Jinhe, *Wei Jin Sui Tang hunyin xingtai yanjiu* (Jinan: Qi Lu shushe, 2005), 28–29.

50. Li, *Wei Jin Sui Tang hunyin xingtai yanjiu*, 35, 37, 62.

51. Liu, *Shih-shuo Hsin-yü*, 75 (2.100); Liu, *Shishuo xinyu huijiao jizhu*, 2:139.

52. Knapp, *Selfless Offspring*, 13.

53. Dennis Grafflin, "Social Order in the Early Southern Dynasties: The Formation of Eastern Chin" (PhD diss., Harvard University, 1980), 49. Most historians researching this era use the term "clan," but Grafflin describes these kinship groupings as "lineages."

54. Wang Yi-t'ung, "Slaves and Other Comparable Social Groups during the Northern Dynasties (386–618)," *Harvard Journal of Asiatic Studies* 16, nos. 3/4 (1953): 300–301; Mao Han-kuang, "The Evolution in the Nature of the Medieval Genteel Families," in *State and Society in Early Medieval China*, ed. Albert E. Dien (Stanford: Stanford University Press, 1990), 78; Wang Renlei, "Wei Jin nanbeichao jiating yu jiazu, zongzu guanxi chutan," *Beifang luncong* 6 (2011): 78–80. Shen, *Songshu*, 92:2270, mentions a man who shared so much wealth with his fellow clan members that his wife and children were often cold and hungry. People considered his behavior virtuous.

55. Song Qirui, *Bei Wei nüzhu lun* (Beijing: Zhongguo shehui kexue, 2006), 14–16. Not every region had important clans. In Shandong, for example, affine relationships between individual families took priority over their blood ties to extended relatives. Holmgren, "The Making of an Elite," 56.

56. Deng Miaoci, "Cong Shishuo xinyu kan Wei Jin shiren de hun yu huan," *Mingzuo xinshang* 11 (2011): 40–44.

57. Dusanka D. Misevic, "Oligarchy or Social Mobility: A Study of the Great Clans of Early Medieval China," *The Museum of Far Eastern Antiquities* 65 (1993): 214.

58. Liao Jianqi, "Beichao shehui hunyin zhuangkuang chuyi," *Shixue yuekan* 2 (1998): 69–70. Li, *Wei Jin Sui Tang hunyin xingtai yanjiu*, provides a table of forty-four spouses from gentry families and gives the background of each, demonstrat-

ing the extent of intermarriage among the aristocracy. Holmgren, "The Making of an Elite," 12–13, focuses on the marriages of one prominent family. Literature also documents elite intermarriage. Zhao Liheng, "Jiu Shishuo xinyu kan Wei Jin nanbeichao de hunyin wenhua," *Xuchang Xueyuan xuebao* 1 (2007): 40–41; Zhang Ya'nan and Wang Tiantong, "Soushenji yu Wei Jin hunyin sangzang lisu," *Shandong Jiaoyu Xueyuan xuebao* 1 (2008): 44.

59. Zhang Yange and Zhao Guohua, "Wei Jin shiqi Yingchuan Xun shi hungou kaoshu," *Shehui jingwei* 9 (2014): 165–67, describes the effects of marriage on status by analyzing the marriage strategy of one important family in detail.

60. Xie Baofu, *Beichao hunsang lisu yanjiu* (Beijing: Shoudu Shifan Daxue, 1998), 16–17; Li, *Wei Jin Sui Tang hunyin xingtai yanjiu*, 170–77.

61. Ochi Shigeaki, *Gi Shin Nanchō no kizoku sei* (Tokyo: Kenbun, 1982), 183–93; Li, *Wei Jin Sui Tang hunyin xingtai yanjiu*, 65–67; Nakamura Keiji, *Rikuchō seiji shakai shi kenkyū* (Tokyo: Kyuko shoin, 2013), 335–53.

62. Li, *Wei Jin Sui Tang hunyin xingtai yanjiu*, 73.

63. Zhao, "Jiu Shishuo xinyu kan Wei Jin nanbeichao de hunyin wenhua," 41; Dien, "Everyday Life," 442; Zhang Bangwei, *Songdai hunyin jiazu shilun* (Beijing: Renmin chubanshe, 2003), 2.

64. Lee, "Women and Marriage," 62–63.

65. Li, *Wei Jin Sui Tang hunyin xingtai yanjiu*, 177–81.

66. Li, *Wei Jin Sui Tang hunyin xingtai yanjiu*, 73.

67. Richard B. Mather, "Intermarriage as a Gauge of Family Status in the Southern Dynasties," in *State and Society in Early Medieval China*, ed. Albert E. Dien (Stanford: Stanford University Press, 1990), 219.

68. Jennifer Holmgren, "Social Mobility in the Northern Dynasties: A Case Study of the Feng of Northern Yen," *Monumenta Serica* 35 (1981–1983): 30–31.

69. Jennifer Holmgren, "The Lu Clan of Tai Commandary and Their Contribution to the To-pan State of Northern Wei in the Fifth Century," *T'oung Pao* 69, nos. 4–5 (1983): 300.

70. Xu Hui, Qiu Min, and Hu Axian, *Liuchao wenhua* (Nanjing: Jiangsu guji chubanshe, 2001), 531–34.

71. Jin Wudi issued an edict that if a girl's parents had not married her off by age seventeen, local officials were to arrange a match. Fang, *Jinshu*, 3:63.

72. Zhu Dawei, Liu Chi, Liang Mancang, and Chen Yong, *Wei Jin nanbeichao shehui shenghuo shi* (Beijing: Zhongguo shehui kexue chubanshe, 1998), 256–57. The custom of holding posthumous weddings dates back to high antiquity.

73. Zhang Chengzong and Sun Li, "Wei Jin Nanbeichao hunsu chutan," *Zhejiang xuekan* 95, no. 6 (1995): 102.

74. All ages in this book age are given in *sui*, according to the traditional Chinese system of reckoning. Wang Wanying, "Beichao funü hunjia shulun," *Datong Gaodeng Zhuanke Xuexiao xuebao* 13, no. 4 (1999): 9–10.

75. Birrell, *Chinese Love Poetry*, 271; Xu, *Jianzhu yutai xinyong*, 9:1b.

76. Chen Shanshan, "Qianxi Wei Jin nanbeichao de zaohun xianxiang jiqi chengyin," *Lanzhou Jiaoyu Xueyuan xuebao* 29, no. 10 (2013): 14, notes that in the Western Jin era, men were believed to marry at about age sixteen *sui* and women at fourteen. Liao, "Beichao shehui hunyin zhuangkuang chuyi," 70, asserts that in the northern dynasties, men often married at fifteen and women at thirteen.

Zhang, *Jiating shihua*, 40, estimates that grooms were usually fifteen or sixteen and brides between thirteen and fifteen. Zhang Chengzong and Chen Qun, *Zhongguo funü tongshi: Wei Jin nanbei chao juan* (Hangzhou: Hangzhou chubanshe, 2010), 361–62, estimates the average early medieval marriage age as between thirteen and fifteen. Ping Yao notes that epitaphs from the Eastern Wei and Northern Qi put the average age of marriage of women mentioned in these records at 16.5. Epitaphs from the Western Wei and Northern Zhou have an average female marriage age of fourteen. The average age of elite women in northern Wei was 19.33. Yao, "Women in Portraits, 164–66.

77. Lee, "Women and Marriage," 131, estimates the average age of marriage for women as thirteen to eighteen *sui*. The table on p. 140 shows that the average age of elite women recorded in epitaphs was 17.6. The table on p. 141 shows that husbands were 9.1 years older than wives on average.

78. Li, *Beishi*, 34:1268. This seems to have been similar to the classical pinning ceremony. Cho-yun Hsu and Katheryn M. Linduff, *Western Chou Civilization* (New Haven, CT: Yale University Press, 1988), 374.

79. Zhang, "Wei Jin nanbeichao shiqi yu funü xiangguan de falü wenti ji sifa anjian," 25.

80. Zhu et al., *Wei Jin nanbeichao shehui shenghuo shi*, 242–46, 253–54; Feng Sumei, "Wei Jin nanbeichao shiqi de zaohun xianxiang," *Jinyang xuekan* 6 (2000): 63; Zhang, "Lun beichao minjian 'hunlian' geci," 115–16; Chen, "Qianxi Wei Jin nanbeichao de zaohun xianxiang jiqi chengyin," 14–15.

81. Feng, "Wei Jin nanbeichao shiqi de zaohun xianxiang," 65; Lee, "Women and Marriage," 80.

82. Epitaphs report wives who married very young and died at the age of eleven or twelve *sui*. Yao, "Women in Portraits, 164–65.

83. Wei, *Weishu*, 71:1580.

84. Patricia Buckley Ebrey, "Shifts in Marriage Finance from the Sixth to the Thirteenth Century," in *Women and the Family in Chinese History*, ed. Patricia Buckley Ebrey (London: Routledge, 2003), 64–65.

85. Katsuyama Minoru, *Chūgoku Sō—Min dai ni okeru konin no gakusaiteki kenkyū* (Tokyo: Tōhoku Daigaku shuppankai, 2007), 132–35; Wang, "Beichao funü hunjia shulun," 12; Zhang and Sun, "Wei Jin Nanbeichao hunsu chutan," 102; Li, *Wei Jin Sui Tang hunyin xingtai yanjiu*, 80–82; Zhang, *Liuchao funü*, 136–39.

86. Wei, *Weishu*, 4B:103.

87. Ebrey, "Shifts in Marriage Finance from the Sixth to the Thirteenth Century," 98–99; David R. Knechtges, "Marriage and Social Status: Shen Yue's 'Impeaching Wang Yuan,'" in *Early Medieval China: A Sourcebook*, ed. Wendy Swartz, Robert Ford Campany, Yang Lu, and Jessey J. C. Choo (New York: Columbia University Press, 2014), 166–75.

88. Zhang and Wang, "Soushenji yu Wei Jin hunyin sangzang lisu," 45.

89. Lee, "Women and Marriage," 88–89.

90. Keith Knapp, "The Ru Reinterpretation of *Xiao*," *Early China* 20 (1995): 200–202; Donald Holzman, "The Place of Filial Piety in Ancient China," *Journal of the American Oriental Society* 118, no. 2 (1998): 1–15.

91. Henry Rosemont Jr. and Roger T. Ames, *The Chinese Classic of Family Reverence: A Philosophical Translation of the* Xiaojing (Honolulu: University of Hawaii

Press, 2009), 107; Jian Zhaoliang, ed., *Xiaojing jizhu shushu—fu dushutang dawen*, annotated by Zhou Chunjian (Shanghai: Huadong Shifan Daxue chubanshe, 2011), 5:37.

92. Knapp, *Selfless Offspring*, 164–65.

93. Kate A. Lingley, "Lady Yuchi in the First Person: Patronage, Kinship, and Voice in the Guyang Cave," *Early Medieval China* 18 (2012): 25.

94. Wei, *Weishu*, 92:1990, 1994. A married woman had the responsibility of looking after the health of her in-laws. Li Zhende, "Han Tang zhijian jiating zhong de jiankang zhaogu yu xingbie," in *Disanjie guoji hanxue huiyi lunwenji lishizu, xingbie yu yiliao* (Taipei: Institute of History and Philology, 2002), 9–10.

95. Kenneth DeWoskin and J. I. Crump Jr., trans., *In Search of the Supernatural: The Written Record* (Stanford: Stanford University Press, 1996), 139–40 (11.297).

96. Yuet Keung Lo, "Filial Devotion for Women: A Buddhist Testimony from Third-Century China," in *Filial Piety in Chinese Thought and History*, ed. Alan K. L. Chan and Sor-hoon Tan (London: RoutledgeCurzon, 2004), 71–90; Lo Yuet Keung, "Recovering a Buddhist Voice on Daughter-in-Law: The Yuyenü jing," *History of Religions* 44, no. 4 (2005): 318–50. A complete translation of the scripture appears on pp. 347–50.

97. Melvin P. Thatcher, "Marriages of the Ruling Elite in the Spring and Autumn Period," in *Marriage and Inequality in Chinese Society*, ed. Rubie S. Watson and Patricia B. Ebrey (Berkeley: University of California Press, 1991), 44; Wai-yee Li, *The Readability of the Past in Early Chinese Historiography* (Cambridge, MA: Harvard University Asia Center, 2007), 151.

98. For example, they might demand that their daughter divorce her husband and return home. Jessey J. C. Choo, "Adoption and Motherhood: 'The Petition Submitted by Lady [née] Yu,'" in *Early Medieval China: A Sourcebook*, ed. Wendy Swartz, Robert Ford Campany, Yang Lu, and Jessey J. C. Choo (New York: Columbia University Press, 2014), 512.

99. Li Zhende, "Nüren de Zhongguo zhonggushi—xingbie yu Han Tang zhijian de lilü yanjiu," in *Chūgoku no rekishi sekai—tōgō no shisutemu to takenteki hatsuten*, ed. Nihon Chūgokushi gakkai (Tokyo: Kyūko, 2002), 478–81; Hou Xudong and Howard Goodman, "Rethinking Chinese Kinship in the Han and the Six Dynasties: A Preliminary Observation," *Asia Major* 23, no. 1 (2010): 30, 38–47. The kinship system of the Shandong region in particular placed enormous stress on maternal ties. Holmgren, "The Making of an Elite," 56.

100. Fang, *Jinshu*, 60:1633.

101. Li, *Nanshi*, 19:534.

102. Li, "Nüren de Zhongguo zhonggushi," 477–78; Lee, "The Death of a Princess," 16.

103. Ma Yijin, *Wei Jin Nanbeichao de funü yuanzuo* (Taipei: Hua Mulan wenhua chubanshe, 2010); Wang, "Slaves and Other Comparable Social Groups," 310. For some examples see Li, *Beishi*, 32:1182, 36:1340, 68:2383.

104. Li, *Nanshi*, 57:1407.

105. Liu, *Shih-shuo Hsin-yü*, 147 (5.4); Liu, *Shishuo xinyu huijiao jizhu*, 5:250. Also Shen, *Songshu*, 45:1379.

106. Liu, *Shih-shuo Hsin-yü*, 348 (19.13); Liu, *Shishuo xinyu huijiao jizhu*, 19:575.

107. Liu, *Shih-shuo Hsin-yü*, 456 (29.5); Liu, *Shishuo xinyu huijiao jizhu*, 29:725.

108. Liu, *Shih-shuo Hsin-yü*, 355 (19.29); Liu, *Shishuo xinyu huijiao jizhu*, 19:589; Li, *Beishi*, 71:2455.

109. Holmgren, "The Making of an Elite," 16–17, 35.

110. Nevertheless, the bond to paternal relatives usually took precedence. For example, orphans were often raised by the deceased father's brother or paternal grandmother. Li, *Beishi*, 76:2590; Yao, *Liangshu*, 30:441; Shen, *Songshu*, 56:1557; Linghu, *Zhoushu*, 32:562.

111. Liu, *Shih-shuo Hsin-yü*, 75 (2.100); Liu, *Shishuo xinyu huijiao jizhu*, 2:139.

112. Li, *Beishi*, 31:1133.

113. Liu, *Shih-shuo Hsin-yü*, 55 (2.51), 218 (8.22), 298–99 (12.4); Liu, *Shishuo xinyu huijiao jizhu*, 2:102, 8:372, 12:507.

114. Liu, *Shih-shuo Hsin-yü*, 242 (8.139), 398 (24.15); Liu, *Shishuo xinyu huijiao jizhu*, 8:519, 24:646; Li, *Beishi*, 71:2455. For an analysis of the kinship system that gave rise to close ties between maternal uncles and their nephews, see Bret Hinsch, "The Origins of Han-Dynasty Consort Kin Power," *East Asian History* 25/26 (2003): 1–24.

115. For an example of domestic abuse, see Linghu, *Zhoushu*, 9:142.

116. Li, *Nanshi*, 26:698.

117. Sherry J. Mou, *Gentlemen's Prescriptions for Women's Lives: A Thousand Years of Biographies of Chinese Women* (Armonk, NY: M. E. Sharpe, 2004), 114, 183.

118. Howard L. Goodman, *Xun Xu and the Politics of Precision in Third-Century AD China* (Leiden: Brill, 2010), 82–83.

119. Wei, *Weishu*, 97:2132.

120. Shao, *Beichao jiating xingtai yanjiu*, 72.

121. Liu, *Shih-shuo Hsin-yü*, 488 (35.6); Liu, *Shishuo xinyu huijiao jizhu*, 35:767.

122. Liu, *Shih-shuo Hsin-yü*, 434; Liu, *Shishuo xinyu huijiao jizhu*, 26:693.

123. Liu, *Shih-shuo Hsin-yü*, 131 (4.72); Liu, *Shishuo xinyu huijiao jizhu*, 4:228.

124. Zhang and Wang, "Soushenji yu Wei Jin hunyin sangzang lisu," 46.

125. An Jianhua, "Qiantan beichao fufu hezangmu," *Sichuan Daxue xuebao* 1 (2004): 21–22; Zhang and Chen, *Zhongguo funü tongshi*, 649–85; Zhang, *Liuchao funü*, 392–404; Davis, *Entombed Epigraphy and Commemorative Culture in Early Medieval China*, 217–23.

126. An, "Qiantan beichao fufu hezangmu," 22.

127. An, "Qiantan beichao fufu hezangmu," 22. For examples, see Zhao, *Han Wei nanbeichao muzhi huibian*, 133; Shen, *Songshu*, 15:405.

128. Zhang Chengzong, "Wei Jin nanbeichao shiqi de funü danshenzang," *Nanjing Ligong Daxue xuebao* 23, no. 3 (2010): 100; Zhang and Chen, *Zhongguo funü tongshi*, 685–96. For other uncommon modes of female burial, see Zhang and Chen, 698–705.

129. Sun Qin'an, "Guanyu Wei Jin Nanbei chao yanqing wenxue de zucheng ji pingjia," *Shanghai Shehui Kexue yuan xueshu jikan* 36, no. 1 (1994): 189, 191; Chu Tingting, "Cong Wei Jin liuchao nüxing shige kan nüxing shengming yishi de fusu," *Huzhou Shizhuan xuebao* 19, no. 4 (1997): 37–38.

130. Thomas Jansen, "Yutai xinyong," in *Early Medieval Chinese Texts: A Bibliographical Guide*, ed. Cynthia L. Chennault et al. (Berkeley: Institute of East Asian Studies, University of California, 2015), 482.

131. Birrell, *Chinese Love Poetry*, 115; Xu, *Jianzhu yutai xinyong*, 8:9a.

132. Birrell, *Chinese Love Poetry*, 21.

133. Birrell, *Chinese Love Poetry*, 8–10, 19.

134. Birrell, *Chinese Love Poetry*, 296; Xu, *Jianzhu yutai xinyong*, 9:22a.

135. Liu, *Shih-shuo Hsin-yü*, 487 (35.5); Liu, *Shishuo xinyu huijiao jizhu*, 35:766–67; Zhang, "Lun beichao minjian 'hunlian' geci," 117–18.

136. Birrell, *Chinese Love Poetry*, 84; Xu, *Jianzhu yutai xinyong*, 2:8b. I have changed T'ai to Tai. Also see Birrell, 112; Xu, 3:7a. ("Oh beautiful heart of my heart! / Except you, who would hold my heart?")

137. Birrell, *Chinese Love Poetry*, 113; Xu, *Jianzhu yutai xinyong*, 3:7b.

138. Mu-Chou Poo, "The Completion of an Ideal World: The Human Ghost in Early-Medieval China," *Asia Major* 10, nos. 1/2 (1997): 86–89; Wang Tianchan, "Wei Jin liuchao zhiguai xiaoshuo qingai zuopinzhong de nüxing xingxiang," *Fuzhou Shizhuan xuebao* 1 (2002): 17–19, gives many example of romantic woman portrayed in anomaly literature. However, Daniel Hsieh, *Love and Women in Early Chinese Fiction* (Hong Kong: The Chinese University Press, 2008), 25, points out that we should not exaggerate the place of women and female themes in anomaly literature. Women's matters were just one of many topics in this broad genre of writing.

139. Rémi Mathieu, *Démons et Merveilles dans la Littérature Chinoise des Six Dynasties: La Fantastique et l'anecdotique dans le "Soushen Ji" de Gan Bao* (Paris: Éditions You-Feng, 2000), 33–34, 36, 38, 49.

140. Kuroda Mamiko, "Riku chou Tōdai ni okeru yūkontan no tōjō jinbutsu—kankontan to no hikaku," *Nihon Chūgoku gakukaihou* 48 (1996): 119–32.

141. Li Yanong, "Zhouzu de shizu zhidu yu Tuobazu de qianfengjian zhi," in *Li Yanong shi lunji* (Shanghai: Shanghai renmin chubanshe, 1962), 250; Sun Jie, "Cong *Shijing* kan Zhoudai de chuqizhi," *Anhui wenxue* 5 (2007): 63–64.

142. Zhang, *Jiating shihua*, 42.

143. Wang Lihua, *Zhongguo jiatingshi: diyi juan, xian Qin zhi nanbei chao shiqi* (N.p.: Guangdong renmin chubanshe, 2007), 422.

144. Li, *Beishi*, 31:1144.

145. Wei, *Weishu*, 52:1147.

146. Zhang, "Wei Jin nanbeichao shiqi yu funü xiangguan de falü wenti ji sifa anjian," 26–27.

147. Wang, *Zhongguo jiatingshi: diyi juan, xian Qin zhi nanbei chao shiqi*, 420–21.

148. Li, *Nanshi*, 24:654. Also Li, *Beishi*, 92:3053; Shen, *Songshu*, 58:1591.

149. Li, *Beishi*, 15:578.

150. Wang, *Zhongguo jiatingshi: diyi juan, xian Qin zhi nanbei chao shiqi*, 420.

151. Wang and Cao, *A Record of Buddhist Monasteries in Luo-yang*, 173–75.

152. Li, *Beishi*, 17:633.

153. Fang, *Jinshu*, 65:1756.

154. Zeng Xiaoxia, "Dai yan yu zi yu—Wei Jin qifu shiwen tanxi," *Hunan Renwen Keji Xueyuan xuebao* 1 (2013): 82–86. These poems resembled poetry about the palace lady who had lost the ruler's favor, and poems about widowhood. Guo, "Liang Han Wei Jin cifu zhong de xianshi nüxing ticai yu xingbie biaoda," 30–34.

155. Birrell, *Chinese Love Poetry*, 224; Xu, *Jianzhu yutai xinyong*, 7:11a.

156. Birrell, *Chinese Love Poetry*, 111; Xu, *Jianzhu yutai xinyong*, 3:6b–7a.

157. Birrell, *Chinese Love Poetry*, 111; Xu, *Jianzhu yutai xinyong*, 3:6b–7a.

158. Birrell, *Chinese Love Poetry*, 83; Xu, *Jianzhu yutai xinyong*, 2:7a–7b.

159. Birrell, *Chinese Love Poetry*, 77; Xu, *Jianzhu yutai xinyong*, 2:3A.

160. Shao, *Beichao jiating xingtai yanjiu*, 79–80. *Jiqie* was a neologism; Han dynasty records lack this term and refer to concubines simply as *qie*. Liu Zenggui, "Wei Jin Nanbeichao shidai de qie," *Xin shixue* 2, no. 4 (1991): 9–10. The distinction between *qie* and *ji* seems to have been ambiguous.

161. Zhang, "Wei Jin nanbeichao shiqi yu funü xiangguan de falü wenti ji sifa anjian," 25–26. Wei, *Weishu*, 52:1147, describes a man who fell in love with his concubine and abandoned his wife, resulting in mutual recriminations and lawsuits. Shen, *Songshu*, 32:931, quotes the Han dynasty apocryphon *Hongfan Wuxing zhuan* 洪範五行傳 comparing the substitution of concubine for wife as comparable to murder.

162. Liu, *Shih-shuo Hsin-yü*, 471 (33.2); Liu, *Shishuo xinyu huijiao jizhu*, 33:746, describes a woman who thought that she was to become a man's wife. But because he deliberately conducted the wedding ceremony improperly, she ended up his concubine.

163. Holmgren, "Social Mobility in the Northern Dynasties," 27; Shao, *Beichao jiating xingtai yanjiu*, 76–78. Lee, "Women and Marriage," 170, asserts that concubinage was not very popular in the north.

164. Wei, *Weishu*, 40:909.

165. Liu, "Wei Jin Nanbeichao shidai de qie," 12.

166. Liu, "Wei Jin Nanbeichao shidai de qie," 13, 15.

167. Fang, *Jinshu*, 121:3046.

168. Liu, *Shih-shuo Hsin-yü*, 255; Liu, *Shishuo xinyu huijiao jizhu*, 9:442.

169. Li Baiyao, *Bei Qi shu* (Beijing: Zhonghua shuju, 1972), 16:216; 18:235. Slaves were also used sexually. Wei Zheng, *Suishu*, annotated by Linghu Defen and Wang Zhaoying (Beijing: Zhonghua Shuju, 1973), 64:1507.

170. Liu, "Wei Jin Nanbeichao shidai de qie," 8–9. Li, *Beishi*, 53:1902, mentions a man whose eight children were all born to concubines.

171. Wei, *Weishu*, 53:1173; Li, *Beishi*, 33:1222.

172. Liu, "Wei Jin Nanbeichao shidai de qie," 8–9.

173. Harriet Zurndorfer, "Polygamy and Masculinity in China: Past and Present," in *Changing Chinese Masculinities: From Imperial Pillars of State to Global Real Men*, ed. Kam Louie (Hong Kong: Hong Kong University Press, 2016), 17.

174. Wang and Hong, *A Record of Buddhist Monasteries in Luo-yang*, 69.

175. David R. Knechtges, "Estate Culture in Early Medieval China: The Case of Shi Chong," in *Early Medieval China: A Sourcebook*, ed. Wendy Swartz, Robert Ford Campany, Yang Lu, and Jessey J. C. Choo (New York: Columbia University Press, 2014), 531. Quoting *Xuwen zhangzhi* 續文章志.

176. Wei, *Weishu*, 18:423; Li, *Beishi*, 16:609-10.

177. Liu, "Wei Jin Nanbeichao shidai de qie," 27–28.

178. Liu, *Shih-shuo Hsin-yü*, 301 (13.2); Liu, *Shishuo xinyu huijiao jizhu*, 13:510.

179. Shen, *Songshu*, 82:2102. Fang, *Jinshu*, 39: 1146, records the case of a concubine born into an elite family that declined into poverty. Liu, *Shih-shuo Hsin-yü*, 15 (1:28); Liu, *Shishuo xinyu huijiao jizhu*, 1:26, mentions a concubine who came from a prominent northern family that declined after they fled south. Li, *Wei Jin Sui Tang hunyin xingtai yanjiu*, 30, believes that these sorts of cases were rare.

180. Liu, *Shih-shuo Hsin-yü*, 350 (19.18); Liu, *Shishuo xinyu huijiao jizhu*, 19:579–80.

181. Wei, *Weishu*, 18:429.

182. Liu, "Wei Jin Nanbeichao shidai de qie," 16–17; Dien, "Everyday Life," 442–43.

183. Shen, *Songshu*, 74:1920.

184. Li, *Beishi*, 17:633.

185. Liu, *Shih-shuo Hsin-yü*, 488 (35.7); Liu, *Shishuo xinyu huijiao jizhu*, 35:768.

186. Li, *Nanshi*, 20:557.

187. Fang, *Jinshu*, 96:2522–23.

188. Wang, "Slaves and Other Comparable Social Groups," 328.

189. Liu, "Wei Jin Nanbeichao shidai de qie," 18–19.

190. Yen, *Family Instructions for the Yen Clan*, 12; Zhao, "Jiu Shishuo xinyu kan Wei Jin nanbeichao de hunyin wenhua," 41.

191. Fang, *Jinshu*, 3:63; Yen, *Family Instructions for the Yen Clan*, 12–13; Dien, "Everyday Life," 442–43.

192. Fang, *Jinshu*, 49:1364.

193. Li, *Wei Jin Sui Tang hunyin xingtai yanjiu*, 182–85.

194. Wang, "Slaves and Other Comparable Social Groups," 329–30.

195. Liu, "Wei Jin Nanbeichao shidai de qie," 22–23.

CHAPTER 2

1. Wright, *The Sui Dynasty*, 64.

2. Mark Edward Lewis, *China between Empires: The Northern and Southern Dynasties* (Cambridge, MA: The Belknap Press of Harvard University Press, 2009), 189–90.

3. *Mude* 母德: Zhao, *Han Wei nanbeichao muzhi huibian*, 42. *Muyi* 母儀: Zhao, *Han Wei nanbeichao muzhi huibian*, 100, 132, 215, 251, 317, 340, 373, 398, 474.

4. Some authorities demanded that mourning for a divorced mother should be reduced. Zheng Yaru, "Zhonggu shiqi de muzi guanxi—xingbie yu Han Tang zhijian de jiating yanjiu," in *Zhongguo shi xinlun—xingbie shi fence*, ed. Li Zhende (Taipei: Zhongyang yanjiu yuan, 2009), 146.

5. During the Shang dynasty, a mother's rank determined that of her son. Ying Wang, "Rank and Power among Court Ladies at Anyang," in *Gender and Chinese Archaeology*, ed. Katheryn M. Linduff and Yan Sun (Walnut Creek, CA: Altamira Press, 2004), 97, 110. During the Eastern Zhou, a woman's social rank followed that of her husband. Thatcher, "Marriages of the Ruling Elite in the Spring and Autumn Period," 28. This belief remained in force during the medieval era. Li, *Nanshi*, 26:698. Mencius popularized the idea that a widow's rank depended on that of her son. Bryan W. Van Norden, trans., *Mengzi: With Selections from Traditional Commentaries* (Indianapolis: Hackett Publishing, 2008), 31–32 (1B16.1). Han dynasty authorities reasserted this idea. Ban, *Hanshu*, 11:335. This principle was accepted during the Six Dynasties. Wei, *Weishu*, 99:2206; Shen, *Songshu*, 15:397, 15:409, 55:1543. Yao, *Liangshu*, 7:160.

6. Liu, "Wei Jin Nanbeichao shidai de qie," 22–23.

7. Wei, *Weishu*, 92:1979.

8. Wei, *Weishu*, 85:1873.

9. Shen, *Songshu*, 76:1969.

10. Fang, *Jinshu*, 86:2224.

11. Li, *Beishi*, 92:3022. Liu, *Shih-shuo Hsin-yü*, 151 (5.7); Liu, *Shishuo xinyu hui-jiao jizhu*, 5:255, describes two men feasting and drinking in the company of the mother of one of the men. Her presence seems to indicate the intimacy of the bond between these two men.

12. Wei, *Weishu*, 50:1117, 1119. Wei, *Weishu*, 39:893, describes a case in which a mother was exiled to the frontier along with her son as punishment for his crimes. She eventually returned home due to an amnesty.

13. Yao, *Liangshu*, 20:313.

14. Wei, *Weishu*, 61:1360.

15. Wei, *Weishu*, 24:633, mentions a virtuous household that expressed "the way of motherly love and filial piety." And a ward in Luoyang was called Cixiao 慈孝, implying that motherly love and filial piety were considered reciprocal virtues. Wang and Cao, *A Record of Buddhist Monasteries in Luo-yang*, 227.

16. Shimomi Takao, *Bosei izon no shisō—"nijūshi kō" kara kangaeru boshi ittai kannen to kō* (Tokyo: Kenbun, 2002).

17. Lee, "The Death of a Princess," 14, 16.

18. Babies were killed or abandoned if they had bad features or were born on an inauspicious day. Babies born on the fifth day of the fifth month were the most inauspicious. A Liang dynasty woman was said to have given birth to an unnaturally large baby boy who had eyes on the top of his head. He turned out to be a plague demon. After his birth, epidemics struck several areas. Wei, *Suishu*, 23:660. Government functionaries discouraged infanticide. They sometimes punished parents who killed their children and occasionally provided subsidies for childbirth. Scholars condemned childbirth taboos, and some religious institutions raised abandoned children. Li Zhende, "Han Sui zhijian de 'sheng zi bu ju' wenti," *Zhongyang Yanjiuyuan Lishi Yuyan Yanjiusuo jikan* 66, no. 3 (1995): 747–812. Religious texts also warned of retribution for murder. Besides Buddhist works, which forbid killing any living thing, the *Taiping jing* specifically also forbids infanticide. This work argues that a mother who killed her baby became unhappy. This work assumes that girls would be killed more often than boys, so infanticide would not only deplete the population but also unbalance the sex ratio. Barbara Hendrischke, "The Daoist Utopia of Great Peace," *Oriens Extremus* 35, nos. 1/2 (1992): 67, 71.

19. Zhu Mingxun, "Lun Wei Jin liuchao shiqi de Xiaojing yanjiu," *Huazhong Keji Daxue xuebao* 3 (2002): 97–101. For translation and commentary, see Rosemont and Ames, *The Chinese Classic of Family Reverence*.

20. Shimomi Takao, *Juka shakai to bosei—bosei no iroku no kanten de miru Kan Gi Shin Chūgoku josei shi*, rev. ed. (Tokyo: Kenbun shuppan, 2008), 89–90, provides a long list of early medieval *Xiao jing* commentaries. Emperor Wen of Wei enthusiastically promoted the study of *Xiao jing*. At various times this classic was recited at court. Li, *Beishi*, 4:137, 4:148; Li, *Nanshi*, 34:900. Some heirs apparent studied *Xiao jing* to prepare them to rule. Yao, *Liangshu*, 7:165; Li, *Beishi*, 22:829. And one young man gained an emperor's notice because of his proficiency in this text. Li, *Beishi*, 75:2579.

21. Ochi, *Gi Shin Nanchō no kizoku sei*, 359–68.

22. For example, Yao, *Liangshu*, 33:469.

23. Kawakatsu Yoshio, *Rikuchō kizoku sei shakai no kenkyū* (Tokyo: Iwanami, 1982), 292–96.

24. Wei, *Weishu*, 68:1510.

25. Liu Lingdi, "Han Wei liuchao daojiao de xiaodao," *Nandu xuetan* 27, no. 1 (2007): 39–41. Yoshikawa Tadao, *Liuchao jingshen shi yanjiu*, trans. Wang Qifa (Nanjing: Jiangsu renmin chubanshe, 2010), 419–35, documents the popularity of filial piety discourse among Daoists and Buddhists as well as Confucians.

26. Chen Yifeng, "Wei Jin nanbeichao shiqi rufo de xiaodao zhi zheng," *Nandu xuetan* 23, no. 2 (2003): 23–27.

27. Alan Cole, *Mothers and Sons in Chinese Buddhism* (Stanford: Stanford University Press, 1998), 2–3.

28. Zheng, "Zhonggu shiqi de muzi guanxi—xingbie yu Han Tang zhijian de jiating yanjiu," 181–86.

29. Zhang Guogang, "Zhonggu fojiao jielü yu jiating lunli," in *Jiating shi yanjiu de xin shiye*, ed. Zhang Guogang (Beijing: Sanlian shuju, 2004), 51–53.

30. Cole, *Mothers and Sons in Chinese Buddhism*, 42–46.

31. Cole, *Mothers and Sons in Chinese Buddhism*, 57–64.

32. Beata Grant and Wilt L. Idema, trans., *Escape from Blood Pond Hell: The Tales of Mulian and Woman Huang* (Seattle: University of Washington Press, 2011); Cole, *Mothers and Sons in Chinese Buddhism*, 159–91; Robert F. Campany, "Ghosts Matter: The Culture of Ghosts in Six Dynasties Zhiguai," *Chinese Literature* 13 (1991): 19.

33. For filial piety in *Shishuo xinyu*, see Lu Hongping, "Cong Shishuo xinyu kan Wei Jin shiren de zhongxiaoguan," *Lunlixue yanjiu* 1 (2011): 50–56. *Weishu* chapter 86 is devoted to stories of filial sons. Many of these men were lauded for showing devotion to their mothers, demonstrating that people considered filial attention toward a mother as important as that toward a father. Shao Zhengkun, "Lun beichao nüzi de jiating diwei," *Xi'an Ouya Xueyuan xuebao* 2 (2010): 64. *Jinshu* was the first standard history to include a section on filial sons. Also see Keith N. Knapp, "Xiaozi zhuan," in *Early Medieval Chinese Texts: A Bibliographical Guide*, ed. Cynthia L. Chennault et al. (Berkeley: Institute of East Asian Studies, University of California, 2015), 409–13. Two women's biographies in the work are also devoted to filial women. Mou, *Gentlemen's Prescriptions*, 101–2. From the late sixth century onward, epitaphs emphasize not only the virtues of the deceased but also the filial piety of the children who commissioned these memorials. Yao, "Women in Portraits," 169. For the stress on filial regard to mothers, see Wei, *Weishu*, 60:1347

34. Japanese scholars in particular have depicted filial piety as a fundamental organizing principle of early medieval society. Ogata Isamu, *Chūgoku kodai no ie to kokka—kōtei shipaika no chitsujo kekkō* (Tokyo: Iwanami shoten, 1975), 187–97; Ochi Shigeaki, *Gi Shin nanchō no hito to shakai* (Tokyo: Kenbun shuppan, 1985), 41–46, 157–63; Shimomi, *Juka shakai to bosei*, 81–84.

35. Li Jingrong, "Lun Wei Jin shiqi de jimu zi guanxi," *Zhuzhou Shifan Gaodeng Zhuanke Xuexiao xuebao* 10, no. 1 (2005): 45–47.

36. Zhang, "Wei Jin nanbeichao shiqi yu funü xiangguan de falü wenti ji sifa anjian," 25.

37. Wei, *Weishu*, 111:2878.

38. Choo, "Adoption and Motherhood," 512–13. Although this suit failed, it nevertheless shows that a mother assumed that she could sue a wayward son, even if he had been adopted.

39. Shen, *Songshu*, 54:1534; Li, *Nanshi*, 27:727.

40. Wei, *Weishu*, 65:1450.

41. Benjamin E. Wallacker, "Chang Fei's Preface to the Chin Code of Law," *T'oung Pao* 72, nos. 4–5 (1986): 260.

42. Wei, *Weishu*, 88:1909, 1911.

43. Li, *Beishi*, 19:701.

44. Li Zhende, "Han Tang zhijian yishu zhong de shengchan zhi dao," *Zhongyang Yanjiuyuan Lishi Yuyan Yanjiusuo jikan* 67, no. 3 (1996): 533–654; Li Zhende, "Han Tang zhijian qiuzi yifang shitan—jianlun fuke lanshang yu xingbie lunshu," *Zhongyang Yanjiuyuan Lishi Yuyan Yanjiusuo jikan* 68, no. 2 (1997): 283–367; Jen-der Lee, "Childbirth in Early Imperial China," *Nan Nü* 7, no. 2 (2005): 224–45.

45. Wei, *Weishu*, 111:2874.

46. Wei, *Weishu*, 71:1571.

47. Wei, *Weishu*, 75:1672.

48. Yen, *Family Instructions for the Yen Clan*, 4.

49. Zhang, *Jiating shihua*, 39.

50. Fang, *Jinshu*, 51:1409. It was not uncommon for a man to show filial devotion to a surrogate mother such as an aunt, grandmother, or step-mother. Fang, *Jinshu*, 39:1143, 47:1333, 61:1666, 76: 2015; Wei, *Weishu*, 52:1152, 45:1009, 77:1708; Li, *Nanshi*, 30:781, 49:1227. Liu, *Shih-shuo Hsin-yü*, 8 (1.14); Liu, *Shishuo xinyu huijiao jizhu*, 1:14. Buddhists might even extend filial regard to an unrelated woman who simply looked like an elderly mother. Kathryn A. Tsai, *Lives of the Nuns: Biographies of Chinese Buddhist Nuns from the Fourth to Sixth Centuries, A Translation of the* Pi-ch'iu-ni chuan, compiled by Shih Pao-ch'ang (Honolulu: University of Hawaii Press, 1972), 48–49; Shi Baochang, *Biqiuni zhuan jiaozhu*, annotated by Wang Rutong (Taipei: Zhonghua, 2006), 2:75–76.

51. Liu, *Shih-shuo Hsin-yü*, 81 (3.2); Liu, *Shishuo xinyu huijiao jizhu*, 3:146.

52. Shen, *Songshu*, 45:1374.

53. Shen, *Songshu*, 91:2247.

54. Wei, *Weishu*, 70:1561.

55. Keith N. Knapp, "Exemplary Everymen: Guo Shidao and Guo Yuanping as Confucian Commoners," *Asia Major* 23, no. 1 (2010): 87.

56. Knapp, "Exemplary Everymen," 97–98.

57. Li, *Beishi*, 34:1271, 35:1290.

58. Andrew Chittick, "*Song shu*," in *Early Medieval Chinese Texts: A Bibliographical Guide*, ed. Cynthia L. Chennault et al. (Berkeley: Institute of East Asian Studies, University of California, 2015), 320–23.

59. Tsai, *Lives of the Nuns*, 26; Shi, *Biqiuni zhuan jiaozhu*, 1:18.

60. Xiao Zixian, *Nan Qi shu* (Beiing: Zhonghua shuju, 1972), 55:956–58.

61. Wei, *Weishu*, 43:977; 45:1023.

62. Shen, *Songshu*, 46:1389.

63. Li, *Nanshi*, 11:318.

64. Liu, *Shih-shuo Hsin-yü*, 35 (2.13); Liu, *Shishuo xinyu huijiao jizhu*, 2:60.

65. For a poor man who worked hard to feed his mother, see Li, *Nanshi*, 55:1371.

66. Fang, *Jinshu*, 41:1188, 88:2376–77.

67. Fang, *Jinshu*, 81:2113; Li, *Nanshi*, 31:820; Liu, *Shih-shuo Hsin-yü*, 360 (20.7); Liu, *Shishuo xinyu huijiao jizhu*, 20:594.

68. Li, *Nanshi*, 37:961.

69. Lingley, "Lady Yuchi in the First Person," 46. For the Ding Lan tale and its visual representations, see Wu Hung, *The Wu Liang Shrine: The Ideology of Early Chinese Pictorial Art* (Stanford: Stanford University Press, 1989), 168, 185, 272, 274, 282–85; Wei Wenge, "Muzang ziliao zhong suojian ershisi xiao zhi fazhan yan-bian," *Wenwu shijie* 5 (2010): 44; Knapp, *Selfless Offspring*, 34–35, 191–94.

70. Xiao, *Nan Qi shu*, 43:757.

71. Li, *Beishi*, 93:3089.

72. Wei, *Weishu*, 86:1883; Li, *Beishi*, 64:2285.

73. Keith N. Knapp, "Reverent Caring: The Parent-Son Relationship in Early Medieval Tales of Filial Offspring," in *Filial Piety in Chinese Thought and History*, ed. Alan K. L. Chan and Sor-hoon Tan (London: RoutledgeCurzon, 2004), 44–70.

74. Wei, *Weishu*, 43:969. Also Liu, *Shih-shuo Hsin-yü*, 14 (1.26); Liu, *Shishuo xinyu huijiao jizhu*, 1:24.

75. Xiao, *Nan Qi shu*, 27:504.

76. Yao, *Liangshu*, 11:205; Li, *Nanshi*, 56:1381.

77. Tsai, *Lives of the Nuns*, 45, 47; Shi, *Biqiuni zhuan jiaozhu*, 2:72; Robert Ford Campany, *Signs from the Unseen Realm: Buddhist Miracle Tales from Early Medieval China* (Honolulu: University of Hawaii Press, 2012), 213.

78. Liu, *Shih-shuo Hsin-yü*, 22 (1.45); Liu, *Shishuo xinyu huijiao jizhu*, 1:41–42.

79. Fang, *Jinshu*, 33:987. Similarly, Li, *Beishi*, 69:2391.

80. Miranda Brown, "Sons and Mothers in Warring States and Han China, 453 BCE–220 CE," *Nan Nü* 5, no. 2 (2003): 139; Miranda Brown, *The Politics of Mourning in Early China* (Albany: State University of New York Press, 2007), 66, 70, 72–75. Han dynasty historians emphasized the funeral that Confucius performed for his mother, not the one for his father. Ban, *Hanshu*, 36:1953; Fan Ye, *Hou Hanshu*, annotated by Liu Zhao and Li Xian et al. (Beijing: Zhonghua Shuju, 1965), 49:1636.

81. Zheng Yaru, *Qinggan yu zhidu—Wei JIn shidai de muzi guanxi* (Taipei: Guoli Taiwan Daxue, 2001), 21–114.

82. Shen, *Songshu*, 91:2243, 91:2257.

83. Wei, *Weishu*, 62:1388–89.

84. Fang, *Jinshu*, 62:1696.

85. Liu, *Shih-shuo Hsin-yü*, 135 (4.82); Liu, *Shishuo xinyu huijiao jizhu*, 4:133.

86. Liu, *Shih-shuo Hsin-yü*, 372 (23.2); Liu, *Shishuo xinyu huijiao jizhu*, 23:610.

87. Zhang Chengzong, "Wei Jin nanbeichao funü sangzang liyi kao," *Suzhou Daxue xuebao* 2 (2010): 99–102; Wang Weiping, "On Observing Etiquette and Custom—A Case of the Essence of the Funeral and Burial in the Six Dynasties," *Xueshujie* 6 (2015): 298–99.

88. Luo Tonghua, *Tongju gongcai: Tangdai jiating yanjiu* (Taipei: Zhengda chu-banshe, 2015), 483–88.

89. Timothy M. Davis, "Texts for Stabilizing Tombs," in *Early Medieval China: A Sourcebook*, ed. Wendy Swartz, Robert Ford Campany, Yang Lu, and Jessey J. C. Choo (New York: Columbia University Press, 2014), 604–5. Tombs of women as

well as men might also include a land purchase contract for the site of the tomb to ensure that the deceased would not be evicted (pp. 599–60).

90. Wei, *Weishu*, 4B:103; Li, *Beishi*, 2:72.

91. Li, *Beishi*, 46:1691. For the Zhou system of posthumous female names, see Zhang Shuyi, "Zhoudai nüzi de xingshi zhidu," *Shixue jikan* 2 (1999): 68; Cao Zha-olan, *Jinwen yu Yin Zhou nüxing wenhua* (Beijing: Beijing Daxue, 2004), 106; Chen Jie, *Shang Zhou xingshi zhidu yanjiu* (Beijing: Shangwu yinshuguan, 2007), 297–330.

92. Shen, *Songshu*, 15:397–403.

93. Zhang Huanjun, "Lizhi yu renqing de tiaoshi—yi Wei Jin shiqi qianmu de fusang wenti wei zhongxin," *Shanxi Shida xuebao* 1 (2011): 55–59.

94. Zheng Yaru, "Zhonggu shiqi de muzi guanxi," 146.

95. Wei, *Weishu*, 78:1730–31; Fang, *Jinshu*, 67:1835.

96. Chaos: Fang, *Jinshu*, 67:1786. Poverty: Fang, *Jinshu*, 52:1443.

97. Shen, *Songshu*, 92:2263.

98. Wei, *Weishu*, 111:1880.

99. Wei, *Weishu*, 38:872–73.

100. Fang, *Jinshu*, 75:1976.

101. Li, *Nanshi*, 23:625.

102. Fang, *Jinshu*, 40: 1167, 43:1233, 47:1331, 47:1328, 51:1425, 76:2017, 83:2164; Wei, *Weishu*, 36:835.

103. Liu, *Shih-shuo Hsin-yü*, 81 (3.1); Liu, *Shishuo xinyu huijiao jizhu*, 3:146.

104. Wei, *Weishu*, 18:420, 33:773, 33:794, 42:948, 45:1030, 47:1053, 47:1055, 49:1103, 49:1106, 55:1221, 57:1274, 57:1276, 58:1285, 58:1297, 65:1460, 66:1482, 67:1500, 72:1602, 72:1613, 72:1618, 79:1762, 93:1992. This occasionally happened in the south as well. Fang, *Jinshu*, 58:1570. Zheng Yaru, *Qin en nan bao: Tangdai shiren de xiaodao shijian ji qi tizhihua* (Taipei: Taida chuban zhongxin, 2014), 55–60, discusses the early medieval custom of resigning from office to care for a parent.

105. Wei, *Weishu*, 24:615; Liu, *Shih-shuo Hsin-yü*, 12 (1.20); Liu, *Shishuo xinyu huijiao jizhu*, 1:20.

106. Li, *Beishi*, 33:1232; Li, *Nanshi*, 28:755.

107. Li, *Beishi*, 71:2468.

108. Wei, *Weishu*, 56:1238; Wang and Cao, *A Record of Buddhist Monasteries in Luo-yang*, 171.

109. Wei, *Weishu*, 86:1886; Fang, *Jinshu*, 38:1126.

110. Wei, *Weishu*, 52:1152, 65:1450.

111. Liu, *Shih-shuo Hsin-yü*, 23 (1.47); Liu, *Shishuo xinyu huijiao jizhu*, 1:43.

112. Yao, *Liangshu*, 22:354.

113. Tsai, *Lives of the Nuns*, 71; Shi, *Biqiuni zhuan jiaozhu*, 3:128.

114. Wei, *Weishu*, 92:1985.

CHAPTER 3

1. Shen, *Songshu*, 14:336, describes the ideal imperial wedding ceremony, which was based on Zhou dynasty precedents. 14:337–39 describes the rituals used in imperial weddings in the southern dynasties. 14:340–41 describes the wedding ceremony of the heir apparent.

2. Holmgren, "Imperial Marriage in the Native Chinese and Non-Han State," 61.

3. For example, Li, *Nanshi*, 11:317; Shen, *Songshu*, 41:1281.

4. Cynthia L. Chennault, "Lofty Gates or Solitary Impoverishment? Xie Family Members of the Southern Dynasties," *T'oung Pao* 85, nos. 4–5 (1999): 249–327, describes one example of this marriage strategy in great detail. Fang, *Jinshu*, 33:996, documents a similar case.

5. Misevic, "Oligarchy or Social Mobility," 217–21; Bielenstein, "The Six Dynasties, Vol. 2," 17; Robert Joe Cutter, "To the Manner Born? Nature and Nurture in Early Medieval Chinese Literary Thought," in *Culture and Power in the Reconstitution of the Chinese Realm, 200–600*, ed. Scott Pearce, Audrey Spiro, and Patricia Ebrey (Cambridge, MA: Harvard University Asia Center, 2001), 70.

6. Cao Fang 曹芳 was enthroned as emperor of Wei in 239 at age eight. In 254 the strongmen Sima She 司馬師 and Sima Zhao 司馬昭 deposed Cao Fang as emperor and replaced him with Cao Mao 曹髦 at age fourteen. To do so, they used the authority of Empress Dowager Guo 郭, in accordance with Han dynasty precedent. Robert Joe Cutter, "Sex, Politics, and Morality at the Wei (220–265) Court," in *Selected Essays on Court Culture in Cross-Cultural Perspective*, ed. Yaofu Lin (Taipei: National Taiwan University Press, 1999), 106–13.

7. Holmgren, "Imperial Marriage in the Native Chinese and Non-Han State," 60.

8. Mather, "Intermarriage as a Gauge of Family Status," 212–14; Bielenstein, "The Six Dynasties, Vol. 2," 18–22; Misevic, "Oligarchy or Social Mobility," 224, 226, 228–29; Li, *Wei Jin Sui Tang hunyin xingtai yanjiu*, 37, 60–61.

9. Bielenstein, "The Six Dynasties, Vol. 2," 19.

10. Chennault, "Lofty Gates or Solitary Impoverishment?," 258.

11. For example Li, *Nanshi*, 12:347.

12. Li, *Nanshi*, 12:337. For another example, see Fang, *Jinshu*, 38:1122.

13. Li, *Nanshi*, 12:338; Shen, *Songshu*, 41:1283.

14. Wei, *Weishu*, 83A:1820.

15. Xie, *Beichao hunsang lisu yanjiu*, 15; Valentin G. Golavachev, "Matricide among the Tuoba-Xianbei and Its Transformation during the Northern Wei," *Early Medieval China* 8 (2002): 5–7. The Tuoba also sometimes married Han women and those from other ethnicities. For an overview of Tuoba political marriage, see Zhang Jihao, *Cong Tuoba dao Bei Wei—Bei Wei wangchao chuangjian lishi de kaocha* (Banqiao: Daoxiang, 2003), 221, 225–26, 231–32.

16. Zhang, *Cong Tuoba dao Bei Wei*, 20–30, 227–28; Andrew Eisenberg, *Kingship in Early Medieval China* (Leiden: Brill, 2008), 29; Li, *Beishi*, 1:8.

17. Li, *Wei Jin Sui Tang hunyin xingtai yanjiu*, 161–63.

18. Eisenberg, *Kingship in Early Medieval China*, 52.

19. Jennifer Holmgren, "The Harem in Northern Wei Politics—398–498 AD," *Journal of the Economic and Social History of the Orient* 26, no. 1 (1983): 78; Holmgren, "Imperial Marriage in the Native Chinese and Non-Han State," 79–80; Jennifer Holmgren, "Race and Class in Fifth Century China: The Emperor Kaotsu's Marriage Reform," *Early Medieval China* 2 (1995–1996): 92–93.

20. Misevic, "Oligarchy or Social Mobility," 237, 240, 244.

21. Misevic, "Oligarchy or Social Mobility," 245–47.

22. Li, *Beishi*, 1:26; Jennifer Holmgren, "Political Organization of Non-Han States in China: The Role of Imperial Princes in Wei, Liao and Yuan," *Journal of*

Oriental Studies 25, no. 1 (1987): 13; Liu Yongcong, "Wei Jin yihuan shijia dui hou-fei zhuzheng zhi fumian pingjia," in *Zhongguo funüshi lunji sanji*, ed. Bao Jialin (Taipei: Daoxiang, 1993), 29–30.

23. Jennifer Holmgren, "Women and Political Power in the Traditional T'o-pa Elite: A Preliminary Study of the Biographies of Empresses in the Wei-shu," *Monumenta Serica* 35 (1981–1983): 57–58; Eisenberg, *Kingship in Early Medieval China*, 29, 50–51.

24. Most scholars consider matricide a Northern Wei innovation. Golavachev, "Matricide among the Tuoba-Xianbei," 18, 26, argues that matricide was a traditional Tuoba custom predating the establishment of the Northern Wei dynasty. Sanping Chen, "Succession Struggles and the Ethnic Identity of the Tang Imperial House," *Journal of the Royal Asiatic Society*, third series, 6, no. 3 (1996): 395, interprets matricide as a reaction to domineering mothers in steppe culture.

25. For example, Linghu, *Zhoushu*, 9:143, 9:147.

26. Wei, *Weishu*, 83B:1832–33.

27. Linghu, *Zhoushu*, 16:267; Wei, *Weishu*, 83B:1829.

28. Xie, *Beichao hunsang lisu yanjiu*, 17.

29. Jennifer Holmgren, "Northern Wei as a Conquest Dynasty: Current Perceptions, Past Scholarship," *Papers on Far Eastern History* 49 (1989): 23.

30. Barfield, *The Perilous Frontier*, 112, 123, 126. For some examples of how northern emperors used marriage to ally themselves with the Göktürks (Tujue), see Linghu, *Zhoushu*, 5:75, 7:118; Li, *Beishi*, 23:857.

31. Zhang, *Cong Tuoba dao Bei Wei*, 89, 156, theorizes that the Tuoba may have been organized as intermarrying moieties.

32. Holmgren, "Imperial Marriage in the Native Chinese and Non-Han State," 77.

33. Holmgren, "Race and Class in Fifth Century China," 97–102; Holmgren, "Family, Marriage and Political Power in 6th Century China," 1; Li, *Wei Jin Sui Tang hunyin xingtai yanjiu*, 113, 122.

34. Wei, *Weishu*, 75:1664; Wang, *A Record of Buddhist Monasteries in Luo-yang*, 33.

35. Jennifer Holmgren, "A Question of Strength: Military Capacity and Princess Bestowal in Imperial China's Foreign Relations (Han to Ch'ing)," *Monumenta Serica* 39 (1990–1991): 65.

36. Fang, *Jinshu*, 32:971–72.

37. Fang, *Jinshu*, 32:972, 974.

38. Bielenstein, "The Six Dynasties, Vol. 2," 16–24, briefly describes all of the six dynasty empresses whose biographies are known. The Northern Wei had twenty-two empresses. Some died young, and some were only awarded the title of empress posthumously. Almost nothing is recorded about the empresses and other consorts of the first eight Wei rulers. Wei, *Weishu*, 13:321. Four empresses had major political roles: Empress Xianming, Empress Chang (Wenchengzhao), Empress Feng (Wencheng Wenming), and Empress Hu (Xuanwuling). Song, *Bei Wei nüzhu lun*, 46–47. Duan Tali singles out seventy women who participated in politics to some degree in the medieval era, which includes the Sui and Tang. In this era 73.7 percent of powerful women were of steppe extraction. Duan Tali, "Beichao zhi Sui Tang shiqi nüxing canzheng xianxiang toushi," *Jianghai xuekan* 5 (2001): 111. Zhao Yi, *Nianer shi zhaji* (Taipei: Shijie shuju, 1974), 19:252–53, de-

scribes how posthumous names for empresses were constructed in each era, from Han to Tang. When an empress died, she was given a posthumous name. But the emperor's posthumous name was often appended to her name, creating a two character posthumous name for her.

39. Li, *Beishi*, 8:283.

40. Wei, *Weishu*, 56:1238.

41. Holmgren, "Political Organization of Non-Han States," 13; Holmgren, "Women and Political Power in the Traditional T'o-pa Elite," 63; Holmgren, "Imperial Marriage in the Native Chinese and Non-Han State," 79–80.

42. The extended family of Li Chong, a favorite of Empress Wending, became extremely wealthy due to her largesse. Wei, *Weishu*, 53:1189.

43. Fang, *Jinshu*, 31:953.

44. Zhao, *Nianer shi zhaji*, 15:207. For example, Li, *Beishi*, 33:1216.

45. Eisenberg, *Kingship in Early Medieval China*, 161–62; Keith McMahon, *Women Shall Not Rule: Imperial Wives and Concubines in China from Han to Liao* (Lanham, MD: Rowman & Littlefield, 2013), 172.

46. To weaken female power at court, two of six emperors in the fifth century never appointed legal consorts. Holmgren, "The Harem in Northern Wei Politics," 76–77.

47. Li, *Beishi*, 51:1844.

48. Holmgren, "Women and Political Power in the Traditional T'o-pa Elite," 56–57; Wei, *Weishu*, 13:321, 325.

49. Song, *Bei Wei nüzhu lun*, 47.

50. Holmgren, "Women and Political Power in the Traditional T'o-pa Elite," 43.

51. Li, *Beishi*, 10:359. People of the time recognized the possibility of female power. In addition to the precedents of the Eastern Han, rumor also had it that "to the north there is also a kingdom of queens where women rule." However, "no one has ever been there." Wei, *Weishu*, 101:2241.

52. Fang, *Jinshu*, 31:949.

53. Song, *Bei Wei nüzhu lun*, 47.

54. McMahon, *Women Shall Not Rule*, 121–22.

55. Wei, *Weishu*, 108C:2786–87.

56. Wang and Cao, *A Record of Buddhist Monasteries in Luo-yang*, 27.

57. Li, *Beishi*, 52:1876.

58. Song, *Bei Wei nüzhu lun*, 46–47.

59. Mathieu, *Démons et Merveilles*, 125.

60. Early medieval historiography followed Han dynasty precedent in this regard. Ban, *Hanshu*, 1:1–2; Shen, *Songshu*, 27:760–75.

61. Wei, *Weishu*, 1:2–3; Li, *Beishi*, 1:2, 1:36.

62. Liu, *Shih-shuo Hsin-yü*, 35 (2.13); Liu, *Shishuo xinyu huijiao jizhu*, 2:60; Fang, *Jinshu*, 25:773–74.

63. Wu Daoyang was her posthumous title. Her name was Yang Zhi. Lily Xiao Hong Lee, A. D. Stefanowska, and Sue Wiles, eds., *Biographical Dictionary of Chinese Women: Antiquity through Sui, 1600 B.C.E.–618 C.E.* (Hong Kong: Hong Kong University Press, 2007), 374–76; Fang, *Jinshu*, 31:955.

64. Wei, *Weishu*, 67:1493.

65. Fang, *Jinshu*, 31:950; Yao, *Liangshu*, 3:97; Shen, *Songshu*, 41:1282.

66. Fang, *Jinshu*, 31:950, 952; Li, *Nanshi*, 12:338. Shen, *Songshu*, 14:355–56, 17:482, evokes the *Zhou li* as justification. Bret Hinsch, "Textiles and Female Virtue in Early Imperial Chinese Historical Writing," *Nan Nü* 5, no. 2 (2003): 170–202.

67. Zhang Yong, "Lun Wei Jin nanbeichao dasheng fojiao dui funü jingshen fengmao de yingxiang," *Zhongguo Shehui Kexue Xueyuan Yanjiushengyuan xuebao* 1 (2008): 65–66.

68. Wei, *Weishu*, 9:225; McMahon, *Women Shall Not Rule*, 174.

69. Her surname was Hu. Wang and Cao, *A Record of Buddhist Monasteries in Luo-yang*, 261.

70. Yongning temple. Li, *Beishi*, 27:992.

71. Wang and Cao, *A Record of Buddhist Monasteries in Luo-yang*, 15, 17, 59, 157.

72. Bielenstein, "The Six Dynasties, Vol. 2," 24–28.

73. Bielenstein, "The Six Dynasties, Vol. 1," 69. For examples of female regencies, see Li, *Beishi*, 4:144; Fang, *Jinshu*, 76: 2011, 2030. Han dynasty precedent could be used to justify a female regency. Fang, *Jinshu*, 32:973.

74. Wei, *Weishu*, 9:222.

75. Bielenstein, "The Six Dynasties, Vol. 1," 78.

76. Bielenstein, "The Six Dynasties, Vol. 1," 188–89.

77. McMahon, *Women Shall Not Rule*, 142. Wei, *Weishu*, 31:745.

78. McMahon, *Women Shall Not Rule*, 147; Fang, *Jinshu*, 8:191.

79. For example, Fang, *Jinshu*, 8:199.

80. Li, *Beishi*, 55:2011.

81. Fang, *Jinshu*, 1:18; 76:2030, 77:2040; Li, *Beishi*, 4:155.

82. Wei, *Weishu*, 1:10.

83. Fang, *Jinshu*, 2:27–28.

84. Fang, *Jinshu*, 2:34; Wei, *Weishu*, 19B:482, 19B:519.

85. Li, *Beishi*, 5:175; Wei, *Weishu*, 66:1475, 93:1007.

86. Wei, *Weishu*, 9:228.

87. Fang, *Jinshu*, 4:92, 36:1072.

88. Holmgren, "Imperial Marriage in the Native Chinese and Non-Han State," 77; Bielenstein, "The Six Dynasties, Vol. 2," 25, 28.

89. Xiao, *Nan Qi shu*, 22:415.

90. Li, *Nanshi*, 47:1177.

91. For some examples, see Fang, *Jinshu*, 93:2411–15, 2417–18, 2420, 2422.

92. For a comprehensive and well-written biography of Wenming, see Kang Le, "Bei Wei Wenming taihou ji qi shidai (shang pian)" *Shihuo* 15, nos. 11/12 (1986): 461–75; Kang Le, "Bei Wei Wenming taihou ji qi shidai (xia pian)" *Shihuo* 16, nos. 1/2 (1986): 56–66. Also Holmgren, "The Lu Clan of Tai Commandary," 295; Holmgren, "The Harem in Northern Wei Politics," 85–89; Zhou Jianjiang, *Taihe shiwunian—Bei Wei zhengzhi wenhua biange yanjiu* (Guangzhou: Guangdong renmin, 2001), 198–225; Eisenberg, *Kingship in Early Medieval China*, 61–62, 71, 79, 85–88; McMahon, *Women Shall Not Rule*, 139–40; Li Ping, *Bei Wei Pingcheng shidai* (Shanghai: Shanghai guji, 2014), 198–225.

93. He was also known by his Xianbei surname as Yifu Hun.

94. Barfield, *The Perilous Frontier*, 125.

95. Holmgren, "Race and Class in Fifth Century China," 97–102.

96. Harshness: Wei, *Weishu*, 31:741; 44:994. Sexual license: Wei, *Weishu*, 93:1988–90; Li, *Beishi*, 33:1215.

97. Jennifer Holmgren, "Empress Dowager Ling of the Northern Wei and the T'o-pa Sinicization Question," *Papers on Far Eastern History* 18 (1978): 123–70; McMahon, *Women Shall Not Rule*, 143–45.

98. Hui-shu Lee, *Empresses, Art, and Agency in Song Dynasty China* (Seattle: University of Washington Press, 2010), 10–11; Zhou Yin, "Bei Wei Luoyang nüxing zhi fojiao xinyang shijie guanqie," in *Lifa yu xinyang—Zhongguo gudai nüxing yanjiu lunkao*, ed. Pu Muzhou (Hong Kong: Shangwu yinshuguan, 2013), 177–84.

99. Keith McMahon, "The Institution of Polygamy in the Chinese Imperial Palace," *The Journal of Asian Studies* 72, no. 4 (2013): 917–36; McMahon, *Women Shall Not Rule*, 11. Even an aspiring warlord would assemble a large harem to legitimize his authority. Fang, *Jinshu*, 106:2777.

100. Bielenstein, "The Six Dynasties, Vol. 2," 30, 36–37; Patricia Buckley Ebrey, "Rethinking the Imperial Harem: Why Were There So Many Palace Women?" in *Women and the Family in Chinese History*, ed. Patricia Buckley Ebrey (London: Routledge, 2003), 178; Liu, "Wei Jin Nanbeichao shidai de qie," 3.

101. Prominent family: Li, *Beishi*, 21:795; Wei, *Weishu*, 38:878, 47:1053, 56:1243, 63:1412; Fang, *Jinshu*, 31:953; Misevic, "Oligarchy or Social Mobility," 244. Foreign kingdom: Wei, *Weishu*, 60:1346; 100:2217. Beauty and talent: Fang, *Jinshu*, 39:1153, 40:1168; Li, *Beishi*, 10:376.

102. Zhang Chengzong, "Beichao gongnü kaolue," *Suzhou Daxue xuebao* 2 (2006): 107. For examples of Xianbei capturing large numbers of women, see Wei, *Weishu*, 30:723, 731.

103. People believed that an emperor who broke this rule and consorted with his father's concubines had behaved immorally. Liu, *Shih-shuo Hsin-yü*, 342 (19.4); Liu, *Shishuo xinyu huijiao jizhu*, 19:567–68.

104. Bielenstein, "The Six Dynasties, Vol. 2," 38.

105. Wei, *Weishu*, 7A:146, 7B:165; Li, *Beishi*, 3:95.

106. Birrell, *Chinese Love Poetry*, 297–98; Xu, *Jianzhu yutai xinyong*, 9:22b–23a.

107. Li, *Nanshi*, 11:330.

108. Bielenstein, "The Six Dynasties, Vol. 2," 36–37.

109. Shen, *Songshu*, 80:2057–58. For some similar examples, see Shen, *Songshu*, 72:1855–56; Fang, *Jinshu*, 38:1119; Linghu, *Zhoushu*, 13:201. Nor were all sons born to concubines. Sometimes a performer or another lesser occupant of the palace gave birth to a child of the emperor. Li, *Bei Qi shu*, 11:148.

110. Holmgren, "Imperial Marriage in the Native Chinese and Non-Han State," 72.

111. Li, *Nanshi*, 20:557; Bielenstein, "The Six Dynasties, Vol. 2," 31.

112. Scott Pearce, "Nurses, Nurslings, and New Shapes of Power in the Mid-Wei Court," *Asia Major* 22, no. 1 (2009): 287–309.

113. Jen-Der Lee, "The Epitaph of a Third-Century Wet Nurse, Xu Yi," in *Early Medieval China: A Sourcebook*, ed. Wendy Swartz, Robert Ford Campany, Yang Lu, and Jessey J. C. Choo (New York: Columbia University Press, 2014), 459.

114. Zhao, *Nianer shi zhaji*, 14:186.

115. Jen-Der Lee, "Wet Nurses in Early Imperial China," *Nan Nü* 2, no. 1 (2000): 3–4, translates a relevant epitaph.

116. Wei, *Weishu*, 58:1291.
117. Lee, "Wet Nurses in Early Imperial China," 7–8.
118. Wei, *Weishu*, 13:326.
119. Fang, *Jinshu*, 34: 1023. Favoritism toward a former wet nurse was a continuation of Han dynasty norms. Liu, *Shih-shuo Hsin-yü*, 274 (10.1); Liu, *Shishuo xinyu huijiao jizhu*, 10:469.
120. Lee, "The Epitaph of a Third-Century Wet Nurse, Xu Yi," 460.
121. Li, *Bei Wei Pingcheng shidai*, 135–85.
122. Wei, *Weishu*, 5:112, 83A:1817.
123. Lee, "The Epitaph of a Third-Century Wet Nurse, Xu Yi," 459, 461.
124. Yao, *Liangshu*, 7:155.
125. Wu Tianren, *Zhengshi daodu* (Taipei: Taiwan shangwu yinshuguan, 1990), 33; Bielenstein, "The Six Dynasties, Vol. 2," 16.
126. Olivia Milburn, "Palace Women in the Former Han Dynasty (202 BCE–CE 23): Gender and Administrative History in the Early Imperial Era," *Nan Nü* 18, no 2 (2016): 195–223, discusses the evolution of the Western Han system, which served as the basis for subsequent palace ranks. Bielenstein, "The Six Dynasties, Vol. 2," 28–30, provides a cogent overview of these titles and how they changed during the early medieval era. Li, *Nanshi*, 11:316–17, summarizes the fluctuating female titles during the Southern Dynasties and notes when each appellation originated. Also Shen, *Songshu*, 41:1269–79; Xiao, *Nan Qi shu*, 20:389; McMahon, *Women Shall Not Rule*, 145–46. For detailed information on northern palace titles, see Wei, *Weishu*, 13:321; Li, *Beishi*, 4:58–59, 10:370, 35:1317. The Qing dynasty scholar Zhao Yi (1727–1814) notes that during the Han dynasty, palace intrigues and the ambitions of particular women affected the system of palace titles. Zhao, *Nianer shi zhaji*, 4:58–59. A similar dynamic may have been in play during the early medieval era. Besides palace women, under the Northern Wei the mothers and wives of high officials could receive the titles of *jun*, *junjun*, or *furen*. Wei, *Weishu*, 42:946, 32:752, 46:1040.
127. Clothing: Fang, *Jinshu*, 25:773–74; Shen, *Songshu*, 18:505, 18:521. Vehicles: Shen, *Songshu*, 18:495–98; Xiao, *Nan Qi shu*, 17:336, 338. Seals: Shen, *Songshu*, 18:506–8; Xiao, *Nan Qi shu*, 17:342–43. Ritual: Shen, *Songshu*, 15:397–403, 15:407–8, 17:467–68, 17:470–77, 19:537.
128. Wei, *Weishu*, 108D:2805, notes that both minister and wife share the same key virtue of obedience. Lisa Raphals, *Sharing the Light: Representations of Women and Virtue in Early China* (Albany: State University of New York Press, 1998), 12; Paul Rakita Goldin, *The Culture of Sex in Ancient China* (Honolulu: University of Hawaii Press, 2002), 34–35; Xiaorong Li, *Women's Poetry of Late Imperial China* (Seattle: University of Washington Press, 2012), 48.
129. Zhang Chengzong, "Sanguo Liang Jin nanchao gongü kaolue," *Nanjing Xiaozhuang Xueyuan xuebao* 1 (2005): 23.
130. Wei, *Weishu*, 13:321–22.
131. Shen, *Songshu*, 41:1270–79; Zhang, "Sanguo Liang Jin nanchao gongü kaolue," 25–26; Zhang, "Beichao gongnü kaolue," 108–10. For representative epitaphs describing the lives of two high female palace officials, see Zhao, *Han Wei nanbeichao muzhi huibian*, 123–24.
132. Wei, *Weishu*, 35:808.

133. Li, *Beishi*, 40:1465–66.

134. Wei, *Weishu*, 31:746.

135. For an example of nuns conducting the funeral of an empress dowager, see Li, *Beishi*, 4:146.

136. Lily Xiao Hong Lee, "The Emergence of Buddhist Nuns in China and Its Social Ramifications," in *The Virtue of Yin: Studies on Chinese Women* (Canberra: Wild Peony, 1994), 63; Shi, *Biqiuni zhuan jiaozhu*, 9.

137. Tsai, *Lives of the Nuns*, 34; Shi, *Biqiuni zhuan jiaozhu*, 1:35–36.

138. Huang Zhiyan, *Gongzhu zhengzhi: Wei Jin nanbeichao zhengzhishi de xing-bie kaocha* (New Taipei: Daoxiang chubanshe, 2013), 30–47, 59–86, discusses the evolution of the titles of princesses, from the Han through the early medieval era. Pages 47–59 discuss the coming of age ceremonies and wedding ceremonies of princesses. Shen, *Songshu*, 14:341–42, and Li, *Beishi*, 59:2109, also describe the wedding ceremonies of a princess. Huang, *Gongzhu zhengzhi*, 125–203, discusses the income and wealth of princesses, including bathing benefices (*tangmuyi*) and land ownership.

139. Li, *Beishi*, 59:2109, describes a princess allowed to choose her own spouse. She married a man who was attractive and good at riding, archery, singing, dancing, and playing musical instruments.

140. Ban, *Hanshu*, 1B:78, n. 3.

141. Fang, *Jinshu*, 44:1262, 45:1285; Li, *Nanshi*, 29:776.

142. Holmgren, "Imperial Marriage in the Native Chinese and Non-Han State," 79–80; Holmgren, "Race and Class in Fifth Century China," 92. Even ambitious warlords copied this marriage strategy. Li, *Beishi*, 69:2397. Huang, *Gongzhu zhengzhi*, 208–85, discusses how emperors chose their sons-in-law. Pages 286–311 provide a long table that lists princesses and their husbands, showing the backgrounds of imperial sons-in-law. For examples of northern political marriage with foreign leaders and warlords, see Wei Shou, *Weishu*, 1:12, 44:991–92; Li, *Beishi*, 20:757, 22:820.

143. Shi Guangming, "Weishu suojian Bei Wei gongzhu hunyin guanxi yanjiu," *Minzu yanjiu* 5 (1989): 106–7; Li, *Wei Jin Sui Tang hunyin xingtai yanjiu*, 114–16.

144. For example, Wei, *Weishu*, 83A:1815, 1819, 1821; Li, *Beishi*, 20:741, 23:856, 25:912, 28:1016, 29:1047, 29:1049, 58:2085, 60:2131, 62:2209, 62:2213. Most men considered marriage to a princess an excellent opportunity. Wang, *A Record of Buddhist Monasteries in Luo-yang*, 173–75.

145. Holmgren, "Imperial Marriage in the Native Chinese and Non-Han State," 80; Shi, "Weishu suojian Bei Wei gongzhu hunyin guanxi yanjiu," 108–9.

146. Sometimes an emperor deliberately sought out in-laws who would not meddle in politics. Liu, *Shih-shuo Hsin-yü*, 424 (25.60); Liu, *Shishuo xinyu huijiao jizhu*, 25:679.

147. Fang, *Jinshu*, 98:2553–54.

148. Li, *Beishi*, 28:1016.

149. Li, *Beishi*, 32:1190.

150. Wei, *Weishu*, 47:1051. She eventually died from illness, probably smallpox, much to her husband's relief.

151. Wei, *Weishu*, 15:374.

152. Yao, *Liangshu*, 21:321.

153. Wei, *Weishu*, 37:854.

154. Li, *Beishi*, 27:983.

155. Wei, *Weishu*, 46:1036.

156. Bret Hinsch, "Evil Women and Dynastic Collapse: Tracing the Development of an Ideological Archetype," *Quarterly Journal of Chinese Studies* 1, no. 2 (2012): 62–81.

157. *Hou Hanshu* takes an extremely negative view of empresses who participated in politics. Liu, "Wei Jin yihuan shijia dui houfei zhuzheng zhi fumian pingjia," 32.

158. Wei, *Weishu*, 93:1986. Qin Shihuang suspected his mother Zhao Ji of being unchaste. Wang Shaodong, "Qin Shihuang zhenjie funüguan de xinli tanyin," *Nei Menggu Daxue xuebao* 6 (1996): 30–35. Empress Lü, wife of Han Gaozu, seized control of the government, endangering the unstable new dynasty. Hans Van Ess, "Praise and Slander: The Evocation of Empress Lü in the *Shiji* and the *Hanshu*," *Nan Nü* 8, no. 2 (2006): 221–54.

159. Wei, *Weishu*, 48:1073.

160. Fang, *Jinshu*, 32:984.

161. Liu, "Wei Jin yihuan shijia dui houfei zhuzheng zhi fumian pingjia," 30.

162. McMahon, *Women Shall Not Rule*, 143–45.

163. For example, Wei, *Weishu*, 16:405.

164. J. Michael Farmer, "On the Composition of Zhang Hua's 'Nüshi Zhen,'" *Early Medieval China* 10–11, part 1 (2004): 174. This text was written in response to the cruelty of Empress Jia Nanfeng of Jin.

165. Chen Shou, *Sanguozhi*, annotated by Pei Songzhi (Hong Kong: Zhonghua shuju, 1971), 2:80.

166. Liu, "Wei Jin yihuan shijia dui houfei zhuzheng zhi fumian pingjia," 32–33. Liu Hsieh, *The Literary Mind and the Carving of Dragons: A Study of Thought and Pattern in Chinese Literature*, trans. Vincent Yu-chung Shih (New York: Columbia University Press, 1959), 88; Liu Xie, *Wenxin diaolong* (Beijing: Zhonghua shuju, 1985), 4:22–23.

167. Birrell, *Chinese Love Poetry*, 209, 210, 233, 257; Xu, *Jianzhu yutai xinyong*, 6:16b–18a, 7:18b, 8:11b.

CHAPTER 4

1. Shao Zhengkun, "Lun beichao nüzi de jiating diwei," 65.

2. Shūzō Shiga, "Family Property and the Law of Inheritance in Traditional China," in *Chinese Family Law and Social Change in Historical and Comparative Perspective*, ed. David C. Buxbaum (Seattle: University of Washington Press, 1978), 109–10.

3. H. J. Habakkuk, "Family Structure and Economic Change in Nineteenth Century Europe," *Journal of Economic History* 15, no. 1 (1955): 1–12. For example, one official decided a case regarding inheritance by citing the ancient ritual code. Li, *Beishi*, 26:950–51.

4. Susan Carol Rogers and Sonya Salamon, "Inheritance and Social Organization among Family Farmers," *American Ethnologist* 10, no. 3 (1983): 539.

5. Lei Lei, "Wei Jin nanchao funü zai jiatingzhong de jingji diwei," *Xiangfan Xueyuan xuebao* 4 (2007): 76.

6. Lee, "Women and Marriage," 124–25.

7. Li, *Beishi*, 78:2631, describes the case of a poor man who wanted to sell part of his wife's dowry, but she refused. He resented her refusal and later divorced her.

8. Shao, "Lun beichao nüzi de jiating diwei," 65. Li, "Han Tang zhijian nüxing caichanquan shitan," 194–202, outlines the early evolution of dowry.

9. Li Zhende, "Han Tang zhijian nüxing caichanquan shitan," in *Zhongguo shi xinlun—xingbie shi fence*, ed. Li Zhende (Taipei: Zhongyang yanjiu yuan, 2009), 197–99; Lei, "Wei Jin nanchao funü zai jiatingzhong de jingji diwei," 73–74.

10. Yang, *Baopuzi waipian jiaojian*, 25:616.

11. Birrell, *Chinese Love Poetry*, 100; Xu, *Jianzhu yutai xinyong*, 2:20b.

12. Judith Brown, "Note on the Division of Labor by Sex," *American Anthropologist* 72 (1970): 1075–76.

13. Wei, *Weishu*, 92:1977; Mou, *Gentlemen's Prescriptions*, 113–14.

14. Zhang Chengzong, "Liuchao Jiangnan funü de jingji huodong," *Zhejiang Shifan Daxue xuebao* 5 (2006): 48–50; Zhang Chengzong, "Wei Jin nanbeichao funü de jiawu laodong," *Yangzhou Daxue xuebao* 2 (2009): 90–92; Lee, "Women and Marriage," 122.

15. Zhang, "Wei Jin nanbeichao funü de jiawu laodong," 94–95.

16. Lei, "Wei Jin nanchao funü zai jiatingzhong de jingji diwei," 75.

17. Wei, *Weishu*, 47:1056, 56:1255, 110:2849; Li, *Beishi*, 31:1122.

18. Richard von Glahn, *The Economic History of China: From Antiquity to the Nineteenth Century* (Cambridge: Cambridge University Press, 2016), 158, 164, 194–95.

19. Zhang, "Liuchao Jiangnan funü de jingji huodong," 46–48; Zhang, "Wei Jin nanbeichao funü de jiawu laodong," 92–94; Ma Hongliang and Zhou Haiyan, "Wei Jin nanbeichao de nügong shangyezhe," *Xueshu luntan* 11 (2006): 178.

20. Wei, *Sui shu*, 24:678, describes the early medieval land allotment system in idealized terms. During the time for silk making, women aged fifteen *sui* and over were allegedly obligated to move to a camp in the local mulberry grove to raise silkworms and produce silk.

21. Fang, *Jinshu*, 86:2226; Li, *Nanshi*, 11:329; Xiao, *Nan Qi shu*, 20:391; Ma and Zhou, "Wei Jin nanbeichao de nügong shangyezhe," 178.

22. Zhao, *Han Wei nanbeichao muzhi huibian*, 294, 340, 373. Shao, *Beichao jiating xingtai yanjiu*, 264–65.

23. Hinsch, "Textiles and Female Virtue," 170–202.

24. Xu Hui and Jiang Fuya, *Liuchao jingji shi* (Nanjing: Jiangsu guji chubanshe, 1993), 309–18; Gao Min, *Wei Jin nanbeichao jingji shi* (Shanghai: Shanghai renmin chubanshe, 1996), 845–51.

25. Fang, *Jinshu*, 31:952.

26. Li, *Nanshi*, 12:338.

27. Fang, *Jinshu*, 31:950.

28. Fang, *Jinshu*, 96:2512; Liu, *Shih-shuo Hsin-yü*, 19:581–82.

29. Liu, *Shih-shuo Hsin-yü*, 344 (19.8); Liu, *Shishuo xinyu huijiao jizhu*, 19:571.

30. Fang, *Jinshu*, 49:1377.

31. Birrell, *Chinese Love Poetry*, 179; Xu, *Jianzhu yutai xinyong*, 5:19a.

32. Birrell, *Chinese Love Poetry*, 170; Xu, *Jianzhu yutai xinyong*, 5:11a. Another woman spends her time fulling cloth while waiting for her man to return. Birrell, *Chinese Love Poetry*, 213; Xu, *Jianzhu yutai xinyong*, 7:1b. Alan L. Miller, "The Woman Who Married a Horse: Five Ways of Looking at a Chinese Folktale," *Asian Folklore Studies* 54, no. 2 (1995): 275–305, discusses a fourth-century story that creatively associates a wife unhappily separated from her husband with sericulture.

33. Birrell, *Chinese Love Poetry*, 187, 191; Xu, *Jianzhu yutai xinyong*, 6:1a, 6:4a.

34. Birrell, *Chinese Love Poetry*, 218, 224; Xu, *Jianzhu yutai xinyong*, 7:4b, 7:11a.

35. Wang Guofu, "Cong Dadiwan yi, er qi wenhua yicun kan woguo muxi shizu shehui," *Tianshui Shifan Xueyuan xuebao* 6 (2002): 35; Wang, "Rank and Power among Court Ladies at Anyang," 118; Gu Lihua, *Handai funü shenghuo qingkuang* (Beijing: Shehui kexue wenxian, 2012), 147–68, 171–89.

36. Han Guopan, *Sui Tang de juntian zhidu* (Shanghai: Shanghai renmin, 1957), 19, 25, 29, 31; Huang Yunhe, "Juntian yu beichao funü," *Xuchang Shizhuan xuebao* 13, no. 1 (1994): 27–32; Yang Lien-sheng, "Notes on the Economic History of the Chin Dynasty," in *Studies in Chinese Institutional History* (Cambridge, MA: Harvard University Press, 1961), 135–36, 139; Zhou Haiyan, "Wei Jin nanbeichao funü zai nongye zhong de diwei he zuoyong," *Xinxiang Shifan Gaodeng Zhuanke Xuexiao xuebao* 4 (2006): 117–18. Li, "Han Tang zhijian nüxing caichanquan shitan," 228–34, discusses the place of women in early medieval land grant systems. Wei, *Sui shu*, 24:678, describes the ideal early medieval land allotment system. Also Fang, *Jinshu*, 26:790; Wei, *Weishu*, 110:2853–4.

37. von Glahn, *The Economic History of China*, 173–78.

38. Li, *Beishi*, 19:708; 34:11261.

39. The declining reputation of shamanism affected attitudes toward female healers. Jen-der Lee, "Gender and Medicine in Tang China," *Asia Major* 16, no. 2 (2003): 16–17.

40. Lee, "Gender and Medicine in Tang China," 21–23.

41. Li, "Han Tang zhijian jiating zhong de jiankang zhaogu yu xingbie," 3–6, 10–16; Lee, "Gender and Medicine in Tang China," 3–6, 9–16, 24–25.

42. Lee, "Gender and Medicine in Tang China," 16–17.

43. Li Zhende, "Han Tang zhijian de nüxing yiliao zhaoguzhe," *Taida lishi xuebao* 23 (1999): 123–56.

44. Ning Xin, "Tangdai funü de shehui jingji huodong—yi 'Taiping guangji' wei zhongxin," in *Tang Song nüxing yu shehui*, ed. Deng Xiaonan (Shanghai: Shanghai cishu, 2003), 1:244–45.

45. Liu, *Shih-shuo Hsin-yü*, 350–51 (19.19); Liu, *Shishuo xinyu huijiao jizhu*,19:581–82.

46. Zhang, "Liuchao Jiangnan funü de jingji huodong," 50.

47. Ma and Zhou, "Wei Jin nanbeichao de nügong shangyezhe," 179–80.

48. Knechtges, "Estate Culture in Early Medieval China," 532.

49. Entertainers were most often called *ji*. If a concubine had talent at singing or dancing, she might be referred to as a *jiqie*. Liu, "Wei Jin Nanbeichao shidai de qie," 9; Song Dexi, "Tangdai de jinü," in *Zhongguo Funüshi lunji xuji*, ed. Bao Jialin (Taipei: Daoxiang chubanshe, 1991), 68. Xiao Guoliang, *Zhongguo changji shi* (Taipei: Wenjin chubanshe, 1996), 2–3, describes the evolution of the orthography of the characters *ji* and *chang*. Enslaved performers who entertained troops had

a status called *yinghu yueji*. This was a hereditary low caste legally classified as "base" (*jian*). Other terms for the status of enslaved entertainers were *yuehu* and *yingji*. Yan Ming, *Zhongguo mingji yishu shi* (Taipei: Wenjin, 1992), 25–26.

50. Liu, *Shih-shuo Hsin-yü*, 70 (2:86), 465 (31.1); Liu, *Shishuo xinyu huijiao jizhu*, 2:130–31, 31:738; Shen, *Songshu*, 19:547; Li, *Beishi*, 5:174; Wei, *Suishu*, 22:637.

51. Li, *Bei Qi shu*, 11:148; Li, *Beishi*, 52:1880.

52. Enslaved household performers were called *jiaji*. Shao, *Beichao jiating xingtai yanjiu*, 79–80; Wei, *Weishu*, 55:1229. Xiao, *Zhongguo changji shi*, 43–44, provides a table listing prominent people from the Six Dynasties era who kept numerous concubines or entertainers in their homes.

53. Yan, *Zhongguo mingji yishu shi*, 42.

54. Yao, *Liangshu*, 38:548; Yan, *Zhongguo mingji yishu shi*, 30–32, 35–42; Xiao, *Zhongguo changji shi*, 45–48; Zurndorfer, "Polygamy and Masculinity in China," 17.

55. Liu, "Wei Jin Nanbeichao shidai de qie," 10.

56. Li, *Beishi*, 57:2074, 61:2189.

57. Yan, *Zhongguo mingji yishu shi*, 27.

58. Yan, *Zhongguo mingji yishu shi*, 42–43.

59. Zhou Jiren, "Lun Zhongguo gudai biaoyan yishu de shangpinhua wenti," *Zhongguoshi yanjiu* 15, no. 4 (1993): 44–48.

60. Yan, *Zhongguo mingji yishu shi*, 46–51.

61. Birrell, *Chinese Love Poetry*, 232; Xu, *Jianzhu yutai xinyong*, 7:17b–18a. Struck by their beauty, religious rebels declared that these entertainers were water immortals (*shuixian*) and threw more than one hundred of them into water during a religious ritual. Fang, *Jinshu*, 100:2634.

62. Albert E. Dien, *Six Dynasties Civilization* (New Haven: Yale University Press, 2007), 343–44. Also pp. 346, 348–50.

63. An Dong-hwan, "Liuchao yuefu minge zhong de jinü zhi ge," *Shandong Jiaoyu Xueyuan xuebao* 1 (2003): 54–56.

64. Peng Jiepo, "Qin, Han, Wei, Jin shiqi de xiuwu," *Beijing Wudao Xueyuan xuebao* 2 (2009): 14–20.

65. Zheng Yongle, "Xian Qin liang Han Weijin liuchao wudao wenxue yanjiu" (PhD diss., Zhongguo Yishu Yanjiuyuan, 2004), 47–72.

66. Fang, *Jinshu*, 32:983; Zhang, *Liuchao funü*, 360–65.

67. Birrell, *Chinese Love Poetry*, 100; Xu, *Jianzhu yutai xinyong*, 2:20b.

68. Wang and Cao, *A Record of Buddhist Monasteries in Luo-yang*, 64–67.

69. Wei, *Weishu*, 57:1270, 111:1880; Li, *Beishi*, 32:1179; Wang, "Slaves and Other Comparable Social Groups," 313.

70. Li, *Beishi*, 32:1182.

71. Wei, *Weishu*, 30:723, 30:731, 35:819; Li, *Beishi*, 61:2187, 78:2644; Yao, *Liangshu*, 5:135; Linghu, *Zhoushu*, 6:104.

72. According to Wei law, kidnapping and enslaving a man or woman was punishable by death. Wei, *Weishu*, 111:2881.

73. Zhang and Chen, *Zhongguo funü tongshi*, 233–63, 266.

74. Yang, *Baopuzi waipian jiaojian*, 25:616.

75. Liu, *Shih-shuo Hsin-yü*, 259 (30.2); Liu, *Shishuo xinyu huijiao jizhu*, 30:728.

76. Li, *Beishi*, 39:1429.

77. Wang, "Slaves and Other Comparable Social Groups," 322–23.

78. Liu, *Shih-shuo Hsin-yü*, 458 (30.1); Liu, *Shishuo xinyu huijiao jizhu*, 30:727.

79. Wang, "Slaves and Other Comparable Social Groups," 359.

80. Wei, *Weishu*, 61:1369–70.

81. Wei, *Weishu*, 71:1571.

82. Wang, "Slaves and Other Comparable Social Groups," 327.

83. Li, *Beishi*, 14:524, 14:525.

84. Fang, *Jinshu*, 49:1364.

85. Wei, *Weishu*, 73:1633; Li, *Beishi*, 44:1620.

86. DeWoskin and Crump, *In Search of the Supernatural*, 94 (7.193).

87. Zheng Yanqin, "Liang Han Wei Jin nanbeichao shiqi nüxing 'wushihua' xianxiang chutan," *Nanjing Xiaozhuang Xueyuan xuebao* 4 (2010): 22–24.

88. An Ran, "Wei Jin nanbeichao wenxuezhong yongwu nüxing xingxiang tanxi," *Huaihai Gongxueyuan xuebao* 14, no. 1 (2016): 39–41.

89. Wei, *Weishu*, 92:1980.

90. Fang, *Jinshu*, 96:2511.

91. Fang, *Jinshu*, 2:34.

92. Zhou Zhaowang, "Wei Jin nanbeichao shiqi de nübing," *Jiangxi shehui kexue* 2 (1997): 63.

93. Shen, *Songshu*, 63:1675; Li, *Nanshi*, 23:625.

94. Fang, *Jinshu*, 81:2133; Li, *Beishi*, 73:2513.

95. Zhou, "Wei Jin nanbeichao shiqi de nübing," 60–61; Zhang and Chen, *Zhongguo funü tongshi*, 552–66. This was not a new custom. Sun Wenbo, "Qin Han de nüzi canzhan yu qinshu suijun," in *Lifa yu xinyang—Zhongguo gudai nüxing yanjiu lunkao*, ed. Pu Muzhou (Hong Kong: Shangwu yinshuguan, 2013), 52–74, discusses women supporting and accompanying armies during the Han dynasty.

96. Zhang Chengzong, "Wei Jin nanbeichao funü congjun kao," *Nantong Daxue xuebao* 21, no. 1 (2005): 99–100.

97. Li, *Beishi*, 79:2651, shows that rulers knew that they were violating ritual regulations by forcing women to participate in war.

98. Zhou, "Wei Jin nanbeichao shiqi de nübing," 61.

99. Zhang, "Wei Jin nanbeichao shiqi yu funü xiangguan de falü wenti ji sifa anjian," 26–27; Zhang, "Wei Jin nanbeichao funü congjun kao," 101.

100. Jorit Wintjes, "'Keep the Women Out of the Camp!': Women and Military Institutions in the Classical World," in *A Companion to Women's Military History*, ed. by Barton C. Hacker and Margaret Vining (Leiden: Brill, 2012), 25.

101. Zhang, "Wei Jin nanbeichao funü congjun kao," 99.

102. von Glahn, *The Economic History of China*, 157–58; Zhou, "Wei Jin nanbeichao funü zai nongye zhong de diwei he zuoyong," 117; Zhang, "Wei Jin nanbeichao funü congjun kao," 101, 103.

103. Fang, *Jinshu*, 42:1208.

104. Sufen Sofia Lai, "From Cross-Dressing Daughter to Lady Knight-Errant: The Origin and Evolution of Chinese Women Warriors," in *Presence and Presentation: Women in the Chinese Literati Tradition*, ed. Sherry J. Mou (New York: St. Martin's Press, 1999), 81–82; Lan Dong, *Mulan's Legend and Legacy in China and the United States* (Philadelphia: Temple University Press, 2011).

CHAPTER 5

1. Lu Ting, "Han Wei liuchao fuzhong de Nü Wa xingxiang yu wenxue muti de xingcheng," *Yuwen jiaoxue tongxun* 10 (2014): 73–75, discusses the outpouring of devotional poetry about Nü Wa. Wang Qing, "Wei Jin shiqi de Xiwangmu chuanshuo yi ji chansheng Beijing," *Nanjing Shida xuebao* 3 (1997): 118–22, describes early medieval stories about Xiwangmu. Because these narratives followed Han dynasty prototypes, they often featured Emperor Han Wudi as a major character, as he allegedly met the goddess.

2. Ma Yan, "Wei Jin nanbeichao Hannü xingxiang de shanbian guocheng gouchen," *Yunyang Shifan Gaodeng Zhuanke Xuexiao xuebao* 35, no. 1 (2015): 44–47; DeWoskin and Crump, *In Search of the Supernatural*, 16–18 (1.31).

3. Zhang Chengzong, "Wei Jin nanbeichao de zongjiao xinyang," *Nantong Daxue xuebao* 22, no. 2 (2006): 94–95; Wu Congxiang, *Handai nüxing lijiao yanjiu* (Jinan: Qilu, 2013), 223–45.

4. Jia Erqiang, *Shen jie gui yu: Tangdai minjian xinying toushi* (Xi'an: Shaanxi renmin jiaoyu, 2000), 59–61; Zhang, "Wei Jin nanbeichao de zongjiao xinyang," 94–95; Philip Clart, "Ceshen: Spirit of the Latrine," in *The Routledge Encyclopedia of Taoism, Volume I: A–L*, ed. Fabrizio Pregadio (London: Routledge, 2008), 245.

5. Wei, *Weishu*, 103:2307.

6. Wei, *Weishu*, 1:2–3.

7. Campany, "Ghosts Matter," 23–30, classifies the various types of ghosts.

8. For example, Wang and Cao, *A Record of Buddhist Monasteries in Luo-yang*, 227–29.

9. Miyakawa Hisayuki, *Rikuchōshi kenkyū: shūkyō hen* (Tokyo: Heirakudera shoten, 1964), 342–55.

10. Zhang, "Wei Jin nanbeichao de zongjiao xinyang," 91.

11. Liu Chunxiang, "Wei Jin nanbeichao shiqi de wuxi yu yinsi," *Xuchang Xueyuan xuebao* 6 (2006): 27–30; Zhang and Chen, *Zhongguo funü tongshi*, 319–22; Edward H. Schafer, "Ritual Exposure in Ancient China," *Harvard Journal of Asiatic Studies* 14, nos. 1/2 (1951): 135–36. Xiao, *Nan Qi shu*, 42:744, states that many people believed in the powers of female and male shamans. Dong Tao, "Xian Qin Qin Han shehui wuzhe de xingbie kaocha," in *Lifa yu xinyang—Zhongguo gudai nüxing yanjiu lunkao*, ed. Pu Muzhou (Hong Kong: Shangwu yinshuguan, 2013), 93–110, discusses the gender of ancient and early imperial shamans. An edict uses ancient terminology in referring to male shamans as *xi* and female shamans as *wu*. Li, *Beishi*, 61:2167.

12. Stephan N. Kory, "Presence in Variety: De-Trivializing Female Diviners in Medieval China," *Nan Nü* 18, no. 1 (2016): 3–48.

13. Jin Xia, "Wei Jin shi de shang wu zhi feng," *Xuchang Xueyuan xuebao* 6 (2003): 40–41; Liu, "Wei Jin nanbeichao shiqi de wuxi yu yinsi," 27; Zhao Rongjun, "Han Wei Jin shi de wushu tezheng kaocha," *Shilin* 4 (2011): 37.

14. Wei, *Weishu*, 108A:2735.

15. Wei, *Weishu*, 97:2140.

16. Fang, *Jinshu*, 31:956.

17. Li, *Beishi*, 3:88; Schafer, "Ritual Exposure in Ancient China," 134; Jin, "Wei Jin shi de shang wu zhi feng," 40–41; Zhao, "Han Wei Jin shi de wushu tezheng

kaocha," 35. Shamans could face other threats as well. Occasionally women were unwillingly exposed to the sun or dunked in water during shamanistic rituals. Fang, *Jinshu*, 100:2634.

18. Zhao Shichuang, *Daojiao yu nüxing* (Shanghai: Shanghai guji chubanshe, 1990), 44–53.

19. Lee, "Women and Marriage," 281.

20. Roger T. Ames, "Taoism and the Androgynous Ideal," in *Women in China: Current Directions in Historical Scholarship*, ed. Richard W. Guisso and Stanley Johannesen (Youngstown, NY: Philo Press, 1981), 43.

21. Lu Jingqing, "Xian Qin funü yu Wei Jin funü 'da' de butong tixian," *Guangxi shehui kexue* 4 (2004): 139–41.

22. For examples of female believers, see Zhang, "Wei Jin nanbeichao de zongjiao xinyang," 93.

23. Suzanne Cahill, *Transcendence and Divine Passion: The Queen Mother of the West in Medieval China* (Stanford: Stanford University Press, 1993).

24. Suzanne E. Cahill, "Sublimation in Medieval China: The Case of the Mysterious Woman of the Nine Heavens," *Journal of Chinese Religions* 20 (1992): 91, 98.

25. Edward H. Schafer, "The Jade Woman of Greatest Mystery," *History of Religions* 17, nos. 3–4 (1978): 390–91.

26. Chi-Tim Lai, "Ko Hung's Discourse of Hsien-Immortality: A Taoist Configuration of an Alternate Ideal Self-Identity," *Numen* 45, no. 2 (1998): 183–220.

27. Paul W. Kroll, "The Divine Songs of the Lady of Purple Tenuity," in *Studies in Early Medieval Chinese Literature and Cultural History in Honor of Richard B. Mather & Donald Holzman*, ed. Paul W. Kroll and David R. Knechtges (Provo, UT: T'ang Studies Society, 2003), 149–211.

28. Catherine Despeux and Livia Kohn, *Women in Daoism* (Cambridge, MA: Three Pines Press, 2003), 87–93, 111–13, 121–22.

29. Daoist nuns were originally called *nüguan* 女官 (literally "female officials"). During the Tang eras they gradually switched to the homophonous appellation 女冠 to distinguish them from female officials in the palace. Livia Kohn, *Monastic Life in Medieval Daoism: A Cross Cultural Perspective* (Honolulu: University of Hawaii Press, 2003), 81. Female clerics were also called *nüshi* ("female masters")

30. Catherine Despeux, "Women in Taoism," in *The Routledge Encyclopedia of Taoism, Volume I: A–L*, ed. Fabrizio Pregadio (London: Routledge, 2008), 171–13.

31. Despeux, "Women in Taoism," 387–18.

32. Although Daoist texts discuss sexual techniques for cultivation, Daoists approached these methods with caution and never emphasized them as the primary means for achieving transcendence. Russell Kirkland, "Fangzhong Shu: 'Arts of the Bedchamber'; Sexual Techniques," in *The Routledge Encyclopedia of Taoism, Volume I: A–L*, ed. Fabrizio Pregadio (London: Routledge, 2008), 409–11.

33. Lee, *Empresses, Art, and Agency in Song Dynasty China*, 10–11. She paid for one temple by reducing official salaries. Li, *Beishi*, 27:992. For another example, see Wang and Cao, *A Record of Buddhist Monasteries in Luo-yang*, 157.

34. Wang and Cao, *A Record of Buddhist Monasteries in Luo-yang*, 171.

35. For example, the Yaoguang Nunnery in Luoyang. Wang and Cao, *A Record of Buddhist Monasteries in Luo-yang*, 59, 63.

36. Wei, *Weishu*, 77:1703; Li, *Beishi*, 4:146.

37. Stephanie Balkwill, "When Renunciation Is Good Politics: The Women of the Imperial Nunnery of the Northern Wei," *Nan Nü* 18, no. 2 (2016): 232–33, 239, 243.

38. Zhang, "Zhonggu fojiao jielü yu jiating lunli," 55–56.

39. Nancy Schuster, "Striking a Balance: Women and Images of Women in Early Chinese Buddhism," in *Women, Religion, and Social Change*, ed. Yvonne Yazbeck Haddad and Ellison Banks Findly (Albany: State University of New York Press, 1985), 89–91; Zhang, "Lun Wei Jin nanbeichao dasheng fojiao dui funü jingshen fengmao de yingxiang," 64–66.

40. Schuster, "Striking a Balance," 95.

41. For example, the nun Zhu Daoxing was adept at secular Pure Conversation (*qingtan*) as well as being an expert in the *Prajñāpāramitā* scriptures. Shi, *Biqiuni zhuan jiaozhu*, 1:25–27; Tsai, *Lives of the Nuns*, 29. Buddhism also absorbed Daoist ideas about the importance of diet, and many medieval nuns were strict vegetarians. Tsai, *Lives of the Nuns*, 19.

42. Kenneth Ch'en, "Anti-Buddhist Propaganda during the Nan-Ch'ao," *Harvard Journal of Asiatic Studies* 15, nos. 1/2 (1952): 187.

43. Chen, "Wei Jin nanbeichao shiqi rufo de xiaodao zhi zheng," 23–27.

44. Bret Hinsch, "Confucian Filial Piety and the Construction of the Ideal Chinese Buddhist Woman," *Journal of Chinese Religions* 30 (2003): 49–76.

45. Van Norden, *Mengzi*, 98, 101.

46. Zhao, *Han Wei nanbeichao muzhi huibian*, 146–47.

47. Before Tanbei (324–396) became a nun, she lived with her widowed mother whom she served so well that her relatives commended her filial piety. Shi, *Biqiuni zhuan jiaozhu*, 1:18–20; Tsai, *Lives of the Nuns*, 26.

48. Shi, *Biqiuni zhuan jiaozhu*, 1:12–14; Tsai, *Lives of the Nuns*, 23.

49. Most famously, a man named Mulian used Buddhist practice to rescues his deceased mother from hell. Grant and Idema, *Escape from Blood Pond Hell*; Campany, "Ghosts Matter," 19.

50. Shi, *Biqiuni zhuan jiaozhu*, 1:7–10; Tsai, *Lives of the Nuns*, 20; Arthur F. Wright, "Biography of the Nun An-Ling-Shou," *Harvard Journal of Asiatic Studies* 15, nos.1/2 (1952): 193–96.

51. Li Yuzhen, *Tangdai de biqiuni* (Taipei: Xuesheng shuju, 1989), 39; Jiao Jie, "Fojiao xinyang yu Tangdai nüxing shenghuo xingtai zaitan—yi Tangdai muzhi ziliao wei zhongxin," *Tangshi luncong* 20 (2015): 219–21.

52. Tang Jia and Song Xiaoqing, "Beichao beike suojian nüxing Mile, Guanyin xinyang tanxi," *Guizhou shehui kexue* 12 (2012): 83–84.

53. Wang and Cao, *A Record of Buddhist Monasteries in Luo-yang*, 123.

54. Zhao, *Han Wei nanbeichao muzhi huibian*, 319.

55. Wang and Cao, *A Record of Buddhist Monasteries in Luo-yang*, 64–67.

56. Campany, *Signs from the Unseen Realm*, xiii.

57. Wei, *Weishu*, 71:1571.

58. Lingley, "Lady Yuchi in the First Person," 26, 30–31, 39–41.

59. Lin Yanzhi, "Tang wudai shiqi Dunhuang diqu de nüren jieshe," *Zhongguo wenhua yuekan* 6 (2000): 32–50; Hao Chunwen, "Zai lun beichao zhi Sui Tang wudai Songchu de nüren jieshe," *Dunhuang yanjiu* 6 (2006): 104–5.

60. Kate A. Lingley, "Naturalizing the Exotic: On the Changing Meanings of Ethnic Dress in Medieval China," *Ars Orientalis* 38 (2010): 66.

61. As this book was compiled in the south during the era of division, it focuses mostly on southern women. Shi, *Biqiuni zhuan jiaozhu*, 2–7, gives a detailed textual history for *Biqiuni zhuan*. Li, *Tangdai de biqiuni*, 10–38, has a long table that summarizes key information about each biography in the work. Liu Yao, *Wei Jin nanbeichao shijia zhuanji yanjiu—Shi Baochang yu Biqiuni zhuan* (Changsha: Yuelu shushe, 2009), 123–69, discusses the sources for the contents of these biographies. Little is known about Baochang. For his biography see Yao, *Wei Jin nanbeichao shijia zhuanji yanjiu*, 10–72. Although this collection has long been attributed to Baochang, Tom de Rauw, "Baochang: Sixth-Century Biographer of Buddhist Monks . . . and Nuns?" *Journal of the American Oriental Society* 125, no. 2 (2005): 203–18, convincingly argues that he did not write *Biqiuni zhuan*. Also see Suzuki Keizō, "Shaku Hōshō Bikuniden ni kansuru gigi," *Shikan* 89 (1973): 48–59; John Kieschnick, "Biqiuni zhuan," in *Early Medieval Chinese Texts: A Bibliographical Guide*, ed. Cynthia L. Chennault et al. (Berkeley: Institute of East Asian Studies, University of California, 2015), 28–31. This book was probably written by someone else, initially had very limited circulation, and was later erroneously attributed to Baochang because he was the most famous hagiographer of that era. *Biqiuni zhuan* was not unique. Other books about nuns were written in the early medieval era but have not been transmitted down to the present. Zhang Chengzong, "Dong Jin nanchao nigu shiji kao," *Nanjing Ligong Daxue xuebao* 2 (2011): 99.

62. Kathryn A. Tsai, "The Chinese Buddhist Monastic Order for Women: The First Two Centuries," in *Women in China: Current Directions in Historical Scholarship*, ed. Richard W. Guisso and Stanley Johannesen (Youngstown, NY: Philo Press, 1981), 5–6, 8. Ann Heirman, "Chinese Nuns and their Ordination in Fifth Century China," *Journal of the International Association of Buddhist Studies* 24, no. 2 (2001): 275–304, discusses the earliest ordination methods for women and the translation of *vinaya* texts for nuns.

63. Shi, *Biqiuni zhuan jiaozhu*, 1:1–6; Tsai, *Lives of the Nuns*, 18–19; Zhao Rongxiang, *Zhongguo diyi biqiuni Jingjian zhuan* (Beijing: Zongjiao wenhua chubanshe, 2008).

64. For a discussion of the daily life of nuns, including their clothing, food, dwellings, and daily activities, see Cai Hongsheng, *Nigu tan* (Guangzhou: Zhongshan Daxue chubanshe, 1996). Gao Erwang, "Beichao zangli zhi 'nili' tanxi," *Ningxia shehui kexue* 3 (2008): 98–101, describes the funerals of nuns during the northern dynasties. Rites for nuns were similar to those for commoners, but they tended to be buried in different places from laypeople.

65. Tsai, *Lives of the Nuns*, 6–7.

66. Li, *Tangdai de biqiuni*, 39. On pp. 49–73, Li analyzes various cases of gentry women who became nuns. Miyakawa, *Rikuchōshi kenkyū*, 327–330, discusses northern empresses who became nuns.

67. Tsai, *Lives of the Nuns*, 6–7; Tsai, "The Chinese Buddhist Monastic Order for Women," 9; Shi, *Biqiuni zhuan jiaozhu*, 8–9; Qiu Shaoping and Zhang Yanxia, "Cong Biqiuni zhuan kan Dong Jin zhi nanchao shiqi funü chujia de yuanyin," *Hunan Chengshi Xueyuan xuebao* 30, no. 3 (2009): 30–31. Song Rentao, "Qianyi Wei Jin nanbeichao shiqi nüxing chujia de xianxiang," *Jiangnan Shehui Xueyuan xuebao* 4, no. 3 (2002): 54, discusses the phenomenon of women becoming nuns to escape taxation.

68. *Biqiuni zhuan* only covers the period up to the year 516. After that, Buddhist miracle tales constitute major source material for the lives of nuns. Although these narratives focus on miracles, they depict nuns engaging in a wide range of ordinary religious activities as well. Valentina Georgieva, "Representation of Buddhist Nuns in Chinese Edifying Miracle Tales during the Six Dynasties and the Tang," *Journal of Chinese Religions* 24 (1996): 47–96.

69. Campany, *Signs from the Unseen Realm*, 104–6, 224.

70. Campany, *Signs from the Unseen Realm*, 127.

71. Tsai, *Lives of the Nuns*, 9–10.

72. Zhao Jibin, "Fahua jing yu liuchao zhi biqiuni guanxi luekao," *Zhonghua wenhua luntan* 2 (2014): 126–30.

73. Georgieva, "Representation of Buddhist Nuns," 55–57; Liu Yao, "Biqiuni zhuan zhong biqiuni chanxiu zhuangkuang luelun," *Huanggang Zhiye Jishu Xueyuan xuebao* 5 (2010): 73–75; Zhou Yuru, "Liuchao Jiangnan biqiuni chanxiu kaolun," *Renwen zazhi* 12 (2014): 14–20.

74. During the W. Wei dynasty (535–557), male and female escapees were tattooed to identify and shame them. Also Brian E. McKnight, *Law and Order in Sung China* (Cambridge: Cambridge University Press, 1992), 349, 387–88. James A. Benn, *Burning for the Buddha: Self-Immolation in Chinese Buddhism* (Honolulu: A Kuroda Institute Book, University of Hawaii Press, 2007), 22, 42–44, describes the spiritual dimensions of Buddhist self-mutilation and suicide.

75. Zhao, "Fahua jing yu liuchao zhi biqiuni guanxi luekao," 127.

76. Tsai, "The Chinese Buddhist Monastic Order for Women," 12–13; Tsai, *Lives of the Nuns*, 7.

77. Spade, "The Education of Women," 21.

78. Li, *Beishi*, 40:1465–66.

79. Tsai, *Lives of the Nuns*, 10–11.

80. Spade, "The Education of Women," 22.

81. Tsai, *Lives of the Nuns*, 33–34; Shi, *Biqiuni zhuan jiaozhu*, 1:35–36.

82. Li, *Tangdai de biqiuni*, 91.

83. Xie Chongguang and Bai Wengu, *Zhongguo sengguan zhidu shi* (Xining: Qinghai renmin chubanshe, 1990), 28–32.

84. Tsai, *Lives of the Nuns*, 34; Shi, *Biqiuni zhuan jiaozhu*, 1:35–36; Zhou Yuru, "Liuchao Jiankang biqiuni canzheng xianxiang tanxi," *Shandong Nüzi Xueyuan xuebao* 6, no. 94 (2010): 47–51.

CHAPTER 6

1. Dorothy Ko, "Pursuing Talent and Virtue: Education and Women's Culture in Seventeenth and Eighteenth Century China," *Late Imperial China* 13, no. 1 (1992): 9.

2. Mou, *Gentlemen's Prescriptions*, 66.

3. Wang Chaoxia, "Rujia suzao de nüxing lixiang renge dui Wei Jin shinü hua de yingxiang," *Beifang meishu* 1 (2013): 60–61.

4. Li, *Nanshi*, 29:773; Li, *Beishi*, 26:948, 28:1018, 33:1222; Fang, *Jinshu*, 31:948, 31:952, 32:975; Wei, *Weishu*, 92:1978; Xiao, *Nan Qi shu*, 34:611.

5. Huang Ying, "*Jinshu—Lienüzhuan* zhong de nüxing," *Sichuan Daxue xuebao* 19 (2004): 19; Liu Shuli, *Xian Qin Han Wei Jin funüguan yu wenxuezhong de nüxing* (Beijing: Xueyuan, 2008), 300–330; Xing Peishun, "'Wei Jin fengliu' xia de liang Jin funü—yi Jinshu *Lienüzhuan* wei zhuyao lizheng," *Changji Xueyuan xuebao* 4 (2011): 21–25.

6. Jennifer Holmgren, "Widow Chastity in the Northern Dynasties: The Lieh-nu Biographies in the Wei-shu," *Papers on Far Eastern History* 23 (1981): 176–77.

7. Lu Jingqing, "Tantan Wei Jin shangceng funü de 'da,'" *Zhaoqing Xueyuan xuebao* 25, no. 4 (2004): 35–37.

8. Jiao Jie, "*Lienü zhuan* yu Zhou Qin Han Tang fude biaozhun," *Shaanxi Shifan Daxue xuebao* 32, no. 6 (2003): 94–96; Yang Shupeng, "*Shishuo xinyu—Xianyuan* xuanlu tese tanxi," *Taiyuan Shifan Xueyuan xuebao* 5, no. 1 (2006): 97.

9. Zhao, *Liu chao shehui wenhua xintai*, 58–59.

10. Raphals, *Sharing the Light*, 250–52.

11. Yamazaki Junichi, "Chō Ka Jōshi shin o megutte—Go Kan kōki Gi Shin aida kōkyū jōsei kunkō," *Chūgoku koten kenkyū* 29 (1984): 20, 37; Farmer, "On the Composition of Zhang Hua's 'Nüshi Zhen,'" 151–54.This book inspired Gu Kaizhi's famous painting of female paragons.

12. Zhang, *Liuchao funü*, 353–60; Shao, *Beichao jiating xingtai yanjiu*, 266.

13. Lee, "Women and Marriage," 119–21.

14. Chen Liping, "Lienü tu de liuxing yu Han Wei liuchao nüxing de jiaohua," *Jinyang xuekan* 2 (2010): 114–16. A woman's epitaph describes the study of paintings as a respected mode of learning. Zhao, *Han Wei nanbeichao muzhi huibian*, 156.

15. Audrey Spiro, "Of Noble Ladies and Notable Conventions: The Search for Gu Kaizhi," in *Studies in Early Medieval Chinese Literature and Cultural History in Honor of Richard B. Mather & Donald Holzman*, ed. Paul W. Kroll and David R. Knechtges (Provo, UT: T'ang Studies Society, 2003), 213–57, discusses the authenticity of these paintings. Also Wen-chien Cheng, "The Pictorial Portrayal of Women and Didactic Messages in the Han and Six Dynasties," *Nan Nü* 19 (2017): 155–212.

16. Wu Can, "Fuzhi: dui liuchao lienü ticai huihua de yizhong jiedu," *Chuangzuo yu pinglun* 10 (2014): 109. A chart on p. 108 records what is known about these thirty-three paintings. Also Goodman, *Xun Xu*, 125, n. 9.

17. Zhao, *Han Wei nanbeichao muzhi huibian*, 55.

18. Zhao, *Han Wei nanbeichao muzhi huibian*, 52, 71, 73, 120, 251. Fang, *Jinshu*, 96:2521–22. In this era, the terms *li* (rites) and *jiao* (teaching) came together to form a compound term that emphasized the importance of the ritual canon as an intellectual discipline. Wu, *Handai nüxing lijiao yanjiu*, 3–4. Patricia Ebrey, "Education Through Ritual: Efforts to Formulate Family Rituals During the Sung Period," in *Neo-Confucian Education: The Formative Stage*, ed. William Theodore de Bary and John Chaffee (Berkeley: University of California Press, 1989), 277, distinguishes between molding and schooling, seeing the teaching of ritual as central to molding children's behavior.

19. Zhao, *Han Wei nanbeichao muzhi huibian*, 124, 382. Wei, *Weishu*, 62:1399; Li, *Nanshi*, 12:338.

20. Wei, *Weishu*, 31:746; Yao, *Chenshu*, 7:126. Female education in classical poetry continued Han dynasty norms for female learning. In the household of

the Eastern Han classicist Zheng Xuan (127–200), even female slaves could quote *Shijing*. Liu, *Shih-shuo Hsin-yü*, 94 (3.3).

21. Birrell, *Chinese Love Poetry*, 29, 33; Xu, *Jianzhu yutai xinyong*, introduction, 2A–B.

22. Liu, *Shih-shuo Hsin-yü*, 487 (35.5); Liu, *Shishuo xinyu huijiao jizhu*, 35:766–67.

23. Zhao, *Han Wei nanbeichao muzhi huibian*, 180, 215. Zhuang Shuai (475–527) edited an encyclopedia in 100 fascicles consisting of references to female matters, created by imperial mandate for consultation by ladies in the inner palace. Xiaofei Tian, *Beacon Fire and Shooting Star: The Literary Culture of the Liang (502–557)* (Cambridge, MA: Harvard University Asia Center, 2007), 109, 191.

24. For example, a prolific Liang dynasty writer named Xu Mian (465–535) wrote a book called *Women's Collection (Furen ji)* in ten fascicles, which has been mostly lost. Chen Xiangqian, "Nanchao *Furen ji* luekao," *Hubei Gongye Daxue xuebao* 17, no. 1 (2012): 126–30, discusses the textual history and contents of this work. Du Yu wrote a book called *Nüren zan*, which has since been lost. Fang, *Jinshu*, 34:1031–32. Shimomi, *Juka shakai to bosei*, 96, lists the names of books about women during the early medieval era. Yamazaki, "Chō Ka Jōshi shin o megutte," 19, lists some early medieval books about women discussed in his article. On pp. 39–42 he provides a chart of thirty-one books that deal with female matters, written during the Eastern Han and early medieval era, giving bibliographic information for each book.

25. Fang, *Jinshu*, 51:1408–19, relates Huangfu Mi's biography. Xu Chuanwu, "Huangfu Mi zunian xinkao," *Zhongguo wenzhe yanjiu jikan* 10 (1997): 91–104, investigates the date of Huangfu's death. Scholars traditionally accept 282 as his date of death, but Xu argues that Huangfu might have died in 293. In addition to his collection of narratives about women, Huangfu compiled four other biographical collections as well, so he was deeply interested in the genre.

26. Wei, *Suishu*, 33:978; Liu Xu et al., *Jiu Tang shu*, annotated by Liu Jie and Chen Naiqian (Beijing: Zhonghua shuju, 1975), 46:2006; Ouyang Xiu and Song Qi, *Xin Tang shu*, annotated by Dong Jiazun et al. (Beijing: Zhonghua shuju, 1975), 58:1486. For descriptions of the work, see Yong Rong, *Siku quanshu zongmu tiyao* (Shanghai: Shangwu, 1933), 57:1265; Xiong Ming, "Luelun Huangfu Mi zazhuan de xiaoshuo pinge," *Jinzhou Shifan Xueyuan xuebao* 24, no. 2 (2002): 26–29.

27. Chen, *Sanguo zhi*, 9:293, n. 1; 25:702–3, n. 1. The narrative in Chen, *Sanguo zhi*, 18:548–50, n. 1, also appears in Liu Zhen, *Dongguan Hanji xiaozhu*, annotated by Wu Shuping (Zhengzhou: Zhongzhou Guji, 1987), 18:836, n. 4. Brief phrases of this narrative are preserved in Fan, *Hou Hanshu*, 23:3544, and Shen, *Songshu*, 29:875, n. 11, and Ouyang Xun, *Yiwen leiju* (Taipei: Wenguang, 1974), 18:335–37. Different versions of some of these narratives appear in Chang Qu, *Huayang guozhi jiaobu tuzhu*, annotated by Ren Naiqiang (Shanghai: Guji, 1987), 3:550–51, 8:592–93, and Li Fang et al., *Taiping yulan* (Taipei: Taiwan Shangwu, Sibu congkan ed., n.d.), 181:1010, 367:1819, 440:2155–56, 440:2159, 441:2159, 482:2336. Different versions of some of these narratives appear in Liu Xiang, *Lienü zhuan* (Taipei: Taiwan Zhonghua shuju, Sibu beiyao ed., 1981) 5:112–14; Albert Richard O'Hara, *The Position of Woman in Early China: According to the Lieh Nü Chuan "The Biographies of Chinese Women"* (Taipei: Mei Ya, 1971), 150–52; Fan, *Hou Hanshu*, 84:2795; Li, *Taiping yulan*, 441:2158–52. A phrase summing up the story, attributed to Huangfu Mi,

appears in Yan Kejun, ed., *Quan shanggu sandai Qin Han sanguo liuchao wen* (Beijing: Zhonghua Shuju, 1958), 1064–61. This narrative appears in a rewritten form in Sima Guang, *Zizhi tongjian* (Shanghai: Guji, 1956), 66:2122 –3, which includes some useful explanatory notes. Anonymous, *Wuchao xiaoshuo daguan* (Shanghai: Saoye shanfang, 1926), 4:120a–b. Other versions of some of these narratives appear in Liu, *Lienü zhuan*, 1:1, 1:6, 1:19–23, 2:42–43, 4:81, 6:116–18; O'Hara, *Position of Woman in Early China*, 13–17, 21–22, 39–42, 66–68, 113–15, 155–57; Ouyang, *Yiwen leiju*, 35:635; Lai Yanyuan, annotator, *Hanshi waizhuan* (Taipei: Taiwan Shangwu, 1991), 2:40, 9:365; James Robert Hightower, *Han Shih Wai Chuan: Han Ying's Illustrations of the Didactic Application of the Classic of Songs* (Cambridge: Harvard University Press, 1952), 39–40, 290.

28. Mou, *Gentlemen's Prescriptions*, 13–14.

29. Yen, *Family Instructions for the Yen Clan*, xi.

30. Yen, *Family Instructions for the Yen Clan*, xiv–xxv, gives a biography of Yan Zhitui. Also Albert E. Dien, "Yanshi jiaxun," in *Early Medieval Chinese Texts: A Bibliographical Guide*, ed. Cynthia L. Chennault et al. (Berkeley: Institute of East Asian Studies, University of California, 2015), 436–41.

31. Lewis, "Writing the World in the Family Instructions of the Yan Clan," 38–42.

32. Raphals, *Sharing the Light*, 250–52.

33. Yen, *Family Instructions for the Yen Clan*, 108.

34. Yen, *Family Instructions for the Yen Clan*, 9–10.

35. Yen, *Family Instructions for the Yen Clan*, 12. For example, Liu, *Shih-shuo Hsin-yü*, 450 (28.1); Liu, *Shishuo xinyu huijiao jizhu*, 28:717.

36. Shao, *Beichao jiating xingtai yanjiu*, 70–71.

37. Wu Zhenglan, *Liuchao Jiangdong shizu de jiaxue menfeng* (Nanjing: Nanjing Daxue chubanshe, 2003), documents the high educational standards of aristocratic families in the Jiangdong region in great detail.

38. Ping Wang, "The Art of Poetry Writing: Liu Xiaochuo's 'Becoming the Number-One Person for the Number-One Position," in *Early Medieval China: A Sourcebook*, ed. Wendy Swartz, Robert Ford Campany, Yang Lu, and Jessey J. C. Choo (New York: Columbia University Press, 2014), 248.

39. Holcombe, "The Exemplar State," 96–106.

40. Liu, *Shih-shuo Hsin-yü*, 64 (2.71); Liu, *Shishuo xinyu huijiao jizhu*, 2:119.

41. Zhang, *Liuchao funü*, 368–72.

42. Wang Lianru, *Han Wei liuchao Langya Wangshi jiazu zhengzhi yu hunyin wenhua yanjiu* (Beijing: Zhongguo shehui kexue, 2013), 175–220.

43. Zhao Jing, "Wei Jin nanbeichao Langya Wang shi jiating wenhua yu wenxue yanjiu" (PhD diss., Shandong Shifan daxue, 2011), 103–12; Wang, *Han Wei liuchao Langya Wangshi jiazu*, 253–98.

44. Yang Xiaoping, "Shijia nüzi duo fengliu—Wei Jin nanbeichao shufa shijiazhong de nüxing shujia guankui," *Shufa* 3 (2014): 34–36.

45. Zhuang Xinxia, "Han Wei liuchao nüxing zhushu kaolun" (PhD diss., Shandong Daxue, 2007), 58–127, introduces female authors of the early medieval era, giving basic information about each known woman writer from the period.

46. Fang, *Jinshu*, 96:2516–17. Also 96:2510.

47. Liu, *Shih-shuo Hsin-yü*, 349 (19.16); Liu, *Shishuo xinyu huijiao jizhu*, 19:578.

48. Tian, *Beacon Fire and Shooting Star*, 109. In addition to *Yutai xinyong*, a lost collection entitled *Zawen* was also written for a female readership. Yin Chun (403–434) compiled *Furen ji* in thirty fascicles. Xu Mian (466–535), a Liang dynasty official, compiled a comparable collection of women's poetry in ten fascicles.

49. McMahon, *Women Shall Not Rule*, 120–21.

50. Lee, *Empresses, Art, and Agency in Song Dynasty China*, 4–6; Wang Chi-chen, "A Gift of a Chinese Painting," *Metropolitan Museum of Art Bulletin* 29, no. 3 (1934): 44–46.

51. Zhao Minli, "Reflections on the Proposition that 'Literary Consciousness Arose in the Wei and Jin Dynasties,'" *Social Sciences in China* 26, no. 2 (2005): 74–79.

52. Shu Hongxia and Yang Dongxia, "Wei Jin renxing zijue dui Songdai nüzuo-jia de yingxiang," *Dalian Daxue xuebao* 1 (2006): 30–33.

53. Fang, *Jinshu*, 40:1172; Liu, *Shih-shuo Hsin-yü*, 349 (19:14); Liu, *Shishuo xinyu huijiao jizhu*, 19:577.

54. Antje Richter, *Letters & Epistolary Culture in Early Medieval China* (Seattle: University of Washington Press, 2013), 140.

55. Lee, "Women and Marriage," 128.

56. Constance Cook, "Education and the Way of the Former Kings," in *Writing & Literacy in Early China: Studies from the Columbia Early China Seminar*, ed. Li Feng and David Prager Branner (Seattle: University of Washington Press, 2011), 334. During the Western Han, learning shifted away from performance to become primarily textual. See p. 307.

57. Lisa Raphals, "Arguments by Women in Early Chinese Texts," *Nan Nü* 3, no. 2 (2001): 157–95; Yiqun Zhou, "Virtue and Talent: Women and *Fushi* in Early China," *Nan Nü* 5, no. 1 (2003): 1–3.

58. Cook, "Education and the Way of the Former Kings," 307.

59. Robert Ashmore, "The Art of Discourse: Xi Kang's 'Sound Is without Sadness or Joy," in *Early Medieval China: A Sourcebook*, ed. Wendy Swartz, Robert Ford Campany, Yang Lu, and Jessey J. C. Choo (New York: Columbia University Press, 2014), 202.

60. Liu, *Shih-shuo Hsin-yü*, 354 (19.24), 355 (19.27); Liu, *Shishuo xinyu huijiao jizhu*, 19:586, 588.

61. Tsai, *Lives of the Nuns*, 17. Shi, *Biqiuni zhuan jiaozhu*, 1:1.

62. Li, *Beishi*, 40:1465–66.

63. Li, *Nanshi*, 12:348.

64. Hinsch, "Textiles and Female Virtue," 170–202.

65. Fang, *Jinshu*, 31:950.

66. Liu, *Shih-shuo Hsin-yü*, 344 (19.8); Liu, *Shishuo xinyu huijiao jizhu*, 19:571.

67. Liu, *Shih-shuo Hsin-yü*, 347 (19.12); Liu, *Shishuo xinyu huijiao jizhu*, 19:575.

68. Xiao, *Nan Qi shu*, 20:390.

69. Dell R. Hales, "Dreams and the Daemonic in Traditional Chinese Short Stories," in *Critical Essays on Chinese Literature*, ed. William H. Nienhauser et al. (Hong Kong: The Chinese University of Hong Kong, 1976), 71–87.

70. For example, DeWoskin and Crump, *In Search of the Supernatural*, 118 (10.251), 120–21 (10.258). Mathieu, *Démons et Merveilles*, 87–99.

71. Fang, *Jinshu*, 102:2657, 113:2883, 121:3035, 127:3161; Li, *Bei Qi shu*, 9:124, 15:193.

72. Wei, *Weishu*, 92:1978; Li, *Beishi*, 15:564; Li, *Nanshi*, 30:793; Wang and Cao, *A Record of Buddhist Monasteries in Luo-yang*, 231.

73. Spade, "The Education of Women," 19–20.

74. Holmgren, "The Making of an Elite," 64.

75. Holmgren, "Widow Chastity in the Northern Dynasties," 174.

76. Fang, *Jinshu*, 96:2509.

77. Lin Suzhen, *Wei Jin Nanbeichao jiaxun zhi yanjiu* (Hua Mulan wenhua chubanshe, 2008), 76–79; Wang Yongping, "Wei Jin nanchao shizu shehui zhi nüjiao yu 'mujiao'—cong yige cemian kan zhonggu shizu wenhua zhi chuancheng," *Hebei xuekan* 36, no. 2 (2016): 60–62.

78. Wei, *Weishu*, 43:978, 92:1980; Li, *Beishi*, 39:1423.

79. Liu, *Shih-shuo Hsin-yü*, 350–51 (19.19); Liu, *Shishuo xinyu huijiao jizhu*, 19:581–82.

80. Liu, *Shih-shuo Hsin-yü*, 344 (19.8); Liu, *Shishuo xinyu huijiao jizhu*, 19:571.

81. Liu, *Shih-shuo Hsin-yü*, 344–45; Liu, *Shishuo xinyu huijiao jizhu*, 19:573.

82. Raphals, *Sharing the Light*, 246–49; Mou, *Gentlemen's Prescriptions*, 116.

83. Fang, *Jinshu*, 122:3068.

84. Liu, *Shih-shuo Hsin-yü*, 343–44 (19.7); Liu, *Shishuo xinyu huijiao jizhu*, 19:570–71.

85. Fang, *Jinshu*, 96:2508.

86. Liu, *Shih-shuo Hsin-yü*, 349–50 (19.17); Liu, *Shishuo xinyu huijiao jizhu*, 19:578.

87. Nanxiu Qian, "Women's Roles in Wei-Chin Character Appraisal as Reflected in the Shih-shuo hsin-yü," in *Studies in Medieval Chinese Literature and Cultural History: In Honor of Richard B. Mather and Donald Holzman*, ed. Paul W. Kroll and David R. Knechtges (Provo, UT: T'ang Studies Society, 2003), 259–61.

88. Paul F. Rouzer, *Articulated Ladies: Gender and the Male Community in Early Chinese Texts* (Cambridge: Harvard University Press, 2001), 99–100.

89. Ōhashi Yoshiharu, "Seisetsu shingo to Shindai bunka—setsuwa ni miru jinbutsu hyōka no jitsusō," *Daitō Bunka Daigaku kangaku kaishi* 45 (2006): 75–82.

90. Qian, "Women's Roles in Wei-Chin Character Appraisal," 276–77, 286–88.

91. Hou Weidong, "Wei Jin qingtan zhi feng dui nüxing de yingxiang," *Ningxia Daxue xuebao* 5 (2005): 66–69.

92. Liu, *Shih-shuo Hsin-yü*, 346–47 (19.11); Liu, *Shishuo xinyu huijiao jizhu*, 19:574.

93. Xing, "'Wei Jin fengliu' xia de liang Jin funü," 21–25.

94. Lu Rong, "Wei Jin nanbeichao funü de wenxue piping," *Suzhou Daxue xuebao* 2 (2008): 70–74.

CHAPTER 7

1. Li, *Beishi*, 44:1620.

2. Yang, *Baopuzi waipian jiaojian*, vol. 1, 25:614–16.

3. Li, *Beishi*, 29:1056; Wang and Cao, *A Record of Buddhist Monasteries in Luo-yang*, 91, 123.

4. Liu, *Shih-shuo Hsin-yü*, 374 (23.7); Liu, *Shishuo xinyu huijiao jizhu*, 23:612.

5. Liu, *Shih-shuo Hsin-yü*, 374 (23.8); Liu, *Shishuo xinyu huijiao jizhu*, 23:612.

6. Liu, *Shih-shuo Hsin-yü*, 487 (35.5); Liu, *Shishuo xinyu huijiao jizhu*, 35:766–67.

7. For example, Xiao, *Nan Qi shu*, 20:393. Xie Baofu, "Beichao Wei, Qi, Zhou zongshi nüxing de tonghun guanxi yanjiu," *Guangxi Shifan Daxue xuebao* 1 (1998): 78–83.

8. Zhuang Huafeng, "Beichao shidai Xianbei funü de shenghuo fengqi," *Minzu yanjiu* 6 (1994): 62–64.

9. Wei, *Weishu*, 19A:443; Li, *Beishi*, 18:673–74.

10. Wang, "Beichao funü hunyin shulun," 10.

11. Birrell, *Chinese Love Poetry*, 132–34; Xu, *Jianzhu yutai xinyong*, 4:2a–4a, is a long poem relating the story of Qiu Hu. Birrell, *Chinese Love Poetry*, 221; Xu, *Jianzhu yutai xinyong*, 7:7b, criticizes a wastrel by calling him a Qiu Hu. Also Birrell, *Chinese Love Poetry*, 91–92, 134; Xu, *Jianzhu yutai xinyong*, 2:13b–14a, 4:4a.

12. Wei, *Weishu*, 46:1036.

13. Li, *Beishi*, 27:983.

14. Wei, *Weishu*, 45:1015.

15. Wei, *Weishu*, 60:1337; Li, *Beishi*, 40:1444.

16. Li, *Beishi*, 35:1309, 43:1605.

17. Scholars have taken various views of the strength of chastity in the early medieval era. Some believe that chastity ideals strengthened in this era, others that they weakened, while a third group emphasizes the variety of views toward chastity among people of different social strata. Yang Yinglin, "Wei Jin Nanbei chao shiqi de zhenjieguan," *Qiusuo* 4 (2003): 252–54.

18. Fang, *Jinshu*, 32:979.

19. For example, Liu, *Shih-shuo Hsin-yü*, 163 (5.25); Liu, *Shishuo xinyu huijiao jizhu*, 5:275.

20. Liu, *Shih-shuo Hsin-yü*, 446 (27.10); Liu, *Shishuo xinyu huijiao jizhu*, 27:711–12.

21. Lee, "Women and Marriage," 192–93, 203–7; Wang, *Zhongguo jiatingshi*, 423–26; Xie Baofu, "Beichao de zaijia, houqu yu qieji," *Zhongguo Shehui Kexue Yuan Yanshengyuan xuebao* 4 (2002): 51–53; Zhang Xinyi, "Funü de shouji yu zaijia kan Wei Jin Nanbei chao de zhenjie," *Zhongzheng lishi xuekan* 7 (2004): 182–90; Zhang, *Jiating shihua*, 42–43.

22. Shi, "Weishu suojian Bei Wei gongzhu hunyin," 106–12.

23. Zhao Zhijian, "Beichao funü zaijia kaoshu," *Minsu yanjiu* 1 (1995): 72–73; Li Cong and Zhao Zhijian, "Wei Jin nanchao funü hunyin sanlun," *Qi Lu xuekan* 5 (1997): 76–77; Yang, "Wei Jin nanbei chao shiqi de zhenjieguan," 253.

24. Zhang and Sun, "Wei Jin Nanbeichao hunsu chutan," 102; Lee, "Women and Marriage," 203.

25. Zhao Zhijian, "Wei Jin nanbeichao funü zaijia kaoshu," *Shandong daxue xuebao* 1 (1995): 22; Xue Ruize, "Jianlun Wei Jin nanbeichao de cihun," *Qinghai shehui kexue* 5 (2000): 81–83.

26. Wei, *Weishu*, 30: 712.

27. Wei, *Weishu*, 30:723. The Wei emperors also gave supporters large numbers of female slaves. Wei, *Weishu*, 31:737.

28. Li, *Beishi*, 55:1984.

29. Linghu, *Zhoushu*, 6:99.

30. Li, *Beishi*, 38:1393. Nuns who had been raped were ridiculed for having failed to preserve their chastity. Wang and Cao, *A Record of Buddhist Monasteries in Luo-yang*, 63.

31. Li, *Beishi*, 22:811, describes an attempt to control the most flagrant abuses.

32. Liu, *Shih-shuo Hsin-yü*, 441 (27.1); Liu, *Shishuo xinyu huijiao jizhu*, 27:705.

33. Wei, *Weishu*, 30:712; Li, *Beishi*, 20:751.

34. Wei, *Weishu*, 19A:448.

35. Lu, "Tuoba shi yu zhongyuan shizu de hunyin guanxi," 246–48.

36. Yang, "Notes on the Economic History of the Chin Dynasty," 125.

37. Zhao, "Beichao funü zaijia kaoshu," 76; Zhuang Huafeng, "Wei Jin Nanbeichao shiqi de funü zaikai," *Anhui Shida xuebao* 19, no. 3 (1991): 343, 346.

38. Linghu, *Zhoushu*, 5:83. Also Fang, *Jinshu*, 3:63.

39. Zhao, "Wei Jin nanbeichao funü zaijia kaoshu," 23; Zhao, "Beichao funü zaijia kaoshu," 75.

40. Xue Ruize and Zhang Zhihong, "Shilun Wei Jin nanbeichao zaihun wenti," *Sixiang zhanxian* 2 (2002): 133. For the ancient Chinese version of this custom, see Xie Weiyang, *Zhoudai jiating xingtai* (Beijing: Zhongguo shehui kexue chubanshe, 1990), 72–74. For Tuoba levirate, see Zhao, "Wei Jin nanbeichao funü zaijia kaoshu," 23; Sun Tongxun, "Some Hints on the Marriage Custom of Early Toba," in *Tuoba shi de Hanhua ji qita—Bei Wei shilun wenji* (Taipei: Daoxiang chubanshe, 2005), 241–48.

41. Lee, "Women and Marriage," 192–93.

42. Wang and Cao, *A Record of Buddhist Monasteries in Luo-yang*, 233.

43. Birrell, *Chinese Love Poetry*, 224; Xu, *Jianzhu yutai xinyong*, 7:11a.

44. Linghu, *Zhoushu*, 6:91.

45. Shen, *Songshu*, 91:2247.

46. Fu Xueqin, "Lun Wei Jin 'Guafu fu' de xiezuo moshi yu xingbie biaoda," *Liaodong Xueyuan xuebao* 18, no. 1 (2016): 1–8.

47. Some critics believe that the poem attributed to the wife of Ding Yi was also written by a man while others accept the traditional ascription, so the authorship of this poem remains contested. Many passages of Pan Yue's poem were modeled after the poem attributed to the wife of Ding Yi. Fu, "Lun Wei Jin 'Guafu fu' de xiezuo" 3–5.

48. Li Jianzhong, "Shennü yu guafu—dui Wei Jin wenxue zhong lianglei nüxing xingxiang de wenhua shenshi," *Zhongnan Minzu Daxue xuebao* 2 (2002): 73–77.

49. Zhang, "Funü de shouji yu zaijia," 172, gives the numbers and percentages of biographies of chaste women from each of the early medieval dynasties. These statistics show that most chastity narratives describe southern women. Each of the standard histories was compiled after the period it describes, so some aspects might express values prevalent in the era of the historian rather than the earlier period under discussion. Holmgren, "Widow Chastity in the Northern Dynasties," 165–66, 169. J. Michael Farmer, "Chastity, Suicide, Art, and History: Changing Conceptions of Female Remarriage in Early Medieval Shu," in *Willow Catkins: Festschrift for Dr. Lily Xiao Hong Lee*, ed. Shirley Chan, Barbara Hendrischke, and Sue Wiles (Sydney: Oriental Society of Australia, 2014), 43–75, argues that during the Eastern Han, widow chastity was largely a regional custom most emphasized by the elites in the Shu (Sichuan) region. In the early medieval era, chastity discourse became mainstream in other places as well.

50. Moreover, the thirty-five narratives about female martyrs from the early medieval era make up only 0.3 percent of the total in the compendium. Dong Jia-

zun, "Lidai jielie funü de tongji," in *Zhongguo funüshi lunji*, ed. Bao Jialin (Taipei: Daoxiang, 1988), 112–13.

51. Yang, "Wei Jin Nanbeichao shiqi de zhenjieguan," 253.

52. Holmgren, "Widow Chastity in the Northern Dynasties," analyzes female biographies in *Weishu* in great detail, providing a methodological model that ought to be applied to the study of female biographies in the other standard histories. She classifies the biographies according each woman's social background and era. Most chastity stories date from the latter half of the dynasty and describe women who belonged to minor or local gentry families. This might reflect a change in behavior, the greater availability of materials, or the biases of the historians who compiled this work. Holmgren suspects that the historians focused on women from lower backgrounds during the latter era because stories about these women illustrated virtues that Northern Qi historians held in esteem.

53. Birrell, *Chinese Love Poetry*, 132; Xu, *Jianzhu yutai xinyong*, 4:2a–2b.

54. Birrell, *Chinese Love Poetry*, 123; Xu, *Jianzhu yutai xinyong*, 3:14a–15a, describes a widow's decision to remain chaste in emotionally charged terms.

55. D. L. Davis and R. G. Whitten, "The Cross-Cultural Study of Human Sexuality," *Annual Review of Anthropology* 16 (1987): 75.

56. Lu, "Tuoba shi yu zhongyuan shizu de hunyin guanxi," 236.

57. Yen, *Family Instructions for the Yen Clan*, 12.

58. Li Zhende, "Cong 'dufu ji' tanqi," *Funü yu liangxing jikan* 3 (1994): 12–15, defines the main concepts related to jealousy. The Liu Song emperor Ming commissioned Yu Tongzhi to write a book on the topic of jealousy titled either *Dufu ji* or *Du ji* for princesses to read in the hope that they would become more tolerant. Only some scattered fragments of this work remain.

59. Niu Zhiping, "Tangdai dufu shulun," in *Zhongguo Funüshi lunji xuji*, ed. Bao Jialin (Taipei: Daoxiang chubanshe, 1991), 61–62; Ōzawa Masāki, *Tō Sō jidai no kazoku, konin, josei—tsuma wa tsuyoku* (Tokyo: Akashi, 2005), 120, 128. Lee, "Women and Marriage," 210–13, gives tables with details of various cases of jealousy. Also Jen-der Lee, "Querelle des femmes? Les femmes jalouses et leur contrôle au début de la Chine médiévale," in *Éducation et Instruction en Chine III. Aux Marges de l'orthodoxie*, ed. Christine Nguyen Tri and Catherine Despeux (Paris: Éditions Peeters, 2004), 70–76.

60. Ban, *Hanshu*, 22:1027.

61. Liu, "Wei Jin Nanbeichao shidai de qie," 27–28.

62. Zhao, "Jiu Shishuo xinyu kan Wei Jin nanbeichao de hunyin wenhua," 41–42.

63. Fang, *Jinshu*, 32:972.

64. Birrell, *Chinese Love Poetry*, 112; Xu, *Jianzhu yutai xinyong*, 3:7b.

65. Birrell, *Chinese Love Poetry*, 14. For example, Birrell, *Chinese Love Poetry*, 84, 248; Xu, *Jianzhu yutai xinyong*, 2:8b, 8:5a.

66. Ōsawa Masāki, "'Dufu,' 'hanqi' yi ji 'junei'—Tang Song biangeqi de hunyin yu jiating de bianhua," in *Tang Song nüxing yu shehui*, ed. Deng Xiaonan (Shanghai: Shanghai cishu, 2003), 2:829, 835–36; Zhang Yunhua, "Lun Bei Wei funü de duhan fengqi," *Shixue jikan* 6 (2008): 99–104; Zhang Xiaowen, "Nüxing ziwo yishi de juexing: Wei Jin nanbeichao hunyin lunli de yipe weidu," *Lunlixue yanjiu* 2 (2014): 31–33.

67. Ōsawa, *Tō Sō jidai no kazoku, konin, josei*, 118.

68. Lee, "Women and Marriage," 164.

69. Wei, *Weishu*, 53:1177.

70. Fang, *Jinshu*, 31:953.

71. McMahon, *Women Shall Not Rule*, 152.

72. Liu, *Shih-shuo Hsin-yü*, 352–53 (19.21); Liu, *Shishuo xinyu huijiao jizhu*, 19:584; Wang, "Slaves and Other Comparable Social Groups," 322, 325.

73. Fang, *Jinshu*, 82:2150.

74. Liu, *Shih-shuo Hsin-yü*, 486 (35.3); Liu, *Shishuo xinyu huijiao jizhu*, 35:765; Fang, *Jinshu*, 40:1170.

75. Li, *Nanshi*, 341–42. Also see Liu, *Shih-shuo Hsin-yü*, 430–31 (26.6); Liu, *Shishuo xinyu huijiao jizhu*, 26:687.

76. Wei, *Weishu*, 59:1311; Li, *Beishi*, 29:1049; Lee, "Women and Marriage," 233–37; Lee, "The Death of a Princess," 3–8; Jen-der Lee, "Crime and Punishment: The Case of Liu Hui in the *Weishu*," in *Early Medieval China: A Sourcebook*, ed. Wendy Swartz, Robert Ford Campany, Yang Lu, and Jessey J. C. Choo (New York: Columbia University Press, 2014), 156–65.

77. Li, *Beishi*, 68:2383; Jia Shaowan, "Wei Jin nanbeichao shiqi nanbeifang funü diwei de chayi ji yuanyin tanjiu," *Jincheng Zhiye Jishu Xueyuan xuebao* 1 (2016): 89.

78. Liu, *Shih-shuo Hsin-yü*, 447–48 (27.12); Liu, *Shishuo xinyu huijiao jizhu*, 27:714.

79. Lee, "Querelle des femmes?," 85–91.

80. Li, *Beishi*, 28:1016.

81. Zhao, *Han Wei nanbeichao muzhi huibian*, 374; Shao, *Beichao jiating xingtai yanjiu*, 264.

82. Wei, *Weishu*, 100:2222.

83. Lee, "Querelle des femmes?," 77–78.

84. Lee, "Querelle des femmes?," 83–85.

85. Li, *Nanshi*, 12:339.

86. Clart, "Ceshen: Spirit of the Latrine," 245.

87. Lee, "Women and Marriage," 139, 142.

88. Wei, *Weishu*, 92:1982.

89. Wei, *Weishu*, 92:1982.

90. Knapp, *Selfless Offspring*, 171–72.

91. Lee, "Women and Marriage," 253–54.

92. Wei, *Weishu*, 92:1990, 92:1994; Mou, *Gentlemen's Prescriptions*, 117–18.

93. Holmgren, "Widow Chastity in the Northern Dynasties," 170–71; Knapp, *Selfless Offspring*, 185. Wei-hung Lin, "Chastity in Chinese Eyes—Nan-Nu Yu-Pieh," *Hanxue yanjiu* 12 (1991): 13–40, describes the evolution of terms related to chastity.

94. Holmgren, "Widow Chastity in the Northern Dynasties," 168, 170–71.

95. Liu, *Shih-shuo Hsin-yü*, 355; Liu, *Shishuo xinyu huijiao jizhu*, 19:589.

96. Liu, *Shih-shuo Hsin-yü*, 325; Liu, *Shishuo xinyu huijiao jizhu*, 17:547.

97. Kristofer Schipper, "Purity and Strangers Shifting Boundaries in Medieval Taoism," *T'oung Pao* 80, nos. 1/3 (1994): 69, 78.

98. Zhang, "Lun Wei Jin nanbeichao dasheng fojiao," 64–67.

99. Zhang, "Zhonggu Fojiao jielü yu jiating lunli," 53–54.

100. Yuet Keung Lo, "Conversion to Chastity: A Buddhist Catalyst in Early Imperial China," *Nan Nü* 10, no. 1 (2008): 23–24.

101. Lo, "Conversion to Chastity," 47.

102. Wei, *Weishu*, 43:969.

103. Li, *Tangdai de biqiuni*, 75–82.

104. Li, *Beishi*, 39:1435; Li, *Tangdai de biqiuni*, 74–75.

105. Tsai, *Lives of the Nuns*, 20; Shi, *Biqiuni zhuan jiaozhu*, 1:7.

106. Tsai, *Lives of the Nuns*, 22; Shi, *Biqiuni zhuan jiaozhu*, 1:10–11.

107. Tsai, *Lives of the Nuns*, 28; Shi, *Biqiuni zhuan jiaozhu*, 1:22–23.

108. Benn, *Burning for the Buddha*.

109. Tsai, *Lives of the Nuns*, 65–66, 92–93; Shi, *Biqiuni zhuan jiaozhu*, 2:115, 4:182–84.

110. Lu Jianrong, "Cong nanxing shuxie cailiao kan san zhi qi shiji nüxing de shehui xingxiang suzao," *Guoli Taiwan Shifan Daxue lishi xuebao* 26 (1998): 21–31. The number of mutilations varied considerably over time. For example, only one of the female biographies in *Weishu* describes self-mutilation. Holmgren, "Widow Chastity in the Northern Dynasties," 168, 172–74.

111. Fang, *Jinshu*, 96:2512–13; Fang, *Jinshu*, 96:2513.

112. Fang, *Jinshu*, 96:2512. Similarly 96:2523–24.

113. Fang, *Jinshu*, 96:2515, 96:2520.

114. Holmgren, "Widow Chastity in the Northern Dynasties," 183.

115. In one of the nonviolent narratives, the woman simply returns home. Another features crying. In five of these narratives a woman swears never to remarry. Zhang, "Funü de shouji yu zaijia," 175.

116. Lu, "Cong nanxing shuxie cailiao," 36.

117. Lee, "Women and Marriage," 202.

118. Li, *Beishi*, 4:141; Lou Jin, "Zhengsheng yuannian chi yu Nanbeichao zhi Tangdai de jingbiao xiaoyi zhi zhidu—jian lun S.1344 hao Lundun canjuan de dingming wenti," *Zhejiang xuekan* 1 (2014): 13–17; Lee, "Women and Marriage," 205–6.

119. Yang, "Wei Jin nanbei chao shiqi de zhenjieguan," 254.

120. Louise Edwards, "Policing the Modern Woman in Republican China," *Modern China* 26, no. 2 (2000): 120; Yang, "Wei Jin Nanbei chao shiqi de zhenjieguan," 252.

121. Susan Mann, "Widows in the Kinship, Class, and Community Structures of Qing Dynasty China," *Journal of Asian Studies* 46, no. 1 (1987): 49.

122. Michael Herzfeld, "Honour and Shame: Problems in the Comparative Analysis of Moral Systems," *Man* 15 (1980): 342–43.

123. Li, *Beishi*, 20:736.

124. Li, *Beishi*, 18:678.

125. Wei, *Weishu*, 57:1276.

126. Mann, "Widows in the Kinship, Class, and Community Structures," 47–48.

127. Wang and Cao, *A Record of Buddhist Monasteries in Luo-yang*, 229–31.

CHAPTER 8

1. Shanxi Sheng Datong Shi Bowuguan and Shanxi Sheng Gongzuo Weihuanhui, "Shanxi Datong Shijiazhai Bei Wei Sima Jinlong mu," *Wenwu* 190 (1972): 25–26.

Some epitaphs also compare the deceased to virtuous female paragons of the past. Zhao, *Han Wei nanbeichao muzhi huibian*, 421, 440.

2. Zhao, *Han Wei nanbeichao muzhi huibian*, 419.

3. Ye Huichang and Lang Ruiping, "Lun beichao bentu wenren shizhong nüxing xingxiang de yihua," *Tianshui Shifan Xueyuan xuebao* 25, no. 4 (2005): 60–63.

4. Li Zhende, "Han Tang zhijian yifang zhong ji jian furen yu nüti wei yao," *Xin shixue* 13, no. 4 (2002): 6, 11, 15–19, 22–26.

5. Fusheng Wu, *The Poetics of Decadence: Chinese Poetry of the Southern Dynasties and Late Tang Periods* (Albany: State University of New York Press, 1998), 5.

6. David R. Knechtges, "Culling the Weeds and Selecting Prime Blossoms: The Anthology in Early Medieval China," in *Culture and Power in the Reconstitution of the Chinese Realm, 200–600*, ed. Scott Pearce, Audrey Spiro, and Patricia Ebrey (Cambridge, MA: Harvard University Asia Center, 2001), 209–10.

7. Cutter, "To the Manner Born?," 69.

8. Ma Lili, "Wei Jin meinü fu zhi yanbian," *Guizhou Minzu Daxue xuebao* 6 (2013): 88–90.

9. Knechtges, "Culling the Weeds," 201–2.

10. Han dynasty exegetes often interpreted ancient love poetry as symbolizing the intense and unequal relationship between ruler and minister. Jowen R. Tung, *Fables for the Patriarchs: Gender Politics in Tang Discourse* (Lanham, MD: Rowman & Littlefield, 2000), 33–40.

11. Wu, *The Poetics of Decadence*, 26; Ann-Marie Hsiung, "The Images of Women in Early Chinese Poetry: The Book of Songs, Han Ballads and Palace Style Verse of the Liang Dynasty," *Chinese Culture* 35, no. 4 (1994): 86–87.

12. Wu, *The Poetics of Decadence*, 4.

13. Graham Sanders, "I Read They Said He Sang What He Wrote: Orality, Writing, and Gossip in Tang Poetry Anecdotes," in *Idle Talk: Gossip and Anecdote in Traditional China*, ed. Jack. W. Chen and David Schaberg (Berkeley: Global, Area, and International Archive and University of California Press, 2014), 88.

14. Hsiung, "The Images of Women," 81, 83–86.

15. Wu, *Handai nüxing lijiao yanjiu*, 194–95.

16. Tian, *Beacon Fire and Shooting Star*, 188–90, 194–95.

17. Franklin Perkins, *Heaven and Earth Are Not Humane: The Problem of Evil in Classical Chinese Philosophy* (Bloomington: Indiana University Press, 2014), 117–18, 125.

18. Wu, *The Poetics of Decadence*, 2.

19. Zhang Yinan, "Wo jian you ling—Tangdai nüshiren de Qi Liang ti chuang-zuo," *Wenshi zhishi* 3 (2014): 112–13.

20. Grace S. Fong, "Wu Wenying's Yongwu Ci: Poem as Artifice and Poem as Metaphor," *Harvard Journal of Asiatic Studies* 45, no. 1 (1985): 323–35.

21. Li, *Women's Poetry of Late Imperial China*, 26; Robert Joe Cutter, "To Make Her Mine: Women and the Rhetoric of Property in Early and Early Medieval Fu," *Early Medieval China* 19 (2013): 39, 45, 47, 50, 53.

22. For detailed analysis of the blazon and related rhetorical techniques, see David Hillman and Carla Mazzio, eds., *The Body in Parts: Fantasies of Corporeality in Early Modern Europe* (New York: Routledge, 1997).

23. Birrell, *Chinese Love Poetry*, 88; Xu, *Jianzhu yutai xinyong*, 2:11a–11b.

24. Birrell, "Introduction," in *Chinese Love Poetry*, 8. Maureen Robertson, "Voicing the Feminine: Constructions of the Gendered Subject in Lyric Poetry by Women of Medieval and Late Imperial China," *Late Imperial China* 13, no. 1 (1992): 69, 71. Only about ten of the poets in *Yutai xinyong* are women. Li, *Women's Poetry of Late Imperial China*, 22.

25. Wu, *The Poetics of Decadence*, 46.

26. Birrell, *Chinese Love Poetry*, 222; Xu, *Jianzhu yutai xinyong*, 7:9a–9b.

27. Birrell, *Chinese Love Poetry*, 225; Xu, *Jianzhu yutai xinyong*, 7:12a.

28. Perkins, *Heaven and Earth Are Not Humane*, 43–44.

29. Wu, *The Poetics of Decadence*, 71; Hsiung, "The Images of Women," 90.

30. Victor Turner, "Symbols in Ndembu Ritual," in *The Forest of Symbols: Aspects of Ndembu Ritual* (Ithaca: Cornell University Press, 1967), 29.

31. Hsiung, "The Images of Women in Early Chinese Poetry," 87, 89.

32. Cai, "A Historical Overview of Six Dynasties Aesthetics," 21.

33. Chu, "Cong Wei Jin liuchao nüxing shige," 36; Jing Jing, "Shijing zhong meiren guannian dui Zhongguo shinühua de yingxiang," *Yishu baijia* 7 (2011): 223–25. For example, Zhao, *Han Wei nanbeichao muzhi huibian*, 419.

34. Nanxiu Qian, *Spirit and Self in Medieval China: The Shih-shuo hsin-yü and Its Legacy* (Honolulu: University of Hawaii Press, 2001), 162–63.

35. Jing Nan, "Shixi Wei Jin fengdu dui Wei Jin shiqi nüxing de yingxiang—cong *Shishuo xinyu*—Xianyuan pian tanqi," *Shehui kexuejia* 6 (2007): 71. For example, Zhao, *Han Wei nanbeichao muzhi huibian*, 70; Yang, "'Shishuo xinyu—Xianyuan' xuanlu tese tanxi," 99.

36. Birrell, *Chinese Love Poetry*, 132; Xu, *Jianzhu yutai xinyong*, 4:2a–2b.

37. Wang Xiulin, *Wei Jin shiren zhi shentiguan* (Taipei: Hua Mulan wenhua chubanshe, 2009), 153–55.

38. Liu, *Shih-shuo Hsin-yü*, 343 (19.6); Liu, *Shishuo xinyu huijiao jizhu*, 19:569.

39. Liu, *Shih-shuo Hsin-yü*, 484 (35.1); Liu, *Shishuo xinyu huijiao jizhu*, 35:763.

40. Liu, *Shih-shuo Hsin-yü*, 349 (19.15); Liu, *Shishuo xinyu huijiao jizhu*, 19:577.

41. Lu, "Cong nanxing shuxie cailiao," 14–21.

42. Mary H. Fong, "Tang Tomb Murals Reviewed in the Light of Tang Texts on Painting," *Artibus Asiae* 45, no. 1 (1984): 54–55.

43. Spiro, "Of Noble Ladies and Notable Conventions," 228, 247; Birrell, *Chinese Love Poetry*, 173; Xu, *Jianzhu yutai xinyong*, 5:14b.

44. Yang, *Baopuzi waipian jiaojian*, vol. 1, 25:620; Chen Dongyuan, *Zhongguo funü shenghuo shi* (Shanghai: Shangwu Yinshuguan, 1937), 77–79; Wei, *Weishu*, 65:1442; Wang and Cao, *A Record of Buddhist Monasteries in Luo-yang*, 197.

45. Ellen Johnston Laing, "Chinese Palace-Style Poetry and the Depiction of a Palace Beauty," *The Art Bulletin* 72, no. 2 (1990): 286–89.

46. Although these plants are called plums in English, *Prunus mume* is not the same species as the Western plum. Maggie Bickford, *Bones of Jade, Soul of Ice: The Flowering Plum in Chinese Art* (New Haven, CT: Yale University Art Gallery, 1985).

47. Shen, *Songshu*, 43:1004–9, gives accounts of strange occurrences involving women. Many involve physical transformations.

48. Wu Congxiang, "Dangfu yu zhennü—Wei Jin nanbeichao zhiguai xiaoshuo zhong de nüxing xingxiang jiedu," *Tianzhong xuekan* 23, no. 4 (2008): 58–61.

49. Pierre Bourdieu, *Outline of a Theory of Practice* (Cambridge: Cambridge University Press, 1977), 195. Bourdieu refers to this as "body habitus."

50. Michael Carter, *Fashion Classics: From Carlyle to Barthes* (Oxford: Berg, 2003), 156; Roland Barthes, *The Language of Fashion*, trans. Andy Stafford, ed. Andy Stafford and Michael Carter (London: Bloomsbury, 2004), 37–38; Rosemary A. Joyce, "Archaeology of the Body," *Annual Review of Anthropology* 34 (2005): 140, 142, 146.

51. Carter, *Fashion Classics*, 2.

52. Elvin Hatch, "Theories of Social Honor," *American Anthropologist* 91, no. 2 (1989): 341–34; Carter, *Fashion Classics*, 46, 47.

53. Hatch, "Theories of Social Honor," 346–47.

54. Birrell, "Introduction," in *Chinese Love Poetry*, 12, 21.

55. Carter, *Fashion Classics*, 49.

56. Zhou Zhaowang and Hou Yonghui, "Wei Jin nanbeichao funü de fushi fengmao," *Jiangxi shehui kexue* 3 (1995): 97–102; Chang Qing, "Wei Jin nanbeichao funü fushi kao," *Jiamusi Jiaoyu Xueyuan xuebao* 4 (2003): 31–34; Li Ya, *Zhongguo lidai zhuangshi* (Beijing: Zhongguo fangzhi chubanshe, 2004), 57–72; Dien, *Six Dynasties Civilization*, 312–24; Zhang and Chen, *Zhongguo funü tongshi*, 481–509.

57. Zhang and Chen, *Zhongguo funü tongshi*, 515–21.

58. Lingley, "Naturalizing the Exotic," 50–80.

59. Birrell, "Introduction," in *Chinese Love Poetry*, 8, 10. For example, Birrell, *Chinese Love Poetry*, 80; Xu, *Jianzhu yutai xinyong*, 2:5a.

60. Shen, *Songshu*, 18:505, 18:521.

61. Zhang and Chen, *Zhongguo funü tongshi*, 509–15. Women were expected to forgo cosmetics while in mourning. Zhang, "Wei Jin nanbeichao funü sangzang liyi kao," 100.

62. Wang Qiyue, "'Wei Jin fengdu' xia de nanxing meirong xianxiang tantao," *Chongqing Keji Xueyuan xuebao* 2 (2009): 176–77.

63. Carter, *Fashion Classics*, 69.

64. Wu, *The Poetics of Decadence*, 65, 73.

65. Li, *Bei Qi shu*, 16:216; 18:235.

66. Liu, *Shih-shuo Hsin-yü*, 485 (35.2); Liu, *Shishuo xinyu huijiao jizhu*, 35:764; Howard L. Goodman, "Sites of Recognition: Burial, Mourning, and Commemoration in the Xun Family of Yingchuan, AD 140–305," *Early Medieval China* 15 (2009): 71–72; Goodman, *Xun Xu and the Politics of Precision*, 61. Scholars have also posited 209–238 and other timeframes for Xun Xu's lifespan.

CONCLUSION

1. Yang, *Baopuzi waipian jiaojian*, 25:601.

2. Zhao, "Reflections on the Proposition," 74, 80–82; Zou Min, "Hanmo Weichu shiwenlun zhongxin de zhuanyi yu wenxue jiazhi de faxian—shilun Lingmu Huxiong zijue de neihan ji qi panduan yiju," *Xibei Nonglin Keji Daxue xuebao* 1 (2010): 130–34. Zhao tempers Suzuki's argument, pointing out that Han literature was not entirely utilitarian and showed budding self-consciousness.

3. Shimomi, *Juka shakai to bosei*, 106, 111.

4. Chu, "Cong Wei Jin liuchao nüxing shige," 36.

5. Kawakatsu, *Rikuchō kizoku sei shakai no kenkyū*, 284–87.

6. Xing, "'Wei Jin fengliu' xia de liang Jin funü," 21–25.

7. Liu Zhao, "*Shishuo xinyu* suo miaohui zhi Wei Jin nüxing fengliu zhiyi," *Xiangfan Xueyuan xuebao* 9 (2008): 46–48.

8. Wu, *Handai nüxing lijiao yanjiu*, 196–201; Zhang, "Nüxing ziwo yishi de juexing," 32–33.

9. Li and Zhao, "Wei Jin nanchao funü hunyin sanlun," 74–75.

10. Mou, *Gentlemen's Prescriptions*, 77.

11. Nanxiu Qian, "*Lienü* versus *Xianyuan*: The Two Biographical Traditions in Chinese Women's History," in *Beyond Exemplar Tales: Women's Biography in Chinese History*, ed. Joan Judge and Hu Ying (Berkeley: University of California Press, 2011), 70, 73–76; Qian, *Spirit and Self in Medieval China*, 143–44.

12. Qian, *Spirit and Self in Medieval China*, 162–63.

13. Zhang Chengzong, "Wei Jin nanbeichao funü de shejiao huodong," *Xiangfan Xueyuan xuebao* 3 (2005): 90–93.

14. Qian, *Spirit and Self in Medieval China*, 146.

15. Robertson, "Voicing the Feminine," 76.

16. Shu and Yang, "Wei Jin renxing zijue," 30–33.

17. Nanxiu Qian, "Milk and Scent: Works About Women in the Shishuo Xinyu Genre," *Nan Nü* 1, no. 2 (1999): 189–90.

Bibliography

Ames, Roger T. "Taoism and the Androgynous Ideal." In *Women in China: Current Directions in Historical Scholarship*, edited by Richard W. Guisso and Stanley Johannesen, 21–45. Youngstown, NY: Philo Press, 1981.

An Dong-hwan 安東煥 (안동환). "Liuchao yuefu minge zhong de jinü zhi ge" 六朝樂府民歌中的妓女之歌. *Shandong Jiaoyu Xueyuan xuebao* 山東教育學院學報 1 (2003): 54–56.

An Jianhua 安劍華. "Qiantan beichao fufu hezangmu" 淺談北朝夫婦合葬墓. *Sichuan Daxue xuebao* 四川大學學報 1 (2004): 21–23.

An Ran 安然. "Wei Jin nanbeichao wenxuezhong yongwu nüxing xingxiang tanxi" 魏晉南北朝文學中勇武女性形象探析. *Huaihai Gongxueyuan xuebao* 淮海工學院學報 14, no. 1 (2016): 39–41.

Anonymous. *Wuchao xiaoshuo daguan* 五朝小說大觀. Shanghai: Saoye shanfang, 1926.

Ashmore, Robert. "The Art of Discourse: Xi Kang's 'Sound Is without Sadness or Joy." In *Early Medieval China: A Sourcebook*, edited by Wendy Swartz, Robert Ford Campany, Yang Lu, and Jessey J. C. Choo, 201–29. New York: Columbia University Press, 2014.

Balkwill, Stephanie. "When Renunciation Is Good Politics: The Women of the Imperial Nunnery of the Northern Wei." *Nan Nü* 18, no. 2 (2016): 224–56.

Ban Gu 班固. *Hanshu* 漢書. Annotated by Yan Shigu 顏師古. Beijing: Zhonghua, 1962.

Barfield, Thomas J. *The Perilous Frontier: Nomadic Empires and China, 221 BC to AD 1757*. Cambridge, MA: Blackwell Publishers, 1989.

Barthes, Roland. *The Language of Fashion*. Translated by Andy Stafford. Edited by Andy Stafford and Michael Carter. London: Bloomsbury, 2004.

Benn, James A. *Burning for the Buddha: Self-Immolation in Chinese Buddhism*. Honolulu: A Kuroda Institute Book, University of Hawaii Press, 2007.

Bickford, Maggie. *Bones of Jade, Soul of Ice: The Flowering Plum in Chinese Art.* New Haven, CT: Yale University Art Gallery, 1985.

Bielenstein, Hans. "The Six Dynasties, Vol. 1." *Museum of Far Eastern Antiquities Bulletin* 68 (1996): 5–324.

———. "The Six Dynasties, Vol. 2." *Museum of Far Eastern Antiquities Bulletin* 69 (1997): 11–191.

Birrell, Anne. *Chinese Love Poetry: New Songs from a Jade Terrace, A Medieval Anthology.* London: Penguin Books, 1986.

Bourdieu, Pierre. *Outline of a Theory of Practice.* Cambridge: Cambridge University Press, 1977.

Brown, Judith. "Note on the Division of Labor by Sex." *American Anthropologist* 72 (1970): 1075–76.

Brown, Miranda. *The Politics of Mourning in Early China.* Albany: State University of New York Press, 2007.

———. "Sons and Mothers in Warring States and Han China, 453 BCE–220 CE." *Nan Nü* 5, no. 2 (2003): 137–69.

Cahill, Suzanne E. "Sublimation in Medieval China: The Case of the Mysterious Woman of the Nine Heavens." *Journal of Chinese Religions* 20 (1992): 91–102.

———. *Transcendence and Divine Passion: The Queen Mother of the West in Medieval China.* Stanford: Stanford University Press, 1993.

Cai Hongsheng 蔡鴻生. *Nigu tan* 尼姑譚. Guangzhou: Zhongshan Daxue chubanshe, 1996.

Cai, Zong-qi. "A Historical Overview of Six Dynasties Aesthetics." In *Chinese Aesthetics: The Ordering of Literature, the Arts, and the Universe in the Six Dynasties,* edited by Zong-qi Cai, 1–23. Honolulu: University of Hawaii Press, 2004.

Campany, Robert F. "Ghosts Matter: The Culture of Ghosts in Six Dynasties Zhiguai." *Chinese Literature* 13 (1991): 15–34.

———. *Signs from the Unseen Realm: Buddhist Miracle Tales from Early Medieval China.* Honolulu: University of Hawaii Press, 2012.

Cao Zhaolan 曹兆蘭. *Jinwen yu Yin Zhou nüxing wenhua* 金文與殷周女性文化. Beijing: Beijing Daxue, 2004.

Carter, Michael. *Fashion Classics: From Carlyle to Barthes.* Oxford: Berg, 2003.

Chang Qing 常倩. "Wei Jin nanbeichao funü fushi kao" 魏晉南北朝婦女服飾考. *Jiamusi Jiaoyu Xueyuan xuebao* 佳木斯教育學院學報 4 (2003): 31–34.

Chang Qu 常璩. *Huayang guozhi jiaobu tuzhu* 華陽國志校補圖注. Annotated by Ren Naiqiang 任乃強. Shanghai: Guji, 1987.

Chen Dongyuan 陳東原. *Zhongguo funü shenghuo shi* 中國婦女生活史. Shanghai: Shangwu Yinshuguan, 1937.

Chen Jie 陳絜. *Shang Zhou xingshi zhidu yanjiu* 商周姓氏制度研究. Beijing: Shangwu yinshuguan, 2007.

Ch'en, Kenneth. "Anti-Buddhist Propaganda during the Nan-Ch'ao." *Harvard Journal of Asiatic Studies* 15, nos. 1/2 (1952): 166–92.

Chen Liping 陳麗平. "Lienü tu de liuxing yu Han Wei liuchao nüxing de jiaohua" 列女圖的流行與漢魏六朝女性教化. *Jinyang xuekan* 晉陽學刊 2 (2010): 114–16.

Chen, Sanping. "'Age Inflation and Deflation' in Medieval China." *Journal of the American Oriental Society* 133, no. 3 (2013): 527–33.

———. "Succession Struggles and the Ethnic Identity of the Tang Imperial House." *Journal of the Royal Asiatic Society*, third series, 6, no. 3 (1996): 379–405.

Chen Shanshan 陳姍姍. "Qianxi Wei Jin nanbeichao de zaohun xianxiang jiqi chengyin" 淺析魏晉南北朝時期的早婚現象及其成因. *Lanzhou Jiaoyu Xueyuan xuebao* 蘭州教育學院學報 29, no. 10 (2013): 14–15.

Chen Shou 陳壽. *Sanguozhi*三國志. Annotated by Pei Songzhi 裴松之. Hong Kong: Zhonghua shuju, 1971.

Chen Xiangqian 陳祥謙. "Nanchao *Furen ji* luekao" 南朝婦人集略考. *Hubei Gongye Daxue xuebao* 湖南工業大學學報 17, no. 1 (2012): 126–30.

Chen Yifeng 陳一風. "Wei Jin nanbeichao shiqi rufo de xiaodao zhi zheng" 魏晉南北朝時期儒佛的孝道之爭. *Nandu xuetan* 南都學壇 23, no. 2 (2003): 23–27.

Chen Yun 陳韻. "Wei Jin Hunli yanjiu" 魏晉婚禮研究. MA thesis, Guoli Taiwan Shifan Daxue, 1980.

Cheng, Wen-chien. "The Pictorial Portrayal of Women and Didactic Messages in the Han and Six Dynasties." *Nan Nü* 19 (2017): 155–212.

Chennault, Cynthia L. "Lofty Gates or Solitary Impoverishment? Xie Family Members of the Southern Dynasties." *T'oung Pao* 85, nos. 4–5 (1999): 249–327.

Chittick, Andrew. "*Song shu*" 宋書. In *Early Medieval Chinese Texts: A Bibliographical Guide*, edited by Cynthia L. Chennault et al., 320–23. Berkeley: Institute of East Asian Studies, University of California, 2015.

Choo, Jessey J. C. "Adoption and Motherhood: 'The Petition Submitted by Lady [née] Yu.'" In *Early Medieval China: A Sourcebook*, edited by Wendy Swartz, Robert Ford Campany, Yang Lu, and Jessey J. C. Choo, 511–29. New York: Columbia University Press, 2014.

———. "Between Imitation and Mockery: The Southern Treatments of Northern Cultures." In *Early Medieval China: A Sourcebook*, edited by Wendy Swartz, Robert Ford Campany, Yang Lu, and Jessey J. C. Choo, 60–76. New York: Columbia University Press, 2014.

Chu Tingting 褚婷婷. "Cong Wei Jin liuchao nüxing shige kan nüxing shengming yishi de fusu" 從魏晉六朝女性詩歌看女性生命意識的復蘇. *Huzhou Shizhuan xuebao* 湖州師專學報19, no. 4 (1997): 36–39.

Clart, Philip. "Ceshen: Spirit of the Latrine." In *The Routledge Encyclopedia of Taoism*, Volume I: *A–L*, edited by Fabrizio Pregadio, 245. London: Routledge, 2008.

Cole, Alan. *Mothers and Sons in Chinese Buddhism*. Stanford: Stanford University Press, 1998.

Cook, Constance. "Education and the Way of the Former Kings." In *Writing & Literacy in Early China: Studies from the Columbia Early China Seminar*, edited by Li Feng and David Prager Branner, 302–36. Seattle: University of Washington Press, 2011.

Crowell, William G. "Social Unrest and Rebellion in Jiangnan during the Six Dynasties." *Modern China* 9, no. 3 (1983): 319–54.

Cutter, Robert Joe. "To Make Her Mine: Women and the Rhetoric of Property in Early and Early Medieval Fu." *Early Medieval China* 19 (2013): 39–57.

———. "Sex, Politics, and Morality at the Wei (220–265) Court." In *Selected Essays on Court Culture in Cross-Cultural Perspective*, edited by Yaofu Lin, 79–113. Taipei: National Taiwan University Press, 1999.

————. "To the Manner Born? Nature and Nurture in Early Medieval Chinese Literary Thought." In *Culture and Power in the Reconstitution of the Chinese Realm, 200–600*, edited by Scott Pearce, Audrey Spiro, and Patricia Ebrey, 53–71. Cambridge, MA: Harvard University Asia Center, 2001.

Davis, D. L., and R. G. Whitten. "The Cross-Cultural Study of Human Sexuality." *Annual Review of Anthropology* 16 (1987): 69–98.

Davis, Timothy M. *Entombed Epigraphy and Commemorative Culture in Early Medieval China: A History of Early Muzhiming*. Leiden: Brill, 2015.

————. "Ranking Men and Assessing Talent: Xiahou Xuan's Response to an Inquiry by Sima Yi." In *Early Medieval China: A Sourcebook*, edited by Wendy Swartz, Robert Ford Campany, Yang Lu, and Jessey J. C. Choo, 125–46. New York: Columbia University Press.

————. "Texts for Stabilizing Tombs." In *Early Medieval China: A Sourcebook*, edited by Wendy Swartz, Robert Ford Campany, Yang Lu, and Jessey J. C. Choo, 592–612. New York: Columbia University Press, 2014.

de Rauw, Tom. "Baochang: Sixth-Century Biographer of Buddhist Monks . . . and Nuns?" *Journal of the American Oriental Society* 125, no. 2 (2005): 203–18.

Deng Miaoci 鄧妙慈. "Cong Shishuo xinyu kan Wei Jin shiren de hun yu huan" 從世說新語看魏晉士人的婚與宦. *Mingzuo xinshang* 名作欣賞 11 (2011): 40–44.

Despeux, Cathrine. "Women in Taoism." In *The Routledge Encyclopedia of Taoism*, Volume I: *A–L*, edited by Fabrizio Pregadio, 171–73. London: Routledge, 2008.

Despeux, Catherine, and Livia Kohn. *Women in Daoism*. Cambridge, MA: Three Pines Press, 2003.

DeWoskin, Kenneth, and J. I. Crump Jr., trans. *In Search of the Supernatural: The Written Record*. Stanford: Stanford University Press, 1996.

Dien, Albert E. "The Bestowal of Surnames under the Western Wei/Northern Chou: A Case of Counter-Acculturation." *T'oung Pao* 63, nos. 2/3 (1977): 137–77.

————. "Everyday Life." In *Early Medieval China: A Sourcebook*, edited by Wendy Swartz, Robert Ford Campany, Yang Lu, and Jessey J. C. Choo, 433–46. New York: Columbia University Press, 2014.

————. *Six Dynasties Civilization*. New Haven, CT: Yale University Press, 2007.

————. "Yanshi jiaxun 顏氏家訓." In *Early Medieval Chinese Texts: A Bibliographical Guide*, edited by Cynthia L. Chennault et al., 436–41. Berkeley: Institute of East Asian Studies, University of California, 2015.

Dong Jiazun 董家遵. "Lidai jielie funü de tongji" 歷代節烈婦女的統計. In *Zhongguo funüshi lunji* 中國婦女史論集, edited by Bao Jialin 鮑家麟, 111–17. Taipei: Daoxiang, 1988.

Dong, Lan. *Mulan's Legend and Legacy in China and the United States*. Philadelphia: Temple University Press, 2011.

Dong Tao 董濤. "Xian Qin Qin Han shehui wuzhe de xingbie kaocha" 先秦秦漢社會巫者的性別考察. In *Lifa yu xinyang—Zhongguo gudai nüxing yanjiu lunkao* 禮法與信仰—中國古代女性研究論考, edited by Pu Muzhou 蒲慕州, 93–110. Hong Kong: Shangwu yinshuguan, 2013.

Duan Tali 段塔麗. "Beichao zhi Sui Tang shiqi nüxing canzheng xianxiang toushi" 北朝至隋唐時期女性參政現象透視. *Jianghai xuekan* 江海學刊 5 (2001): 111–16.

Ebrey, Patricia Buckley. *The Aristocratic Families of Early Imperial China: A Case Study of the Po-Ling Ts'ui Family*. Cambridge: Cambridge University Press, 1978.

———. "Education through Ritual: Efforts to Formulate Family Rituals during the Sung Period." In *Neo-Confucian Education: The Formative Stage*, edited by William Theodore de Bary and John Chaffee, 277–306. Berkeley: University of California Press, 1989.

———. "Rethinking the Imperial Harem: Why Were There So Many Palace Women?" In *Women and the Family in Chinese History*, edited by Patricia Buckley Ebrey, 177–93. London: Routledge, 2003.

———. "Shifts in Marriage Finance from the Sixth to the Thirteenth Century." In *Women and the Family in Chinese History*, edited by Patricia Buckley Ebrey, 97–132. London: Routledge, 2003.

Edwards, Louise. "Policing the Modern Woman in Republican China." *Modern China* 26, no. 2 (2000): 115–47.

Eisenberg, Andrew. *Kingship in Early Medieval China*. Leiden: Brill, 2008.

Fan Ye 范曄. *Hou Hanshu* 後漢書. Annotated by Liu Zhao 劉昭 and Li Xian 李賢 et al. Beijing: Zhonghua Shuju, 1965.

Fang Xuanling 房玄齡 et al. *Jinshu* 晉書. Annotated by Wu Zeyu 吳則虞. Beijing: Zhonghua shuju, 1974.

Farmer, J. Michael. "Chastity, Suicide, Art, and History: Changing Conceptions of Female Remarriage in Early Medieval Shu." In *Willow Catkins: Festschrift for Dr. Lily Xiao Hong Lee*, edited by Shirley Chan, Barbara Hendrischke, and Sue Wiles, 43–75. Sydney: Oriental Society of Australia, 2014.

———. "On the Composition of Zhang Hua's 'Nüshi Zhen.'" *Early Medieval China* 10–11, part 1 (2004): 151–75.

Feng Sumei 馮素梅. "Wei Jin nanbeichao shiqi de zaohun xianxiang" 魏晉南北朝時期的早婚現象. *Jinyang xuekan* 晉陽學刊 6 (2000): 62–66.

Fitzgerald, C. P. "The Chinese Middle Ages in Communist Historiography." *The China Quarterly* 23 (1965): 106–21.

Fong, Grace S. "Wu Wenying's Yongwu Ci: Poem as Artifice and Poem as Metaphor." *Harvard Journal of Asiatic Studies* 45, no. 1 (1985): 323–47.

Fong, Mary H. "Tang Tomb Murals Reviewed in the Light of Tang Texts on Painting." *Artibus Asiae* 45, no. 1 (1984): 35–72.

Fu Xueqin 伏雪芹. "Lun Wei Jin 'Guafu fu' de xiezuo moshi yu xingbie biaoda" 論魏晉寡婦賦的寫作模式與性別表達. *Liaodong Xueyuan xuebao* 遼東學院學報 18, no. 1 (2016): 1–8.

Furth, Charlotte. *A Flourishing Yin: Gender in China's Medical History, 960–1665*. Berkeley: University of California Press, 1999.

Gan Huaizhen 甘懷真. *Tangdai jiamiao lizhi yanjiu* 唐代家廟禮制研究. Taipei: Taiwan shanwu yinshuguan, 1991.

Gao Erwang 高二旺. "Beichao zangli zhi 'nili' tanxi" 北朝葬禮之尼禮探析. *Ningxia shehui kexue* 寧夏社會科學 3 (2008): 98–101.

Gao Min 高敏. *Wei Jin nanbeichao jingji shi* 魏晉南北朝經濟史. Shanghai: Shanghai renmin chubanshe, 1996.

Georgieva, Valentina. "Representation of Buddhist Nuns in Chinese Edifying Miracle Tales during the Six Dynasties and the Tang." *Journal of Chinese Religions* 24 (1996): 47–96.

Guo Jianxun 郭建勛. "Liang Han Wei Jin cifu zhong de xianshi nüxing ticai yu xingbie biaoda" 兩漢魏晉辭賦中的現實女性題材與性別表達. *Zhongguo wenxue yanjiu* 中國文學研究 4 (2003): 30–34.

Golavachev, Valentin G. "Matricide among the Tuoba-Xianbei and Its Transformation during the Northern Wei." *Early Medieval China* 8 (2002): 1–42.

Goldin, Paul Rakita. *The Culture of Sex in Ancient China.* Honolulu: University of Hawaii Press, 2002.

Goodman, Howard L. "Sites of Recognition: Burial, Mourning, and Commemoration in the Xun Family of Yingchuan, AD 140–305." *Early Medieval China* 15 (2009): 49–90.

———. *Xun Xu and the Politics of Precision in Third-Century AD China.* Leiden: Brill, 2010.

Grafflin, Dennis. "The Great Family in Medieval South China." *Harvard Journal of Asiatic Studies* 41, no. 1 (1981): 65–74.

———. "Social Order in the Early Southern Dynasties: The Formation of Eastern Chin." PhD diss., Harvard University, 1980.

Grant, Beata, and Wilt L. Idema, trans. *Escape from Blood Pond Hell: The Tales of Mulian and Woman Huang.* Seattle: University of Washington Press, 2011.

Gu Lihua 顧麗華. *Handai funü shenghuo qingkuang* 漢代婦女生活情況. Beijing: Shehui kexue wenxian, 2012.

Guizot, François. *The History of Civilization in Europe.* Translated by William Hazlitt. London: Penguin, 1997.

Habakkuk, H. J. "Family Structure and Economic Change in Nineteenth Century Europe." *Journal of Economic History* 15, no. 1 (1955): 1–12.

Hales, Dell R. "Dreams and the Daemonic in Traditional Chinese Short Stories." In *Critical Essays on Chinese Literature*, edited by William H. Nienhauser et al., 71–87. Hong Kong: The Chinese University of Hong Kong, 1976.

Han Guopan 韓國磐. *Sui Tang de juntian zhidu* 隋唐的均田制度. Shanghai: Shanghai renmin, 1957.

Hao Chunwen 郝春文. "Zai lun beichao zhi Sui Tang wudai Songchu de nüren jieshe" 再論北朝至隋唐五代宋初的女人結社. *Dunhuang yanjiu* 敦煌研究 6 (2006): 103–8.

Hatch, Elvin. "Theories of Social Honor." *American Anthropologist* 91, no. 2 (1989): 341–53.

Heirman, Ann. "Chinese Nuns and Their Ordination in Fifth Century China." *Journal of the International Association of Buddhist Studies* 24, no. 2 (2001): 275–304.

Hendrischke, Barbara. "The Daoist Utopia of Great Peace." *Oriens Extremus* 35, nos. 1/2 (1992): 61–91.

Herzfeld, Michael. "Honour and Shame: Problems in the Comparative Analysis of Moral Systems." *Man* 15 (1980): 339–51.

Hightower, James Robert. *Han Shih Wai Chuan: Han Ying's Illustrations of the Didactic Application of the Classic of Songs.* Cambridge, MA: Harvard University Press, 1952.

Hillman, David, and Carla Mazzio, eds. *The Body in Parts: Fantasies of Corporeality in Early Modern Europe.* New York: Routledge, 1997.

Hinsch, Bret. "Confucian Filial Piety and the Construction of the Ideal Chinese Buddhist Woman." *Journal of Chinese Religions* 30 (2003): 49–76.

———. "Evil Women and Dynastic Collapse: Tracing the Development of an Ideological Archetype." *Quarterly Journal of Chinese Studies* 1, no. 2 (2012): 62–81.

———. "The Origins of Han-Dynasty Consort Kin Power." *East Asian History* 25/26 (2003): 1–24.

———. "Textiles and Female Virtue in Early Imperial Chinese Historical Writing." *Nan Nü* 5, no. 2 (2003): 170–202.

Holcombe, Charles. "The Exemplar State: Ideology, Self-Cultivation, and Power in Fourth-Century China." *Harvard Journal of Asiatic Studies* 49, no. 1 (1989): 93–139.

———. "Re-Imagining China: The Chinese Identity Crisis at the Start of the Southern Dynasties Period." *Journal of the American Oriental Society* 115, no. 1 (1995): 1–14.

Holmgren, Jennifer. "Empress Dowager Ling of the Northern Wei and the T'o-pa Sinicization Question." *Papers on Far Eastern History* 18 (1978): 123–70.

———. "Family, Marriage and Political Power in 6th Century China: A Study of the Kao Family of Northern Ch'i, c. 520–550." *Journal of Asian History* 16, no. 1 (1982): 1–50.

———. "The Harem in Northern Wei Politics—398–498 AD." *Journal of the Economic and Social History of the Orient* 26, no. 1 (1983): 71–95.

———. "Imperial Marriage in the Native Chinese and Non-Han State, Han to Ming." In *Marriage and Inequality in Chinese Society*, edited by Rubie S. Watson and Patricia Buckley Ebrey, 58–96. Berkeley: University of California Press, 1991.

———. "The Lu Clan of Tai Commandary and Their Contribution to the To-pan State of Norhtern Wei in the Fifth Century." *T'oung Pao* 69, nos. 4–5 (1983): 272–312.

———. "The Making of an Elite: Local Politics and Social Relations in Northeastern China during the Fifth Century A.D." *Papers on Far Eastern History* 30 (1984): 1–74.

———. "Northern Wei as a Conquest Dynasty: Current Perceptions, Past Scholarship." *Papers on Far Eastern History* 49 (1989): 1–50.

———. "Political Organization of Non-Han States in China: The Role of Imperial Princes in Wei, Liao and Yuan." *Journal of Oriental Studies* 25, no. 1 (1987): 1–37.

———. "A Question of Strength: Military Capacity and Princess Bestowal in Imperial China's Foreign Relations (Han to Ch'ing)." *Monumenta Serica* 39 (1990–1991): 31–85.

———. "Race and Class in Fifth Century China: The Emperor Kao-tsu's Marriage Reform." *Early Medieval China* 2 (1995–1996): 86–117.

———. "Social Mobility in the Northern Dynasties: A Case Study of the Feng of Northern Yen." *Monumenta Serica* 35 (1981–1983): 19–32.

———. "Widow Chastity in the Northern Dynasties: The Lieh-nu Biographies in the Wei-shu." *Papers on Far Eastern History* 23 (1981): 165–86.

———. "Women and Political Power in the Traditional T'o-pa Elite: A Preliminary Study of the Biographies of Empresses in the Wei-shu." *Monumenta Serica* 35 (1981–1983): 33–74.

Holzman, Donald. "The Place of Filial Piety in Ancient China." *Journal of the American Oriental Society* 118, no. 2 (1998): 1–15.

Hou Weidong 侯偉東. "Wei Jin qingtan zhi feng dui nüxing de yingxiang" 魏晉清談之風對女性的影響. *Ningxia Daxue xuebao* 寧夏大學學報 5 (2005): 66–70, 88.

Hou Xudong and Howard Goodman. "Rethinking Chinese Kinship in the Han and the Six Dynasties: A Preliminary Observation." *Asia Major* 23, no. 1 (2010): 29–63.

Hsieh, Daniel. *Love and Women in Early Chinese Fiction*. Hong Kong: The Chinese University Press, 2008.

Hsiung, Ann-Marie. "The Images of Women in Early Chinese Poetry: The Book of Songs, Han Ballads and Palace Style Verse of the Liang Dynasty." *Chinese Culture* 35, no. 4 (1994): 81–90.

Hsu, Cho-yun, and Katheryn M. Linduff. *Western Chou Civilization*. New Haven, CT: Yale University Press, 1988.

Huang Ying 黃英. "*Jinshu—Lienüzhuan* zhong de nüxing" '晉書—列女傳' 中的女性. *Sichuan Daxue xuebao* 四川大學學報 19 (2004): 19–20.

Huang Yunhe 黃雲鶴. "Juntian yu beichao funü" 均田制與北朝婦女. *Xuchang Shizhuan xuebao* 許昌師專學報 13, no. 1 (1994): 27–32.

Huang Zhiyan 黃旨彥. *Gongzhu zhengzhi: Wei Jin nanbeichao zhengzhishi de xingbie kaocha* 公主政治 魏晉南北朝政治史的性別考察. New Taipei: Daoxiang chubanshe, 2013.

Jansen, Thomas. "*Yutai xinyong* 玉臺新詠." In *Early Medieval Chinese Texts: A Bibliographical Guide*, edited by Cynthia L. Chennault et al., 482–93. Berkeley: Institute of East Asian Studies, University of California, Berkeley, 2015.

Jia Erqiang 賈二強. *Shen jie gui yu: Tangdai minjian xinying toushi* 神界鬼域: 唐代民間信仰透視. Xi'an: Shaanxi renmin jiaoyu, 2000.

Jia Shaowan 賈少婉. "Wei Jin nanbeichao shiqi nanbeifang funü diwei de chayi ji yuanyin tanjiu" 魏晉南北朝時期南北方婦女地位的差異及原因探究. *Jincheng Zhiye Jishu Xueyuan xuebao* 晉城職業技術學院學報 1 (2016): 89–91.

Jian Zhaoliang 簡朝亮, ed. *Xiaojing jizhu shushu—fu dushutang dawen* 孝經集注述疏—附讀書堂答問. Annotated by Zhou Chunjian 周春健. Shanghai: Huadong Shifan Daxue chubanshe, 2011.

Jiao Jie 焦杰. "Fojiao xinyang yu Tangdai nüxing shenghuo xingtai zaitan—yi Tangdai muzhi ziliao wei zhongxin" 佛教信仰與唐代女性生活型態再探—以唐代墓誌資料為中心. *Tangshi luncong* 唐史論叢 20 (2015): 218–32.

———. "*Lienü zhuan* yu Zhou Qin Han Tang fude biaozhun" 列女傳與周秦漢唐婦德標準. *Shaanxi Shifan Daxue xuebao* 陝西師範大學學報 32, no. 6 (2003): 92–98.

Jin Xia 金霞. "Wei Jin shi de shang wu zhi feng" 魏晉時期的尚巫之風. *Xuchang Xueyuan xuebao* 許昌學院學報 6 (2003): 40–43.

Jing Jing 井精. "Shijing zhong meiren guannian dui Zhongguo shinühua de yingxiang" 詩經中美人觀念對中國仕女畫的影響. *Yishu baijia* 藝術百家 7 (2011): 223–25.

Jing Nan 景楠. "Shixi Wei Jin fengdu dui Wei Jin shiqi nüxing de yingxiang—cong *Shishuo xinyu*—Xianyuan pian tanqi" 試析魏晉風度對魏晉時期女性的影響—從世說新語賢媛篇談起. *Shehui kexuejia* 社會科學家 6 (2007): 71–72, 74.

Joyce, Rosemary A. "Archaeology of the Body." *Annual Review of Anthropology* 34 (2005): 139–58.

Kang Le 康樂. "Bei Wei Wenming taihou ji qi shidai (shang pian)" 北魏文明太后及其時代 (上篇). *Shihuo* 食貨 15, nos. 11/12 (1986): 461–75.

———. "Bei Wei Wenming taihou ji qi shidai (xia pian)" 北魏文明太后及其時代 (下篇). *Shihuo* 食貨 16, nos. 1/2 (1986): 56–66.

Katsuyama Minoru 騰山稔. *Chūgoku Sō—Min dai ni okeru konin no gakusaiteki kenkyū* 中國宋—明代における婚姻の學際的研究. Tokyo: Tōhoku Daigaku shuppankai, 2007.

Kawakatsu Yoshio 川勝義雄. *Rikuchō kizoku sei shakai no kenkyū* 六朝貴租制社會の研究. Tokyo: Iwanami, 1982.

Kieschnick, John. "*Biqiuni zhuan* 比丘尼傳." In *Early Medieval Chinese Texts: A Bibliographical Guide*, edited by Cynthia L. Chennault et al., 28–31. Berkeley: Institute of East Asian Studies, University of California, 2015.

Kirkland, Russell. "Fangzhong Shu: 'Arts of the Bedchamber'; Sexual Techniques." In *The Routledge Encyclopedia of Taoism*, Volume I: *A–L*, edited by Fabrizio Pregadio, 409–11. London: Routledge, 2008.

Knapp, Keith N. "Exemplary Everymen: Guo Shidao and Guo Yuanping as Confucian Commoners." *Asia Major* 23, no. 1 (2010): 87–126.

———. "Reverent Caring: The Parent-Son Relationship in Early Medieval Tales of Filial Offspring." In *Filial Piety in Chinese Thought and History*, edited by Alan K. L. Chan and Sor-hoon Tan, 44–70. London: RoutledgeCurzon, 2004.

———. "The Ru Reinterpretation of *Xiao*." *Early China* 20 (1995): 195–222.

———. *Selfless Offspring: Filial Children and Social Order in Early Medieval China*. Honolulu: University of Hawaii Press, 2005.

———. "*Xiaozi zhuan* 孝子傳." In *Early Medieval Chinese Texts: A Bibliographical Guide*, edited by Cynthia L. Chennault et al., 409–13. Berkeley: Institute of East Asian Studies, University of California, 2015.

Knechtges, David R. "Culling the Weeds and Selecting Prime Blossoms: The Anthology in Early Medieval China." In *Culture and Power in the Reconstitution of the Chinese Realm, 200–600*, edited by Scott Pearce, Audrey Spiro, and Patricia Ebrey, 200–241. Cambridge, MA: Harvard University Asia Center, 2001.

———. "Estate Culture in Early Medieval China: The Case of Shi Chong." In *Early Medieval China: A Sourcebook*, edited by Wendy Swartz, Robert Ford Campany, Yang Lu, and Jessey J. C. Choo, 530–42. New York: Columbia University Press, 2014.

———. "Marriage and Social Status: Shen Yue's 'Impeaching Wang Yuan.'" In *Early Medieval China: A Sourcebook*, edited by Wendy Swartz, Robert Ford Campany, Yang Lu, and Jessey J. C. Choo, 166–75. New York: Columbia University Press, 2014.

Ko, Dorothy. "Pursuing Talent and Virtue: Education and Women's Culture in Seventeenth and Eighteenth Century China." *Late Imperial China* 13, no. 1 (1992): 9–39.

Kohn, Livia. *Monastic Life in Medieval Daoism: A Cross Cultural Perspective*. Honolulu: University of Hawaii Press, 2003.

Kory, Stephan N. "Presence in Variety: De-Trivializing Female Diviners in Medieval China." *Nan Nü* 18, no. 1 (2016): 3–48.

Kroll, Paul W. "The Divine Songs of the Lady of Purple Tenuity." In *Studies in Early Medieval Chinese Literature and Cultural History in Honor of Richard B. Mather & Donald Holzman*, edited by Paul W. Kroll and David R. Knechtges, 149–211. Provo, UT: T'ang Studies Society, 2003.

Kuroda Mamiko黒田 真美子. "Riku chou Tōdai ni okeru yūkontan no tōjō jin-butsu—kankontan to no hikaku" 六朝唐代における幽婚譚の登場人物—神婚譚との比較. *Nihon Chūgoku gakukaihou* 日本中国学会報 48 (1996): 119–32.

Lai, Chi-Tim. "Ko Hung's Discourse of Hsien-Immortality: A Taoist Configuration of an Alternate Ideal Self-Identity." *Numen* 45, no. 2 (1998): 183–220.

Lai, Sufen Sofia. "From Cross-Dressing Daughter to Lady Knight-Errant: The Origin and Evolution of Chinese Women Warriors." In *Presence and Presentation: Women in the Chinese Literati Tradition*, edited by Sherry J. Mou, 77–107. New York: St. Martin's Press, 1999.

Lai Yanyuan 賴炎元, annotator. *Hanshi waizhuan* 韓詩外傳. Taipei: Taiwan Shangwu, 1991.

Laing, Ellen Johnston. "Chinese Palace-Style Poetry and the Depiction of a Palace Beauty." *The Art Bulletin* 72, no. 2 (1990): 284–95.

Lee, Hui-shu. *Empresses, Art, and Agency in Song Dynasty China*. Seattle: University of Washington Press, 2010.

Lee, Jen-der. "Childbirth in Early Imperial China." *Nan Nü* 7, no. 2 (2005): 216–86.

———. "Crime and Punishment: The Case of Liu Hui in the *Weishu*." In *Early Medieval China: A Sourcebook*, edited by Wendy Swartz, Robert Ford Company, Yang Lu, and Jessey J. C. Choo, 156–65. New York: Columbia University Press, 2014.

———. "The Death of a Princess: Codifying Classical Family Ethics in Early Medieval China." In *Presence and Prenetion: Women in the Chinese Literati Tradition*, edited by Sherry J. Mou, 1–38. New York: St. Martin's Press, 1999.

———. "The Epitaph of a Third-Century Wet Nurse, Xu Yi." In *Early Medieval China: A Sourcebook*, edited by Wendy Swartz, Robert Ford Company, Yang Lu, and Jessey J. C. Choo, 458–67. New York: Columbia University Press, 2014.

———. "Gender and Medicine in Tang China." *Asia Major* 16, no. 2 (2003): 1–32.

———. "The Life of Women in the Six Dynasties." *Funü yu liangxing xuekan* 婦女與兩性學刊 4 (1993): 47–80.

———. "Querelle des femmes? Les femmes jalouses et leur contrôle au début de la Chine médiévale." In *Éducation et Instruction en Chine III. Aux Marges de l'orthodoxie*, edited by Christine Nguyen Tri and Catherine Despeux, 67–97. Paris: Éditions Peeters, 2004.

———. "Wet Nurses in Early Imperial China." *Nan Nü* 2, no. 1 (2000): 1–39.

———. "Women and Marriage in China during the Period of Disunion." PhD diss., University of Washington, 1992.

Lee, Lily Xiao Hong. "The Emergence of Buddhist Nuns in China and Its Social Ramifications." In *The Virtue of Yin: Studies on Chinese Women*, 47–64. Canberra: Wild Peony, 1994.

———. "Language and Self-Estimation: The Case of Wei-Jin Women." *Journal of the Oriental Society of Australia* 25–26 (1993–1994): 150–64.

Lee, Lily Xiao Hong, A. D. Stefanowska, and Sue Wiles, eds. *Biographical Dictionary of Chinese Women: Antiquity through Sui, 1600 B.C.E.–618 C.E.* Hong Kong: Hong Kong University Press, 2007.

Lei Lei 雷蕾. "Wei Jin nanchao funü zai jiatingzhong de jingji diwei" 魏晉南朝婦女在家庭中的經濟地位. *Xiangfan Xueyuan xuebao* 襄樊學院學報 4 (2007): 73–76.

Lewis, Mark Edward. *China between Empires: The Northern and Southern Dynasties*. Cambridge, MA: The Belknap Press of Harvard University Press, 2009.

———. "Writing the World in the Family Instructions of the Yan Clan." *Early Medieval China* 13–14, no. 1 (2007): 33–80.

Li Baiyao 李百藥. *Bei Qi shu* 北齊書. Beijing: Zhonghua shuju, 1972.

Li Cong 李聰 and Zhao Zhijian 趙志堅. "Wei Jin nanchao funü hunyin sanlun" 魏晉南朝婦女婚姻散論. *Qi Lu xuekan* 齊魯學刊 5 (1997): 74–78.

Li Fang 李昉 et al. *Taiping yulan* 太平御覽. Taipei: Taiwan Shangwu (Sibu congkan ed.), n.d.

Li Guie 李桂蛾 and Gao Jianxin 高建新. "Cong *Shishuo xinyu* kan Wei Jin shiren jinbu de funüguan" 從世說新語看魏晉士人進步的婦女觀. *Nei Menggu Daxue xuebao* 內蒙古大學學報 35, no. 4 (2003): 48–53.

Li Jianzhong 李建中. "Shennü yu guafu—dui Wei Jin wenxue zhong lianglei nüxing xingxiang de wenhua shenshi 神女與寡婦—對魏晉文學中兩類女性形象的文化審視. *Zhongnan Minzu Daxue xuebao* 中南民族大學學報 2 (2002): 73–77.

Li Jingrong 李靜蓉. "Lun Wei Jin shiqi de jimu zi guanxi" 論魏晉時期的繼母子關係. *Zhuzhou Shifan Gaodeng Zhuanke Xuexiao xuebao* 株洲師範高等專科學校學報 10, no. 1 (2005): 45–47.

Li Jinhe 李金河. *Wei Jin Sui Tang hunyin xingtai yanjiu* 魏晉隋唐婚姻形態研究. Ji-nan: Qi Lu shushe, 2005.

Li Mingren 李明仁. "Tuoba shi zaoqi de hunyin zhengce" 拓跋氏早期的婚姻政策. *Shiyuan* 史原 20 (1997): 89–117.

Li Ping 李憑. *Bei Wei Pingcheng shidai* 北魏平成時代. Shanghai: Shanghai guji, 2014.

Li, Wai-yee. *The Readability of the Past in Early Chinese Historiography*. Cambridge, MA: Harvard University Asia Center, 2007.

Li, Xiaorong. *Women's Poetry of Late Imperial China*. Seattle: University of Washington Press, 2012.

Li Ya 李芽. *Zhongguo lidai zhuangshi* 中國歷代妝飾. Beijing: Zhongguo fangzhi chubanshe, 2004.

Li Yanong 李亞農. "Zhouzu de shizu zhidu yu Tuobazu de qianfengjian zhi" 周族的氏族制度與拓拔族的前封建制. In *Li Yanong shi lunji* 李亞農史論集, 323–96. Shanghai: Shanghai renmin chubanshe, 1962.

Li Yanshou 李延壽. *Beishi* 北史. Beijing: Zhonghua shuju, 1974.

———. *Nanshi* 南史. Beijing: Zhonghua shuju, 1975.

Li Yuzhen 李玉珍. *Tangdai de biqiuni* 唐代的比丘尼. Taipei: Xuesheng shuju, 1989.

Li Zhende 李貞德. "Cong 'dufu ji' tanqi" 從 '妒婦記' 談起. *Funü yu liangxing jikan* 婦女與兩性季刊 3 (1994): 12–15.

———. "Han Tang zhijian de nüxing yiliao zhaoguzhe" 漢唐之間的女性醫療照顧者. *Taida lishi xuebao* 台大歷史學報 23 (1999): 123–56.

———. "Han Tang zhijian yifang zhong ji jian furen yu nüti wei yao" 漢唐之間醫方中德忌見婦人與女體為藥. *Xin shixue* 新史學 13, no. 4 (2002): 1–35.

———. "Han Sui zhijian de 'sheng zi bu ju' wenti" 漢隋之間的 '生子不舉' 問題. *Zhongyang Yanjiuyuan Lishi Yuyan Yanjiusuo jikan* 中央研究院歷史語言研究所集刊 66, no. 3 (1995): 747–812.

———. "Han Tang zhijian jiating zhong de jiankang zhaogu yu xingbie" 漢唐之間家庭中的健康照顧與性別. In *Disanjie guoji hanxue huiyi lunwenji lishizu, xingbie yu yiliao* 第三屆國際漢學會議論文集歷史組, 性別與醫療, 1–49. Taipei: Institute of History and Philology, 2002.

———. "Han Tang zhijian nüxing caichanquan shitan" 漢唐之間女性財產權試探. In *Zhongguo shi xinlun—xingbie shi fence* 中國史新論—性別史分冊, edited by Li Zhende 李貞德, 191–237. Taipei: Zhongyang yanjiu yuan, 2009.

———. "Han Tang zhijian qiuzi yifang shitan—jianlun fuke lanshang yu xingbie lunshu" 漢唐之間求子醫方試探—兼論婦科濫觴與性別論述. *Zhongyang Yanjiuyuan Lishi Yuyan Yanjiusuo jikan* 中央研究院歷史語言研究所集刊 68, no. 2 (1997): 283–367.

———. "Han Tang zhijian yishu zhong de shengchan zhi dao" 漢唐之間醫書中的生產之道. *Zhongyang Yanjiuyuan Lishi Yuyan Yanjiusuo jikan* 中央研究院歷史語言研究所集刊 67, no. 3 (1996): 533–654.

———. "Nüren de Zhongguo zhonggushi—xingbie yu Han Tang zhijian de lilü yanjiu" 女人的中國中古史—性別與漢唐之間的禮律研究. In *Chūgoku no rekishi sekai—tōgō no shisutemu to takenteki hatsuten* 中國の歷史世界—統合のシステムと多元的發展, edited by Nihon Chūgokushi gakkai 日本中國史學會, 469–92. Tokyo: Kyūko, 2002.

Liang Mancang 梁滿倉. *Wei Jin nanbeichao wuli zhidu kaolun* 魏晉南北朝五禮制度考論. Beijing: Shehui kexue wenxian, 2009.

Liao Jianqi 廖健琦. "Beichao shehui hunyin zhuangkuang chuyi" 北朝社會婚姻狀況芻議. *Shixue yuekan* 史學月刊 2 (1998): 69–70.

Lin Suzhen 林素珍. *Wei Jin Nanbeichao jiaxun zhi yanjiu* 魏晉南北朝家訓之研究. Hua Mulan wenhua chubanshe, 2008.

Lin, Wei-hung. "Chastity in Chinese Eyes—Nan-Nu Yu-Pieh." *Hanxue yanjiu* 漢學研究 12 (1991): 13–40.

Lin Yanzhi 林艷枝. "Tang wudai shiqi Dunhuang diqu de nüren jieshe" 唐五代時期敦煌地區的女人結社. *Zhongguo wenhua yuekan* 中國文化月刊 6 (2000): 32–50.

Linghu Defen 令狐德棻. *Zhoushu* 周書. Beijing: Zhonghua shuju, 1995.

Lingley, Kate A. "Lady Yuchi in the First Person: Patronage, Kinship, and Voice in the Guyang Cave." *Early Medieval China* 18 (2012): 25–47.

———. "Naturalizing the Exotic: On the Changing Meanings of Ethnic Dress in Medieval China." *Ars Orientalis* 38 (2010): 50–80.

Liu Chunxiang 劉春香. "Wei Jin nanbeichao shiqi de wuxi yu yinsi" 魏晉南北朝時期的巫覡與淫祀. *Xuchang Xueyuan xuebao* 許昌學院學報 6 (2006): 27–30.

Liu Hsieh. *The Literary Mind and the Carving of Dragons: A Study of Thought and Pattern in Chinese Literature.* Translated by Vincent Yu-chung Shih. New York: Columbia University Press, 1959.

Liu I-ching. *Shih-shuo Hsin-yü: A New Account of Tales of the World.* Commentary by Liu Chün. Translated by Richard B. Mather. Minneapolis: University of Minnesota Press, 1976.

Liu Lingdi 劉玲娣. "Han Wei liuchao daojiao de xiaodao" 漢魏六朝道教的孝道. *Nandu xuetan* 南都學壇 27, no. 1 (2007): 39–41.

Liu Shuli 劉淑麗. *Xian Qin Han Wei Jin funüguan yu wenxuezhong de nüxing* 先秦漢魏晉婦女觀與文學中的女性. Beijing: Xueyuan, 2008.

Liu Xiang 劉向. *Lienü zhuan* 列女傳. Taipei: Taiwan Zhonghua shuju (Sibu beiyao ed.), 1981.

Liu Xie 劉勰, *Wenxin diaolong* 文心雕龍. Beijing: Zhonghua shuju, 1985.

Liu Xu 劉昫 et al. *Jiu Tang shu* 舊唐書. Annotated by Liu Jie 劉節 and Chen Naiqian 陳乃乾. Beijing: Zhonghua shuju, 1975.

Liu Yao 劉飆. "Biqiuni zhuan zhong biqiuni chanxiu zhuangkuang luelun" 比丘尼傳中比丘尼禪修狀況略論. *Huanggang Zhiye Jishu Xueyuan xuebao* 黃岡職業技術學院學報 5 (2010): 73–75.

———. *Wei Jin nanbeichao shijia zhuanji yanjiu—Shi Baochang yu Biqiuni zhuan* 魏晉南北朝釋家傳記研究—釋寶唱與比丘尼傳. Changsha: Yuelu shushe, 2009.

Liu Yiqing 劉義慶. *Shishuo xinyu huijiao jizhu* 世說新語彙校集注. Annotated by Liu Xiaobiao 劉孝標 and Zhu Zhuyu 朱鑄禹. Shanghai: Shanghai guji, 2002.

Liu Yongcong 劉詠聰. "Wei Jin yihuan shijia dui houfei zhuzheng zhi fumian pingjia" 魏晉以還史家對后妃主政之負面評價. In *Zhongguo funüshi lunji sanji* 中國婦女史論集三集, edited by Bao Jialin 鮑家麟, 29–40. Taipei: Daoxiang, 1993.

Liu Zenggui 劉增貴. "Wei Jin Nanbeichao shidai de qie" 魏晉南北朝時代的妾. *Xin shixue* 新史學 2, no. 4 (1991): 1–36.

Liu Zhao 劉釗. "Shishuo xinyu suo miaohui zhi Wei Jin nüxing fengliu zhiyi" 世說新語所描繪之魏晉女性風流質疑. *Xiangfan Xueyuan xuebao* 襄樊學院學報 9 (2008): 46–48.

Liu Zhen 劉珍. *Dongguan Hanji xiaozhu* 東觀漢記校注. Annotated by Wu Shuping 吳樹平. Zhengzhou: Zhongzhou Guji, 1987.

Lo, Yuet Keung. "Conversion to Chastity: A Buddhist Catalyst in Early Imperial China." *Nan Nü* 10, no. 1 (2008): 22–56.

———. "Filial Devotion for Women: A Buddhist Testimony from Third-Century China." In *Filial Piety in Chinese Thought and History*, edited by Alan K. L. Chan and Sor-hoon Tan, 71–90. London: RoutledgeCurzon, 2004.

———. "Recovering a Buddhist Voice on Daughter-in-Law: The Yuyenü jing." *History of Religions* 44, no. 4 (2005): 318–50.

Lou Jin 樓勁. "Zhengsheng yuannian chi yu Nanbeichao zhi Tangdai de jingbiao xiaoyi zhi zhidu—jian lun S.1344 hao Lundun canjuan de dingming wenti" 證聖元年敕與南北朝至唐代的旌表孝義之制度—兼論 S.1344 號倫敦殘卷的定名問題. *Zhejiang xuekan* 浙江學刊 1 (2014): 11–29.

Lu Hongping 魯紅平. "Cong Shishuo xinyu kan Wei Jin shiren de zhongxiaoguan" 從世說新語看魏晉士人的忠孝觀. *Lunlixue yanjiu* 倫理學研究 1 (2011): 50–56.

Lu Jianrong 盧建榮. "Cong nanxing shuxie cailiao kan san zhi qi shiji nüxing de shehui xingxiang suzao" 從男性書寫材料看三至七世紀女性的社會形象塑造. *Guoli Taiwan Shifan Daxue lishi xuebao* 國立台灣師範大學歷史學報 26 (1998): 1–42.

Lu Jingqing 陸靜卿. "Tantan Wei Jin shangceng funü de 'da'" 談談魏晉上層婦女的達. *Zhaoqing Xueyuan xuebao* 肇慶學院學報 25, no. 4 (2004): 35–37.

———. "Xian Qin funü yu Wei Jin funü 'da' de butong tixian" 先秦婦女與魏晉婦女'達'的不同體現. *Guangxi shehui kexue* 廣西社會科學 4 (2004): 139–41.

Lu Rong 盧蓉. "Wei Jin nanbeichao funü de wenxue piping" 魏晉南北朝婦女的文學批評. *Suzhou Daxue xuebao* 蘇州大學學報 2 (2008): 70–74.

Lu Ting 盧婷. "Han Wei liuchao fuzhong de Nü Wa xingxiang yu wenxue muti de xingcheng" 漢魏六朝賦中的女媧形象與文學母體的形成. *Yuwen jiaoxue tongxun* 語文教學通訊 10 (2014): 73–75.

Lu Yaodong 逯耀東. "Tuoba shi yu zhongyuan shizu de hunyin guanxi" 拓拔氏與中原氏族的婚姻關係. In *Cong Pingcheng dao Luoyang* 從平城到洛陽, 149–236. Taipei: Dongda tutu, 2001.

Luo Tonghua 羅彤華. *Tongju gongcai: Tangdai jiating yanjiu* 同居共財: 唐代家庭研究. Taipei: Zhengda chubanshe, 2015.

Ma Hongliang 馬洪良 and Zhou Haiyan 周海燕. "Wei Jin nanbeichao de nügong shangyezhe" 魏晉南北朝的女工商業者. *Xueshu luntan* 學術論壇 11 (2006): 178–80.

Ma Lili 馬黎麗. "Wei Jin meinü fu zhi yanbian" 魏晉美女賦之演變. *Guizhou Minzu Daxue xuebao* 貴州民族大學學報 6 (2013): 88–92.

Ma Yan 馬言. "Wei Jin nanbeichao Hannü xingxiang de shanbian guocheng gouchen" 魏晉南北朝漢女性向的嬗變過程鈎沈. *Yunyang Shifan Gaodeng Zhuanke Xuexiao xuebao* 鄖陽師範高等專科學校學報 35, no. 1 (2015): 44–47.

Ma Yijin 馬以謹. *Wei Jin Nanbeichao de funü yuanzuo* 魏晉南北朝的婦女緣坐. Taipei: Hua Mulan wenhua chubanshe, 2010.

Mann, Susan. "Widows in the Kinship, Class, and Community Structures of Qing Dynasty China." *Journal of Asian Studies* 46, no. 1 (1987): 37–56.

Mao Han-kuang. "The Evolution in the Nature of the Medieval Genteel Families." In *State and Society in Early Medieval China*, edited by Albert E. Dien, 73–109. Stanford: Stanford University Press, 1990.

Mather, Richard B. "Intermarriage as a Gauge of Family Status in the Southern Dynasties." In *State and Society in Early Medieval China*, edited by Albert E. Dien, 211–28. Stanford: Stanford University Press, 1990.

Mathieu, Rémi. *Démons et Merveilles dans la Littérature Chinoise des Six Dynasties: La Fantastique et l'anecdotique dans le "Soushen Ji" de Gan Bao*. Paris: Éditions You-Feng, 2000.

McKnight, Brian E. *Law and Order in Sung China*. Cambridge: Cambridge University Press, 1992.

McMahon, Keith. "The Institution of Polygamy in the Chinese Imperial Palace." *The Journal of Asian Studies* 72, no. 4 (2013): 917–36.

———. *Women Shall Not Rule: Imperial Wives and Concubines in China from Han to Liao*. Lanham, MD: Rowman & Littlefield, 2013.

Milburn, Olivia. "Palace Women in the Former Han Dynasty (202 BCE–CE 23): Gender and Administrative History in the Early Imperial Era." *Nan Nü* 18, no 2 (2016): 195–223.

Miles, Richard. *Carthage Must Be Destroyed: The Rise and Fall of an Ancient Civilization*. London: Penguin Books, 2010.

Miller, Alan L. "The Woman Who Married a Horse: Five Ways of Looking at a Chinese Folktale." *Asian Folklore Studies* 54, no. 2 (1995): 275–305.

Misevic, Dusanka D. "Oligarchy or Social Mobility: A Study of the Great Clans of Early Medieval China." *The Museum of Far Eastern Antiquities* 65 (1993): 5–256.

Miyakawa Hisayuki 宮川尚志. *Rikuchōshi kenkyū: shūkyō hen* 六朝史研究: 宗教篇. Tokyo: Heirakudera shoten, 1964.

Mou, Sherry J. *Gentlemen's Prescriptions for Women's Lives: A Thousand Years of Biographies of Chinese Women*. Armonk, NY: M. E. Sharpe, 2004.

Nakamura Keiji 中村圭爾. *Rikuchō seiji shakai shi kenkyū* 六朝政治社會史研究. Tokyo: Kyuko shoin, 2013.

Ning Xin 寧欣. "Tangdai funü de shehui jingji huodong—yi 'Taiping guangji' wei zhongxin" 唐代婦女的社會經濟活動—以 '太平廣記' 為中心. In *Tang Song nüxing yu shehui* 唐宋女性與社會, edited by Deng Xiaonan 鄧小南, 1:235–51. Shanghai: Shanghai cishu, 2003.

Niu Zhiping 牛志平. "Tangdai dufu shulun" 唐代妒婦述論. In *Zhongguo Funüshi lunji xuji* 中國婦女史論集續集, edited by Bao Jialin 鮑家麟, 55–65. Taipei: Daoxiang chubanshe, 1991.

Ochi Shigeaki 越智重明. *Gi Shin nanchō no hito to shakai* 魏晉南朝の人と社會. Tokyo: Kenbun shuppan, 1985.

———. *Gi Shin Nanchō no kizoku sei* 魏晉南朝の貴族制. Tokyo: Kenbun, 1982.

Ogata Isamu 尾形勇. *Chūgoku kodai no ie to kokka—kōtei shipaika no chitsujo kekkō* 中國古代の家と國家—皇帝支配下の秩序結構. Tokyo: Iwanami shoten, 1975.

O'Hara, Albert Richard. *The Position of Woman in Early China: According to the Lieh Nü Chuan "The Biographies of Chinese Women."* Taipei: Mei Ya, 1971.

Ōhashi Yoshiharu 大橋由治. "Seisetsu shingo to Shindai bunka—setsuwa ni miru jinbutsu hyōka no jitsusō" 世説新語と魏晉文化—説話に見る人物評價の實相. *Daitō Bunka Daigaku kangaku kaishi* 大東文化大学漢学会誌 45 (2006): 65–84.

Oppenheim, A. Leo. *Ancient Mesopotamia: Portrait of a Dead Civilization*, revised edition completed by Erica Reiner. Chicago: University of Chicago Press, 1964.

Ōsawa Masāki 大澤正昭. "'Dufu,' 'hanqi' yi ji 'junei'—Tang Song biangeqi de hunyin yu jiating de bianhua" '妒婦,' '悍妻' 以及 '懼內'—唐宋變革期的婚姻 與家庭之變化. In *Tang Song nüxing yu shehui* 唐宋女性與社會, edited by Deng Xiaonan 鄧小南, 2:829–48. Shanghai: Shanghai cishu, 2003.

———. *Tō Sō jidai no kazoku, konin, josei—tsuma wa tsuyoku* 唐宋時代の家族, 婚姻, 女性—婦は強く. Tokyo: Akashi, 2005.

Ouyang Xiu 歐陽修 and Song Qi 宋祁. *Xin Tang shu* 新唐書. Annotated by Dong Jiazun 董家遵 et al. Beijing: Zhonghua shuju, 1975.

Ouyang Xun 歐陽詢. *Yiwen leiju* 藝文類聚. Taipei: Wenguang, 1974.

Pearce, Scott. "Form and Matter: Archaizing Reform in Sixth-Century China." In *Culture and Power in the Reconstitution of the Chinese Realm, 200–600*, edited by Scott Pearce, Audrey Spiro, and Patricia Ebrey, 149–78. Cambridge, MA: Harvard University Asia Center, 2001.

———. "Nurses, Nurslings, and New Shapes of Power in the Mid-Wei Court." *Asia Major* 22, no. 1 (2009): 287–309.

Peng Jiepo 彭潔波. "Qin, Han, Wei, Jin shiqi de xiuwu" 秦漢魏晉時期的袖舞. *Beijing Wudao Xueyuan xuebao* 北京舞蹈學院學報 2 (2009): 14–20.

Perkins, Franklin. *Heaven and Earth Are Not Humane: The Problem of Evil in Classical Chinese Philosophy*. Bloomington: Indiana University Press, 2014.

Poo, Mu-Chou. "The Completion of an Ideal World: The Human Ghost in Early-Medieval China." *Asia Major* 10, nos. 1/2 (1997): 69–94.

Qian, Nanxiu. "*Lienü* versus *Xianyuan*: The Two Biographical Traditions in Chinese Women's History." In *Beyond Exemplar Tales: Women's Biography in Chinese History*, edited by Joan Judge and Hu Ying, 70–87. Berkeley: University of California Press, 2011.

———. "Milk and Scent: Works about Women in the Shishuo Xinyu Genre." *Nan Nü* 1, no. 2 (1999): 187–236.

———. *Spirit and Self in Medieval China: The Shih-shuo hsin-yü and Its Legacy*. Honolulu: University of Hawaii Press, 2001.

―――. "Women's Roles in Wei-Chin Character Appraisal as Reflected in the Shih-shuo hsin-yü." In *Studies in Medieval Chinese Literature and Cultural History: In Honor of Richard B. Mather and Donald Holzman*, edited by Paul W. Kroll and David R. Knechtges, 259–302. Provo, UT: T'ang Studies Society, 2003.

Qiu Shaoping 邱少平 and Zhang Yanxia 張艷霞. "Cong *Biqiuni zhuan* kan Dong Jin zhi nanchao shiqi funü chujia de yuanyin" 從比丘尼傳看東晉至南朝時期婦女出家的原因. *Hunan Chengshi Xueyuan xuebao* 湖南城市學院學報 30, no. 3 (2009): 30–31.

Quinn, Naomi. "Anthropological Studies on Women's Status." *Annual Review of Anthropology* 6 (1977): 181–225.

Raphals, Lisa. "Arguments by Women in Early Chinese Texts." *Nan Nü* 3, no. 2 (2001): 157–95.

―――. *Sharing the Light: Representations of Women and Virtue in Early China*. Albany: State University of New York Press, 1998.

Richter, Antje. *Letters & Epistolary Culture in Early Medieval China*. Seattle: University of Washington Press, 2013.

Robertson, Maureen. "Voicing the Feminine: Constructions of the Gendered Subject in Lyric Poetry by Women of Medieval and Late Imperial China." *Late Imperial China* 13, no. 1 (1992): 63–110.

Rogers, Susan Carol, and Sonya Salamon. "Inheritance and Social Organization among Family Farmers." *American Ethnologist* 10, no. 3 (1983): 529–50.

Rosemont, Henry, Jr., and Roger T. Ames. *The Chinese Classic of Family Reverence: A Philosophical Translation of the Xiaojing*. Honolulu: University of Hawaii Press, 2009.

Rouzer, Paul F. *Articulated Ladies: Gender and the Male Community in Early Chinese Texts*. Cambridge, MA: Harvard University Press, 2001.

Sanders, Graham. "I Read They Said He Sang What He Wrote: Orality, Writing, and Gossip in Tang Poetry Anecdotes." In *Idle Talk: Gossip and Anecdote in Traditional China*, edited by Jack. W. Chen and David Schaberg, 88–106. Berkeley: Global, Area, and International Archive and University of California Press, 2014.

Schafer, Edward H. "The Jade Woman of Greatest Mystery." *History of Religions* 17, nos. 3–4 (1978): 387–98.

―――. "Ritual Exposure in Ancient China." *Harvard Journal of Asiatic Studies* 14, nos. 1/2 (1951): 130–84.

Schipper, Kristofer. "Purity and Strangers Shifting Boundaries in Medieval Taoism." *T'oung Pao* 80, nos. 1/3 (1994): 61–81.

Schlegel, Alice, and Rohn Eloul. "Marriage Transactions: Labor, Property, Status." *American Anthropologist* 90, no. 2 (1988): 291–309.

Schuster, Nancy. "Striking a Balance: Women and Images of Women in Early Chinese Buddhism." In *Women, Religion, and Social Change*, edited by Yvonne Yazbeck Haddad and Ellison Banks Findly, 87–111. Albany, NY: State University of New York Press, 1985.

Shanxi Sheng Datong Shi Bowuguan 山西省大同市博物館 and Shanxi Sheng Gongzuo Weihuanhui 山西省文物工作委員會. "Shanxi Datong Shijiazhai Bei Wei Sima Jinlong mu" 山西大同石家寨北魏司馬金龍墓. *Wenwu* 文物 190 (1972): 20–33.

Shao Zhengkun 邵正坤. *Beichao jiating xingtai yanjiu* 北朝家庭形態研究. Beijing: Kexue chubanshe, 2008.

———. "Lun beichao nüzi de jiating diwei" 論北朝女子的家庭地位. *Xi'an Ouya Xueyuan xuebao* 西安歐亞學院學報 2 (2010): 64–68.

Shen Yue 沈約. *Songshu* 宋書. Beijing: Zhonghua shuju, 1974.

Shi Baochang 釋寶唱. *Biqiuni zhuan jiaozhu* 比丘尼傳校註. Annotated by Wang Rutong 王儒童. Taipei: Zhonghua, 2006.

Shi Guangming 施光明. "Weishu suojian Bei Wei gongzhu hunyin guanxi yanjiu" 魏書所見北魏公主婚姻關係研究. *Minzu yanjiu* 民族研究 5 (1989): 106–12.

Shiga Shūzō 滋賀秀三. *Chūgoku kazokuhō no genri* 中國家族法の原理. Tokyo: Sōbunsha, 1967.

———. "Family Property and the Law of Inheritance in Traditional China." In *Chinese Family Law and Social Change in Historical and Comparative Perspective*, edited by David C. Buxbaum, 109–50. Seattle: University of Washington Press, 1978.

Shimomi Takao 下見隆雄. *Bosei izon no shisō—"nijūshi kō" kara kangaeru boshi ittai kannen to kō* 母性依存の思想—'二十四孝' から考える母子一体觀念と孝. Tokyo: Kenbun, 2002.

———. *Juka shakai to bosei—bosei no iroku no kanten de miru Kan Gi Shin Chūgoku josei shi* 儒家社會と母性—母性の威力の觀點でみる漢魏晉中國女性史, revised edition. Tokyo: Kenbun shuppan, 2008.

Shu Hongxia 舒紅霞 and Yang Dongxia 楊東霞. "Wei Jin renxing zijue dui Songdai nüzuojia de yingxiang" 魏晉人性自覺對宋代女作家的影響. *Dalian Daxue xuebao* 大連大學學報 1 (2006): 30–33.

Sima Guang 司馬光. *Zizhi tongjian* 資治通鑑. Shanghai: Guji, 1956.

Song Dexi 宋德熹. "Tangdai de jinü" 唐代的妓女. In *Zhongguo Funüshi lunji xuji* 中國婦女史論集續集, edited by Bao Jialin 鮑家麟, 67–121. Taipei: Daoxiang chubanshe, 1991.

Song Qirui 宋其蕤. *Bei Wei nüzhu lun* 北魏女主論. Beijing: Zhongguo shehui kexue, 2006.

Song Rentao 宋仁桃. "Qianyi Wei Jin nanbeichao shiqi nüxing chujia de xianxiang" 淺議魏晉南北朝時期女性出嫁的現象. *Jiangnan Shehui Xueyuan xuebao* 江南社會學院學報 4, no. 3 (2002): 51–54.

Spade, Beatrice. "The Education of Women in China during the Southern Dynasties." *Journal of Asian History* 13, no. 1 (1979): 15–41.

Spiro, Audrey. "Of Noble Ladies and Notable Conventions: The Search for Gu Kaizhi." In *Studies in Early Medieval Chinese Literature and Cultural History in Honor of Richard B. Mather & Donald Holzman*, edited by Paul W. Kroll and David R. Knechtges, 213–57. Provo, UT: T'ang Studies Society, 2003.

Sun Jie 孫潔. "Cong *Shijing* kan Zhoudai de chuqizhi" 從詩經看周代的出妻制. *Anhui wenxue* 安徽文學 5 (2007): 63–64.

Sun Qin'an 孫琴安. "Guanyu Wei Jin Nanbei chao yanqing wenxue de zucheng ji pingjia" 關於魏晉南北朝艷情文學的組成及評價. *Shanghai Shehui Kexue yuan xueshu jikan* 上海社會科學院學術季刊 36, no. 1 (1994): 186–92.

Sun Tongxun 孫同勛. "Some Hints on the Marriage Custom of Early Toba." In *Tuoba shi de Hanhua ji qita—Bei Wei shilun wenji* 拓拔氏的漢化及其他—北魏史論文集, 241–48. Taipei: Daoxiang chubanshe, 2005.

Sun Wenbo 孫聞博. "Qin Han de nüzi canzhan yu qinshu suijun" 秦漢的女子參戰與親屬隨軍. In *Lifa yu xinyang—Zhongguo gudai nüxing yanjiu lunkao* 禮法與信仰—中國古代女性研究論考, edited by Pu Muzhou 蒲慕州, 52–74. Hong Kong: Shangwu yinshuguan, 2013.

Suzuki Keizō 鈴木啟造. "Shaku Hōshō Bikuniden ni kansuru gigi" 釋寶唱撰比丘尼傳に関する疑義." *Shikan* 史觀89 (1973): 48–59.

Swartz, Wendy, Robert Ford Campany, Yang Lu, and Jessey J. C. Choo. "Introduction." In *Early Medieval China: A Sourcebook*, edited by Swartz et al., 1–10. New York: Columbia University Press, 2014.

Tang Jia 唐嘉 and Song Xiaoqing 宋筱清. "Beichao beike suojian nüxing Mile, Guanyin xinyang tanxi" 北朝碑刻所見女性彌勒，觀音信仰探析. *Guizhou shehui kexue* 貴州社會科學 12 (2012): 83–84.

Tanigawa Michio. *Medieval Chinese Society and the Local "Community."* Translated by Joshua A. Fogel. Berkeley: University of California Press, 1985.

Tanigawa Michio and Joshua A. Fogel. "Problems Concerning the Japanese Periodization of Chinese History." *Journal of Asian History* 21, no. 2 (1987): 150–68.

Thatcher, Melvin P. "Marriages of the Ruling Elite in the Spring and Autumn Period." In *Marriage and Inequality in Chinese Society*, edited by Rubie S. Watson and Patricia B. Ebrey, 25–57. Berkeley: University of California Press, 1991.

Tian, Xiaofei. *Beacon Fire and Shooting Star: The Literary Culture of the Liang (502–557)*. Cambridge, MA: Harvard University Asia Center, 2007.

Tsai, Kathryn A. "The Chinese Buddhist Monastic Order for Women: The First Two Centuries." In *Women in China: Current Directions in Historical Scholarship*, edited by Richard W. Guisso and Stanley Johannesen, 1–21. Youngstown, NY: Philo Press, 1981.

———. *Lives of the Nuns: Biographies of Chinese Buddhist Nuns from the Fourth to Sixth Centuries, A Translation of the* Pi-ch'iu-ni chuan, *compiled by Shih Pao-ch'ang.* Honolulu: University of Hawaii Press, 1972.

Tung, Jowen R. *Fables for the Patriarchs: Gender Politics in Tang Discourse.* Lanham, MD: Rowman & Littlefield, 2000.

Turner, Victor. "Symbols in Ndembu Ritual." In *The Forest of Symbols: Aspects of Ndembu Ritual*, 19–47. Ithaca: Cornell University Press, 1967.

Van Ess, Hans. "Praise and Slander: The Evocation of Empress Lü in the *Shiji* and the *Hanshu*." *Nan Nü* 8, no. 2 (2006): 221–54.

Van Norden, Bryan W., trans. *Mengzi: With Selections from Traditional Commentaries.* Indianapolis: Hackett Publishing, 2008.

von Glahn, Richard. *The Economic History of China: From Antiquity to the Nineteenth Century.* Cambridge: Cambridge University Press, 2016.

Wallacker, Benjamin E. "Chang Fei's Preface to the Chin Code of Law." *T'oung Pao* 72, nos. 4–5 (1986): 229–68.

Wang Chaoxia 王朝俠. "Rujia suzao de nüxing lixiang renge dui Wei Jin shinü hua de yingxiang" 儒家塑造的女性理想人格對魏晉仕女畫的影響. *Beifang meishu* 北方美術 1 (2013): 60–61.

Wang Chi-chen. "A Gift of a Chinese Painting." *Metropolitan Museum of Art Bulletin* 29, no. 3 (1934): 44–46.

Wang Guofu 汪國富. "Cong Dadiwan yi, er qi wenhua yicun kan woguo muxi shizu shehui" 從大地灣一，二期文化遺存看我國古代母系氏族社會. *Tianshui Shifan Xueyuan xuebao* 天水師範學院學報 6 (2002): 35–37.

Wang Lianru 王連儒. *Han Wei liuchao Langya Wangshi jiazu zhengzhi yu hunyin wenhua yanjiu* 漢魏六朝琅邪王氏家族政治與婚姻文化研究. Beijing: Zhongguo shehui kexue, 2013.

Wang Lihua 王利華. *Zhongguo jiatingshi: diyi juan, xian Qin zhi nanbei chao shiqi* 中國家庭史: 第一卷, 先秦至南北朝時期. N.p.: Guangdong renmin chubanshe, 2007.

Wang, Ping. "The Art of Poetry Writing: Liu Xiaochuo's 'Becoming the Number-One Person for the Number-One Position.'" In *Early Medieval China: A Sourcebook*, edited by Wendy Swartz, Robert Ford Campany, Yang Lu, and Jessey J. C. Choo, 245–55. New York: Columbia University Press, 2014.

———. "Literary Imagination of the North and South." In *Early Medieval China: A Sourcebook*, edited by Wendy Swartz, Robert Ford Campany, Yang Lu, and Jessey J. C. Choo, 77–87. New York: Columbia University Press, 2014.

Wang Qing 王青. "Wei Jin shiqi de Xiwangmu chuanshuo yi ji chansheng beijing" 魏晉時期的西王母傳說以及產生背景. *Nanjing Shida xuebao* 南京師大學報 3 (1997): 118–22.

Wang Qiyue 王麒越. "'Wei Jin fengdu' xia de nanxing meirong xianxiang tantao" '魏晉風度'下的男性美容現象探討. *Chongqing Keji Xueyuan xuebao* 重慶科技學院學報 2 (2009): 176–77.

Wang Renlei 王仁磊. "Wei Jin nanbeichao jiating yu jiazu, zongzu guanxi chutan" 魏晉南北朝家庭與家族宗族關係初探. *Beifang luncong* 北方論叢 6 (2011): 78–80.

Wang Shaodong 王紹東. "Qin Shihuang zhenjie funüguan de xinli tanyin" 秦始皇貞節婦女觀的心理探因. *Nei Menggu Daxue xuebao* 內蒙古大學學報 6 (1996): 30–35.

Wang Tianchan 王天嬋. "Wei Jin liuchao zhiguai xiaoshuo qingai zuopinzhong de nüxing xingxiang" 魏晉六朝志怪小說情愛作品中的女性形象. *Fuzhou Shizhuan xuebao* 福州師專學報 1 (2002): 17–19.

Wang Wanying 王萬盈. "Beichao funü hunjia shulun" 北朝婦女婚嫁述論. *Datong Gaodeng Zhuanke Xuexiao xuebao* 大同高登專科學校學報 13, no. 4 (1999): 9–16.

Wang Weiping. "On Observing Etiquette and Custom—A Case of the Essence of the Funeral and Burial in the Six Dynasties." *Xueshujie* 學術界 6 (2015): 297–301.

Wang Xiulin 王岫林. *Wei Jin shiren zhi shentiguan* 魏晉士人之身體觀. Taipei: Hua Mulan wenhua chubanshe, 2009.

Wang, Ying. "Rank and Power among Court Ladies at Anyang." In *Gender and Chinese Archaeology*, edited by Katheryn M. Linduff and Yan Sun, 95–113. Walnut Creek, CA: Altamira Press, 2004.

Wang Yitong and Cao Hong, trans. *A Record of Buddhist Monasteries in Luo-yang*. Beijing: Zhonghua Book Company, 2007.

Wang Yi-t'ung. "Slaves and Other Comparable Social Groups during the Northern Dynasties (386–618)." *Harvard Journal of Asiatic Studies* 16, nos. 3/4 (1953): 293–364.

Wang Yongping 王永平. "Wei Jin nanchao shizu shehui zhi nüjiao yu 'mujiao'—cong yige cemian kan zhonggu shizu wenhua zhi chuancheng" 魏晉南朝士族社會之女教與母教—從一個側面看中古士族文化之傳承. *Hebei xuekan* 河北學刊 36, no. 2 (2016): 57–63.

Warner, Rebecca L., Gary R. Lee, and Janet Lee. "Social Organization, Spousal Resources, and Marital Power: A Cross-Cultural Study." *Journal of Marriage and Family* 48, no. 1 (1986): 121–28.

Watson, James L. "Anthropological Overview: The Development of Chinese Descent Groups." In *Kinship Organization in Late Imperial China, 1000–1940,* edited by Patricia Buckey Ebrey and James L. Watson, 274–92. Berkeley: University of California Press, 1986.

Wei Shou 魏收. *Weishu* 魏書. Beijing: Zhonghua, 1974.

Wei Wenge 衛文革. "Muzang ziliao zhong suojian ershisi xiao zhi fazhan yanbian" 墓葬資料中所見二十四孝之發展演變. *Wenwu shijie* 文物世界 5 (2010): 44–49.

Wei Zheng 魏徵. *Suishu* 隋書. Annotated by Linghu Defen 令狐德棻 and Wang Zhaoying 汪紹楹. Beijing: Zhonghua Shuju, 1973.

Wells, Matthew. "*Baopuzi*" 抱朴子. In *Early Medieval Chinese Texts: A Bibliographical Guide,* edited by Cynthia L. Chennault et al., 6–12. Berkeley: Institute of East Asian Studies, University of California, 2015.

Wingjes, Jorit. "'Keep the Women Out of the Camp!': Women and Military Institutions in the Classical World." In *A Companion to Women's Military History,* edited by Barton C. Hacker and Margaret Vining, 17–59. Leiden: Brill, 2012.

Wright, Arthur F. "Biography of the Nun An-Ling-Shou." *Harvard Journal of Asiatic Studies* 15, nos. 1/2 (1952): 193–96.

———. *The Sui Dynasty.* New York: Alfred A. Knopf, 1978.

Wu Can 吳燦. "Fuzhi: dui liuchao lienü ticai huihua de yizhong jiedu" 複製: 對六朝列女題材繪畫的一種解讀. *Chuangzuo yu pinglun* 創作與評論 10 (2014): 107–13.

Wu Chengguo 吳成國. "Lun Dong Jin nanchao hunyin lizhi de diyu chayi" 論東晉南朝婚姻禮制的地域差異. *Hubei Daxue xuebao* 湖北大學學報 3 (1996): 54–58.

Wu Congxiang 吳從祥. "Dangfu yu zhennü—Wei Jin nanbeichao zhiguai xiaoshuo zhong de nüxing xingxiang jiedu" 蕩婦與貞女—魏晉南北朝志怪小說中的女性形象解讀. *Tianzhong xuekan* 天中學刊 23, no. 4 (2008): 58–61.

———. *Handai nüxing lijiao yanjiu* 漢代女性禮教研究. Jinan: Qilu, 2013.

Wu, Fusheng. *The Poetics of Decadence: Chinese Poetry of the Southern Dynasties and Late Tang Periods.* Albany: State University of New York Press, 1998.

Wu Hung. *The Wu Liang Shrine: The Ideology of Early Chinese Pictorial Art.* Stanford: Stanford University Press, 1989.

Wu Tianren 吳天任. *Zhengshi daodu* 正史導讀. Taipei: Taiwan shangwu yinshuguan, 1990.

Wu Zhenglan 吳正嵐. *Liuchao Jiangdong shizu de jiaxue menfeng* 六朝江東士族的家學門風. Nanjing: Nanjing Daxue chubanshe, 2003.

Xiao Guoliang 蕭國亮. *Zhongguo changji shi* 中國娼妓史. Taipei: Wenjin chubanshe, 1996.

Xiao Zixian 蕭子顯. *Nan Qi shu* 南齊書. Beiing: Zhonghua shuju, 1972.

Xie Baofu 謝寶富. "Beichao de zaijia, houqu yu qieji" 北朝的再嫁、後娶與妾妓. *Zhongguo Shehui Kexue Yuan Yanshengyuan xuebao* 中國社會科學院研生院學報 4 (2002): 51–55.

———. *Beichao hunsang lisu yanjiu* 北朝婚喪禮俗研究. Beijing: Shoudu Shifan Daxue, 1998.

———. "Beichao Wei, Qi, Zhou zongshi nüxing de tonghun guanxi yanjiu" 北朝魏，齊，周宗室女性的通婚關係研究. *Guangxi Shifan Daxue xuebao* 廣西師範大學學報 1 (1998): 78–83.

Xie Chongguang 謝重光 and Bai Wengu 白文固. *Zhongguo sengguan zhidu shi* 中國僧官制度史. Xining: Qinghai renmin chubanshe, 1990.

Xie Weiyang 謝維揚. *Zhoudai jiating xingtai* 周代家庭形態. Beijing: Zhongguo shehui kexue chubanshe, 1990.

Xing Peishun 邢培順. "'Wei Jin fengliu' xia de liang Jin funü—yi Jinshu *Lienüzhuan* wei zhuyao lizheng" '魏晉風流'下的兩晉婦女—以晉書烈女傳為主要例證. *Changji Xueyuan xuebao* 昌吉學院學報 4 (2011): 21–25.

Xiong Ming 熊明. "Luelun Huangfu Mi zazhuan de xiaoshuo pinge" 略論皇甫謐雜傳的小說品格. *Jinzhou Shifan Xueyuan xuebao* 錦洲師範學院學報, 24, no. 2 (2002): 26–29.

Xu Chuanwu 徐傳武. "Huangfu Mi zunian xinkao" 皇甫謐卒年新考. *Zhongguo wenzhe yanjiu jikan* 中國文哲研究集刊 10 (1997): 91–104.

Xu Hui 許輝 and Jiang Fuya 蔣福亞. *Liuchao jingji shi* 六朝經濟史. Nanjing: Jiangsu guji chubanshe, 1993.

Xu Hui 許輝, Qiu Min 邱敏, and Hu Axian 胡阿祥. *Liuchao wenhua* 六朝文化. Nanjing: Jiangsu guji chubanshe, 2001.

Xu Ling 徐陵. *Jianzhu yutai xinyong* 箋注玉臺新詠. Annotated by Wu Zhaoyi 吳兆宜. Taipei: Guangwen shuju, 1966.

Xu Zhuoyun 許倬雲. "Handai jiating de daxiao" 漢代家庭的大小. In *Qingzhu Li Ji xiansheng qishi sui lunwenji* 慶祝李濟先生七十歲論文集, edited by Li Fanggui 李方桂 et al., 789–806. Taipei: Qinghua xuebaoshe, 1967.

Xue Ruize 薛瑞澤. "Jianlun Wei Jin nanbeichao de cihun" 簡論魏晉南北朝的賜婚. *Qinghai shehui kexue* 青海社會科學 5 (2000): 81–83.

———. "Wei Jin beichao hunyinzhong de erqi xianxiang" 魏晉北朝婚姻中的二妻現象. *Baoji Lixue Xueyuan xuebao* 寶雞理學院學報 1 (2000): 77–81.

Xue Ruize 薛瑞澤 and Zhang Zhihong 張志紅. "Shilun Wei Jin Nanbeichao zaihun wenti" 試論魏晉南北朝再婚問題. *Sixiang zhanxian* 思想戰線 2 (2002): 132–36.

Yamazaki Junichi 山崎純一. "Chō Ka Jōshi shin o megutte—Go Kan kōki Gi Shin aida kōkyū jōsei kunkō" 張華女史箴をめぐって—後漢後期魏晉閒後宮女性訓考. *Chūgoku koten kenkyū* 中国古典研究 29 (1984): 18–45.

Yan Kejun 嚴可均, ed. *Quan shanggu sandai Qin Han sanguo liuchao wen* 全上古三代秦漢三國六朝文. Beijing: Zhonghua Shuju, 1958.

Yan Ming 嚴明. *Zhongguo mingji yishu shi* 中國名妓藝術史. Taipei: Wenjin, 1992.

Yan Yaozhong 嚴耀中. "Muzhi jiwen zhong de Tangdai funü fojiao xinyang" 墓誌祭文中的唐代婦女佛教信仰. In *Tang Song nüxing yu shehui* 唐宋女性與社會, edited by Deng Xiaonan 鄧小南, 2:467–92. Shanghai: Shanghai cishu, 2003.

Yang Lien-sheng. "Notes on the Economic History of the Chin Dynasty." In *Studies in Chinese Institutional History*, 119–97. Cambridge, MA: Harvard University Press, 1961.

Yang Mingzhao 楊明照. *Baopuzi waipian jiaojian* 抱朴子外篇校箋. Beijing: Xinhua, 1991.

Yang Shupeng 楊淑鵬. "Shishuo xinyu—Xianyuan xuanlu tese tanxi" '世說新語—賢媛' 選錄特色探析. *Taiyuan Shifan Xueyuan xuebao* 太原師範學院學報 5, no. 1 (2006): 97–99.

Yang Xiaoping 楊曉萍. "Shijia nüzi duo fengliu—Wei Jin nanbeichao shufa shiji-azhong de nüxing shujia guankui" 世家女子多風流—魏晉南北朝書法世家中的女性書家管窺. *Shufa* 書法 3 (2014): 34–36.

Yang Yinglin 楊映琳. "Wei Jin Nanbei chao shiqi de zhenjieguan" 魏晉南北朝時期的貞節觀. *Qiusuo* 求索 4 (2003): 252–54.

Yano Chikara 矢野主稅. *Monbatsu shakai seiritsu shi* 門閥社會成立史. Tokyo: Kokusho kankōkai, 1976.

Yao, Ping. "Women in Portraits: An Overview of Epitaphs from Early and Medieval China." In *Overt and Covert Treasures: Essays on the Sources for Chinese Women's History*, edited by Clara Wing-Chung Ho, 157–83. Hong Kong: The City University Press, 2012.

Yao Silian 姚思廉. *Chenshu* 陳書. Beijing: Zhonghua, 1972.

———. *Liangshu* 梁書. Beijing: Zhonghua, 1973.

Yates, Robin D. S. "Medicine for Women in Early China: A Preliminary Survey." *Nan Nü* 7, no. 2 (2005): 127–81.

Ye Huichang 葉會昌 and Lang Ruiping 郎瑞萍. "Lun beichao bentu wenren shizhong nüxing xingxiang de yihua" 論北朝本土文人詩中女性形象的異化. *Tianshui Shifan Xueyuan xuebao* 天水師範學院學報 25, no. 4 (2005): 60–63.

Yen Chih-t'ui. *Family Instructions for the Yen Clan: Yen-shih Chia-hsün.* Translated by Ssu-yü Teng. Leiden: E. J. Brill, 1966.

Yi Jo-lan. "Social Status, Gender Division and Institutions: Sources Relating to Women in Chinese Standard Histories." In *Overt and Covert Treasures: Essays on the Sources for Chinese Women's History*, edited by Clara Wing-Chung Ho, 131–55. Hong Kong: The City University Press, 2012.

Yong Rong 永瑢. *Siku quanshu zongmu tiyao* 四庫全書總目提要. Shanghai: Shangwu, 1933.

Yoshikawa Tadao 吉川忠夫. *Liuchao jingshen shi yanjiu* 六朝精神史研. Translated by Wang Qifa 王啟發. Nanjing: Jiangsu renmin chubanshe, 2010.

Zeng Xiaoxia 曾小霞. "Dai yan yu zi yu—Wei Jin qifu shiwen tanxi" 代言與自喻—魏晉棄婦詩文探析. *Hunan Renwen Keji Xueyuan xuebao* 湖南人文科技學院學報 1 (2013): 82–86.

Zhang Bangwei 張邦煒. *Hunyin yu shehui (Songdai)* 婚姻與社會 (宋代). Chengdu: Sichuan renmin, 1989.

———. *Songdai hunyin jiazu shilun* 宋代婚姻家族史論. Beijing: Renmin chubanshe, 2003.

Zhang Chengzong 張承宗. "Beichao gongnü kaolue" 北朝宮女考略. *Suzhou Daxue xuebao* 蘇州大學學報 2 (2006): 107–11.

———. "Dong Jin nanchao nigu shiji kao" 東晉南朝尼姑事迹考. *Nanjing Ligong Daxue xuebao* 南京理工大學學報 2 (2011): 99–106.

———. *Liuchao funü* 六朝婦女. Nanjing: Nanjing chubanshe, 2012.

———. "Liuchao Jiangnan funü de jingji huodong" 六朝江南婦女的經濟活動. *Zhejiang Shifan Daxue xuebao* 浙江師範大學學報 5 (2006): 46–50.

———. "Sanguo Liang Jin nanchao gongü kaolue" 三國兩晉南朝宮女考略. *Nanjing Xiaozhuang Xueyuan xuebao* 南京曉庄學院學報 1 (2005): 23–29.

———. "Wei Jin nanbeichao de zongjiao xinyang" 魏晉南北朝婦女的宗教信仰. *Nantong Daxue xuebao* 南通大學學報 22, no. 2 (2006): 91–97.

———. "Wei Jin nanbeichao funü congjun kao" 魏晉南北朝婦女從軍考. *Nantong Daxue xuebao* 南通大學學報 21, no. 1 (2005): 99–105.

———. "Wei Jin nanbeichao funü de jiawu laodong" 魏晉南北朝婦女的家務勞動. *Yangzhou Daxue xuebao* 揚州大學學報 2 (2009): 90–95.

———. "Wei Jin nanbeichao funü de shejiao huodong" 魏晉南北朝婦女的社交活動. *Xiangfan Xueyuan xuebao* 襄樊學院學報 3 (2005): 90–93.

———. "Wei Jin nanbeichao funü sangzang liyi kao" 魏晉南北朝婦女喪葬禮儀考. *Suzhou Daxue xuebao* 蘇州大學學報 2 (2010): 99–102.

———. "Wei Jin nanbeichao shiqi de funü danshenzang" 魏晉南北朝時期的婦女單身葬. *Nanjing Ligong Daxue xuebao* 南京理工大學學報 23, no. 3 (2010): 100–106.

———. "Wei Jin nanbeichao shiqi yu funü xiangguan de falü wenti ji sifa anjian" 魏晉南北朝時期與婦女相關的法律問題及司法案件. *Nanjing Ligong Daxue xuebao* 南京理工大學學報 22, no. 2 (2009): 25–30.

Zhang Chengzong 張承宗 and Chen Qun 陳群. *Zhongguo funü tongshi: Wei Jin nanbei chao juan* 中國婦女通史: 魏晉南北朝卷. Hangzhou: Hangzhou chubanshe, 2010.

Zhang Chengzong 張承宗 and Sun Li 孫立. "Wei Jin Nanbeichao hunsu chutan" 魏晉南北朝婚俗初探. *Zhejiang xuekan* 浙江學刊 95, no. 6 (1995): 102–4.

Zhang Guogang 張國剛. *Jiating shihua* 家庭史話. Beijing: Shehui kexue wenxian, 2012.

———. "Zhonggu fojiao jielü yu jiating lunli" 中古佛教戒律與家庭倫理. In *Jiating shi yanjiu de xin shiye* 家庭史研究的新視野, edited by Zhang Guogang, 48–70. Beijing: Sanlian shuju, 2004.

Zhang Huanjun 張煥君. "Lizhi yu renqing de tiaoshi—yi Wei Jin shiqi qianmu de fusang wenti wei zhongxin" 禮制與人情的調適—以魏晉時期前母的服喪問題為中心. *Shanxi Shida xuebao* 山西師大學報 1 (2011): 55–59.

Zhang Jihao 張繼昊. *Cong Tuoba dao Bei Wei—Bei Wei wangchao chuangjian lishi de kaocha* 從拓跋到北魏—北魏王朝創建歷史的考察. Banqiao: Daoxiang, 2003.

Zhang Shuyi 張淑一. "Zhoudai nüzi de xingshi zhidu" 周代女子的姓氏制度. *Shixue jikan* 史學集刊 2 (1999): 67–70.

Zhang Xiaowen 張小穩. "Nüxing ziwo yishi de juexing: Wei Jin nanbeichao hunyin lunli de yipe weidu" 女性自我意識的覺醒: 魏晉南北朝婚姻倫理的一個維度. *Lunlixue yanjiu* 倫理學研究 2 (2014): 31–35.

Zhang Xinyi 張欣怡. "Funü de shouji yu zaijia kan Wei Jin Nanbei chao de zhenjie" 婦女的守節與再嫁看魏晉南北朝的貞節. *Zhongzheng lishi xuekan* 中正歷史學刊 7 (2004): 182–90.

Zhang Ya'nan 張亞南 and Wang Tiantong 王天彤. "Soushenji yu Wei Jin hunyin sangzang lisu" 搜神記與魏晉婚姻喪葬禮俗. *Shandong Jiaoyu Xueyuan xuebao* 山東教育學院學報 1 (2008): 44–46.

Zhang Yange 張艷鴿 and Zhao Guohua 趙國華. "Wei Jin shiqi Yingchuan Xun shi hungou kaoshu" 魏晉時期潁川荀氏婚媾考述. *Shehui jingwei* 社會經緯 9 (2014): 165–67.

Zhang Yinan 張一南. "Wo jian you ling—Tangdai nüshiren de Qi Liang ti chuangzuo" 我見猶怜—唐代女詩人的齊梁體創作. *Wenshi zhishi* 文史知識 3 (2014): 112–17.

Zhang Yong 張勇. "Lun Wei Jin nanbeichao dasheng fojiao dui funü jingshen fengmao de yingxiang" 論魏晉南北朝大乘佛教對婦女精神風貌的影響. *Zhongguo*

Shehui Kexue Xueyuan Yanjiushengyuan xuebao 中國社會科學院研究生院學報 1 (2008): 62–67.

Zhang Yunhua 張雲華. "Lun Bei Wei funü de duhan fengqi" 論北朝婦女的妒悍風氣. *Shixue jikan* 史學集刊 6 (2008): 99–104.

Zhang Zongyuan 張宗原. "Lun beichao minjian 'hunlian' geci" 論北朝民間婚戀歌辭. *Fudan xuebao* 復旦學報 2 (2003): 112–18.

Zhao Chao 趙超. *Han Wei nanbeichao muzhi huibian* 漢魏南北朝墓誌彙編. Tianjin: Tianjin guji chubanshe, 1992.

Zhao Dingchen 趙鼎臣. *Zhuyin jishi ji* 竹隱畸士集. In *Siku jiben bieji shiyi* 四庫輯本別集拾遺, edited by Luan Guiming 欒貴明, 20:178–91. Beijing: Zhonghua shuju, 1983.

Zhao Hui 趙輝. *Liu chao shehui wenhua xintai* 六朝社會文化心態. Taipei: Wenjin, 1996.

Zhao Jibin 趙紀彬. "Fahua jing yu liuchao zhi biqiuni guanxi luekao" 法華經與六朝之比丘尼關係考略. *Zhonghua wenhua luntan* 中華文化論壇 2 (2014): 126–30.

Zhao Jing 趙靜. "Wei Jin nanbeichao Langya Wang shi jiating wenhua yu wenxue yanjiu" 魏晉南北朝琅邪王氏家族文化與文學研究. PhD diss., Shandong Shifan daxue, 2011.

Zhao Liheng 趙麗恆. "Jiu Shishuo xinyu kan Wei Jin nanbeichao de hunyin wenhua" 就世說新語看魏晉南北朝的婚姻文化. *Xuchang Xueyuan xuebao* 許昌學院學報 1 (2007): 40–42.

Zhao Minli. "Reflections on the Proposition that 'Literary Consciousness Arose in the Wei and Jin Dynasties.'" *Social Sciences in China* 26, no. 2 (2005): 73–83.

Zhao Rongjun 趙容俊. "Han Wei Jin shi de wushu tezheng kaocha" 漢魏晉時期的巫術特徵考察. *Shilin* 史林 4 (2011): 32–37.

Zhao Rongxiang 趙榮珦. *Zhongguo diyi biqiuni Jingjian zhuan* 中國第一比丘尼淨檢傳. Beijing: Zongjiao wenhua chubanshe, 2008.

Zhao Shichuang 詹石窗. *Daojiao yu nüxing* 道教與女性. Shanghai: Shanghai guji chubanshe, 1990.

Zhao Yi 趙翼. *Nianer shi zhaji* 廿二史劄記. Taipei: Shijie shuju, 1974.

Zhao Zhijian 趙志堅, "Beichao funü zaijia kaoshu" 北朝婦女再嫁考述. *Minsu yanjiu* 民俗研究 1 (1995): 72–76.

———. "Wei Jin nanbeichao funü zaijia kaoshu" 魏晉南北朝婦女再嫁考述. *Shandong daxue xuebao* 山東大學學報 1 (1995): 19–24, 36.

Zheng Yanqin 鄭彥琴. "Liang Han Wei Jin nanbeichao shiqi nüxing 'wushihua' xianxiang chutan" 兩漢魏晉南北朝時期女性武士化現象初探. *Nanjing Xiaozhuang Xueyuan xuebao* 南京曉庄學院學報 4 (2010): 22–26.

Zheng Yaru 鄭邪如. *Qin en nan bao: Tangdai shiren de xiaodao shijian ji qi tizhihua* 親恩難報: 唐代士人的孝道實踐及其體制化. Taipei: Taida chuban zhongxin, 2014.

———. *Qinggan yu zhidu—Wei Jin shidai de muzi guanxi* 情感與制度—魏晉時代的母子關係. Taipei: Guoli Taiwan Daxue, 2001.

———. "Zhonggu shiqi de muzi guanxi—xingbie yu Han Tang zhijian de jiating yanjiu" 中古時期的母子關係—性別與漢唐之間的家庭史研究. In *Zhongguo shi xinlun—xingbie shi fence* 中國史新論—性別史分冊, edited by Li Zhende 李貞德, 135–90. Taipei: Zhongyang yanjiu yuan, 2009.

Zheng Yongle 鄭永樂. "Xian Qin liang Han Weijin liuchao wudao wenxue yanjiu" 先秦兩漢魏晉六朝舞蹈文學研究. PhD diss., Zhongguo Yishu Yanjiuyuan, 2004.

Zhou Haiyan 周海燕. "Wei Jin nanbeichao funü zai nongye zhong de diwei he zuoyong" 魏晉南北朝婦女在農業中的地位和作用. *Xinxiang Shifan Gaodeng Zhuanke Xuexiao xuebao* 新鄉師範高等專科學校學報 4 (2006): 117–18.

Zhou Jianjiang 周建江. *Taihe shiwunian—Bei Wei zhengzhi wenhua biange yanjiu* 太和十五年—北魏政治文化變革研究. Guangzhou: Guangdong renmin, 2001.

Zhou Jiren 周繼仁. "Lun Zhongguo gudai biaoyan yishu de shangpinhua wenti" 論中國古代表演藝術的商品化問題. *Zhongguoshi yanjiu* 中國史研究15, no. 4 (1993): 44–57.

Zhou Yin 周胤. "Bei Wei Luoyang nüxing zhi fojiao xinyang shijie guanqie" 北魏洛陽女性之佛教信仰世界管窺. In *Lifa yu xinyang—Zhongguo gudai nüxing yanjiu lunkao* 禮法與信仰—中國古代女性研究論考, edited by Pu Muzhou 蒲慕州, 173–99. Hong Kong: Shangwu yinshuguan, 2013.

Zhou, Yiqun. "Virtue and Talent: Women and *Fushi* in Early China." *Nan Nü* 5, no. 1 (2003): 1–42.

Zhou Yuru 周玉茹. "Liuchao Jiangnan biqiuni chanxiu kaolun" 六朝江南比丘尼禪修考論. *Renwen zazhi* 人文雜誌 12 (2014): 14–20.

———. "Liuchao Jiankang biqiuni canzheng xianxiang tanxi" 六朝健康比丘尼參政現象探析. *Shandong Nüzi Xueyuan xuebao* 山東女子學院學報 6, no. 94 (2010): 47–51.

Zhou Zhaowang 周兆望. "Wei Jin nanbeichao shiqi de nübing" 魏晉南北朝時期的女兵. *Jiangxi shehui kexue* 江西社會科學 2 (1997): 59–64.

Zhou Zhaowang 周兆望 and Hou Yonghui 侯永惠. "Wei Jin nanbeichao funü de fushi fengmao" 魏晉南北朝婦女的服飾風貌. *Jiangxi shehui kexue* 江西社會科學 3 (1995): 97–102.

Zhu Dawei 朱大渭, Liu Chi 劉馳, Liang Mancang 梁滿倉, and Chen Yong 陳勇. *Wei Jin nanbeichao shehui shenghuo shi* 魏晉南北朝社會生活史. Beijing: Zhongguo shehui kexue chubanshe, 1998.

Zhu Mingxun 朱明勛. "Lun Wei Jin liuchao shiqi de Xiaojing yanjiu" 論魏晉六朝時期的孝經研究. *Huazhong Keji Daxue xuebao* 華中科技大學學報 3 (2002): 97–101.

Zhuang Huafeng 莊華峰. "Beichao shidai Xianbei funü de shenghuo fengqi" 北朝時代鮮卑婦女的生活風氣. *Minzu yanjiu* 民族研究 6 (1994): 62–68.

———. "Wei Jin Nanbeichao shiqi de funü zaikai" 魏晉南北朝時期的婦女再嫁. *Anhui Shida xuebao* 安徽師大學報 19, no. 3 (1991): 343–48.

Zhuang Lixia 庄麗霞. "Huhua secai de beichao hunli xisu" 胡化色彩的北朝婚禮習俗. *Zhaotong Shifan Gaodeng Zhuangke Xuexiao xueyuan* 昭通師範高等專科學校學報 4 (2006): 36–38.

Zhuang Xinxia莊新霞. "Han Wei liuchao nüxing zhushu kaolun" 漢魏六朝女性著述考論. PhD. diss., Shandong Daxue, 2007.

Zou Min 鄒旻. "Hanmo Weichu shiwenlun zhongxin de zhuanyi yu wenxue jiazhi de faxian—shilun Lingmu Huxiong zijue de neihan ji qi panduan yiju" 漢末魏初詩文論重心的轉移與文學價值的發現—試論鈴木虎雄自覺說的內涵及其判斷依據. *Xibei Nonglin Keji Daxue xuebao* 西北農林科技大學學報 1 (2010): 130–34.

Zurndorfer, Harriet. "Polygamy and Masculinity in China: Past and Present." In *Changing Chinese Masculinities: From Imperial Pillars of State to Global Real Men*, edited by Kam Louie, 13–33. Hong Kong: Hong Kong University Press, 2016.

Index

ASIAN VOICES
An Asia/Pacific/Perspectives Series
Series Editor: Mark Selden